The Rabbi's Atheist Daughter

The Rabbi's Atheist Daughter

Ernestine Rose
International Feminist Pioneer

BONNIE S. ANDERSON

OXFORD
UNIVERSITY PRESS

Oxford University Press is a department of the University of Oxford. It furthers
the University's objective of excellence in research, scholarship, and education
by publishing worldwide. Oxford is a registered trade mark of Oxford University
Press in the UK and certain other countries.

Published in the United States of America by Oxford University Press
198 Madison Avenue, New York, NY 10016, United States of America.

Library of Congress Cataloging-in-Publication Data
Names: Anderson, Bonnie S., author.
Title: The rabbi's atheist daughter : Ernestine Rose, international feminist pioneer /
Bonnie S. Anderson.
Description: New York, NY : Oxford University Press, [2016] |
Includes bibliographical references and index.
Identifiers: LCCN 2016014651 (print) | LCCN 2016014997 (ebook) |
ISBN 978-0-19-975624-7 (hardcover : alk. paper) |
ISBN 978-0-19-062638-9 (Updf) | ISBN 978-0-19-062639-6 (Epub)
Subjects: LCSH: Rose, Ernestine L. (Ernestine Louise), 1810–1892. |
Women social reformers—United States—Biography. |
Feminists—United States—Biography. |
Feminism—United States—History—19th century. |
Women's rights—United States—History—19th century.
Classification: LCC HQ1413.R6 A53 2016 (print) |
LCC HQ1413.R6 (ebook) | DDC 305.42092 [B]—dc23
LC record available at https://lccn.loc.gov/2016014651

1 3 5 7 9 8 6 4 2

Printed by Sheridan Books, Inc., United States of America

For Luise Eichenbaum, who helped me
follow "the buds of desire"

Contents

Acknowledgments

MY INTEREST IN Ernestine Rose began when I read Yuri Suhl's engaging biography of her in the 1970s. Paula Doress-Worters's 2008 collection of Rose's speeches and letters sparked my desire to write my own biography of her. A dinner party of encouraging feminists at Ann Snitow's house ratified this desire. Thanks to my editor, Susan Ferber, for supporting this project throughout the years and to Maya Bringe, my wonderful production manager. Thanks also to Patterson Lamb, the best copy editor I've ever had.

Research took me many places, first to Poland. Thanks to my friend John Graney, MD, for accompanying me there and also for trying to diagnose Ernestine Rose's illnesses. In Poland, I traveled to Rose's birthplace of Piótrkow Trybunalski and did research in Warsaw. Thanks to Agnieszka Klimek, who searched for and translated documents for me, and Małgorzata Witecka, archivist at the Warsaw Central Archives of Historical Research. Additional Polish research and translation was done by Violetta Wiernicka and Lukas Chelminski. Thomas Breitfeld of the Geheimes Staatsarchiv Preussischer Kulturbesitz, Amy Hackett, and Dana Strohscheer helped me with her years in Germany. Regina de Bruijn-Boot and H. J. de Muij-Flenike of the Dutch National Archives in The Hague investigated the account of her alleged time in the Netherlands. In France, my Lyon friend, Claudette Fillard, read every chapter and provided many helpful comments. Nadia Malinovich, my dear relation who is also a historian, educated me in her field of Jewish history, as well as reading and commenting on the sections dealing with Judaism. Sandi Cooper, my colleague at CUNY for many years, let me read her copy of the 1878 Paris peace conference, which I had had trouble finding. In England, Sophie Stewart, archivist at the Co-operative College, Holyoake House, in Manchester, which holds the Robert Owen Papers, was helpful both online and in person. Penny Tinkler enlivened my Manchester stay. Both Jane Rendall and Rebecca Probert helped me with important background material when we met at a German conference in 2011.

The bulk of my research was done in the United States. Thanks to John C. Johnson at the Howard Gotlieb Archival Research Center of Boston University, which houses the Yuri Suhl Papers; Vicki Catozza of the Western Reserve Historical Society in Cleveland for information on Lemuel Barnard; Henry F. Scannell, curator at the Boston Public Library; Nicholas Noyes, collections librarian, and Tiffany Link, research librarian, at the Maine Historical Society in Portland for help with the *Boston Investigator.* Two years of its run are missing from the online version but available in Portland. Thanks also to Henrietta Larou and Belle Graney for housing me during a Maine blizzard. Thanks to Linda Madden at the Mason Library of Keene State College, New Hampshire, for the *Herald of Freedom*; Dean M. Rogers, in Special Collections at the Vassar College Library for both Rose's letters to C. H. Plummer and her speech at the 1871 Robert Owen Centenary; the staff at the University of Michigan Special Collections for Rose's 1879 letter to the Conways, and the staff at the Chicago Historical Society/Chicago History Museum for Rose's 1880 letter to Stanton. I did additional primary research at the New York Public Library, the New York Historical Society, Stirling Memorial Library at Yale University, and the Sophia Smith Collection at Smith College. All the librarians at those institutions were extremely helpful.

The most helpful librarian of all, however, was Professor Helen Georgas of the Brooklyn College Library, who educated me in databases, solved knotty research issues, and cheered me on throughout this project. Thanks also to my former student Marianne LaBatto, Brooklyn College Archivist. She and her helpful staff provided much support, especially in the use of their still-functioning microfilm reader/printer. Jahongir Usmanov researched the New York Municipal Archives for the Roses' homes and helped with the picture permissions. Thanks to Cheryl Olivieri and John Quezada for putting the illustrations in the correct digital format. Thanks also to Celia Braxton for additional *Boston Investigator* research.

Throughout this project, my fellow historians have been immensely helpful and supportive. Thanks to Ted McCormick for the phrase "the rabbi's atheist daughter"; to Mary Louise Roberts for sending me her M.A. thesis on Rose and Wright; to Harriet Alonso, Carol Faulkner, Ann Gordon, and Nancy Hewitt for providing letters about Rose; to Gunja SenGupta for help with anniversary week; to Toba Singer and her family for informing me about orthodox Jewish practices; and to Jocelyn Wills for book loans. The German Women's History Study Group, going strong in New York City since the early 1980s, read and commented on the entire book. Thanks to Dolores Augustine, Marion Berghahn, Renate Bridenthal, Atina Grossmann, Amy

Hackett, Maria Hoehn, Marion Kaplan, Jan Lambertz, Mary Nolan, Krista O'Donnell, Katherine Pence, and Julia Sneeringer for all their work. In addition, a number of friends read and commented on my manuscript. Thanks to Nan Bases, Verna Gillis, Linda Grasso, Cheryl Olivieri, my sister, Jeanie Raben, and especially Stephanie Golden, for their help. My former writing partner and dear friend, Judith Zinsser, provided encouragement through the years. I could not have done my work without support from them and many others.

The Rabbi's Atheist Daughter

Introduction

THE AUDIENCE AT the Second National Woman's Rights Convention that gathered on the morning of October 15, 1851, was so large that the organizers moved the evening session to the city's biggest auditorium. By 7 P.M., close to a thousand people crammed into Worcester, Massachusetts's City Hall, which itself "was crowded long before the hour of the meeting, many being unable to gain access." The evening session began with a clergyman reading a letter from two imprisoned French feminists to their "Sisters in America." After him, Ernestine L. Rose of New York City, the only woman scheduled to lecture that night, mounted the platform to address the crowd. Rose had come to the fore at the first national convention the previous year, where she had spoken frequently, presented resolutions, and become head of an important committee. On this night, Rose gave "an address of an hour in length, which has never been surpassed," a co-worker wrote in an 1870 history of the women's movement.[1]

Her audience, responding to a call "to consider the Rights, Duties and Relations of Woman," confirmed the growing strength of a truly national reform movement for female equality. Only about 300 people had attended the 1848 meeting in the village of Seneca Falls, New York. The same number convened in Worcester in 1850. The city had been chosen because it was a fast-growing center of manufacturing, culture, and reform. When the second National Woman's Rights Convention met there again in 1851, the crowd tripled and women were in the majority. Wide publicity about the first national meeting, even though much was hostile, attracted an impressive audience that had been warned in the announcement summoning participants that "the work contemplated is no child's play. It wars directly with the thought so deeply rooted and so hoary, that Woman is only an appendage, and not an integral part in the fabric of human society. It is in full conflict with the world's teachers, its preachers, its lawgivers, its poets and its painters."[2]

Women speaking in public still shocked a society that wanted to confine respectable females to the home. Men reserved oration for themselves; if women usurped this privilege, condemnations of their shameful, unnatural, unfeminine behavior quickly followed. Public speaking under such conditions took a toll, even for those experienced at it. "I did not rise to make a speech," the abolitionist lecturer Abby Kelley declared at the 1851 convention; "my life has been my speech. For fourteen years I have advocated this cause by my daily life. Bloody feet, Sisters, have worn smooth the path by which you have come up hither." Ernestine Rose had also been lecturing for fourteen years, but she remembered the experience much more positively. "I look back to that time," she wrote in old age. "When a stranger and alone, I went from place to place, in high-ways and by-ways, did the work and paid my bills with great pleasure and satisfaction; for the cause gained ground, and in spite of my heresies I always had good audiences, attentive listeners, and was well-received wherever I went."[3]

Forty-one years old in 1851, Rose was then "in her prime—an excellent lecturer, liberal, eloquent, witty," a radical newspaper later wrote. She "tactfully avoids any appearance of eccentricity," a German reporter approvingly commented, since she never wore the controversial "Bloomer costume"— ankle-length pants under a knee-length dress—which a number of her associates donned in these years to protest the restrictive female clothing of their day. Instead, Ernestine Rose presented herself as a respectable, middle-class woman, in somber-colored, tight-waisted, long-skirted dresses, enlivened by white lace collars and cuffs. "Her costume reflects her personality," the Frenchwoman Jenny d'Héricourt wrote after meeting her a few years later, she "does not pose because she does not try to please . . . she wishes only to persuade and convince." Praising Rose for neither dyeing her hair nor hiding it under a bonnet, d'Héricourt admired her distinctive coiffure of a knot at the back of her head with "long clusters of curls on either side of her face."[4]

Her passionate eloquence distinguished her. Praising a speech she gave at the first Worcester convention, a local newspaper reported that no one could hear her without respecting her talent as an orator, whatever they might think of the merits of her cause, since her "strong, compact, and lucid argument" was "delivered in a manner that few practiced public speakers can equal." "Her eloquence is irresistible," a British sympathizer declared. "It shakes, it awes, it thrills, it melts—it fills you with horror, it drowns you with tears." What most astonished her contemporaries was how well she could engage an audience. "She is far before any woman speaker I ever heard," a female anti-slavery activist wrote in 1853. "She is splendidly clear and logical. But oh! I cannot give any idea of the power and beauty of her speech. I can only stammer about it a little."[5]

Rose began her address at Worcester by segueing gracefully from the oppression suffered by women in post-revolutionary France, where 1848 claims for their rights had been crushed, to the identical situation of American women, "in this far-famed land of freedom." Asserting that either the promise of "life, liberty, and the pursuit of happiness" applied to women, or that American men were hypocrites for denying their female relatives rights they awarded themselves, Rose turned rapidly to her main thesis: that women as human beings deserved equal rights:

> Humanity recognizes no sex—virtue recognizes no sex—mind recognizes no sex—life and death, pleasure and pain, happiness and misery recognize no sex. Like man, woman comes involuntarily into existence; like him she possesses physical and mental and moral powers, on the proper cultivation of which depends her happiness; like him, she is subject to all the vicissitudes of life. . . . Yet she is not recognized as his equal! In the laws of the land she has no rights, in government she has no voice.

Stressing the sexes' common humanity, Rose insisted that women's equality followed from that bond. She challenged the legal "non-existence" of women, especially wives. "From the cradle to the grave she is subject to the power and control of men. Father, guardian, or husband, one conveys her like some piece of merchandise over to the other." Referring to the established Anglo-American doctrine that upon marriage "husband and wife become one person and that person is the husband," Rose unleashed her scorn on this formula for discrimination. "What an inconsistency, that from the moment she enters that compact, in which she assumes the high responsibility of wife and mother, she ceases legally to exist, and becomes a purely submissive being. Blind submission in woman is considered a virtue, while submission to wrong is itself wrong, and resistance to wrong is virtue alike in woman as in man." Employing sarcasm and humor, Rose questioned the familiar arguments that the husband was "presumed" to provide for his wife and be kind to her. "Yes!, he keeps her and so he does a favorite horse; by law they are both considered his property. . . . But what right, I ask, has the law to presume at all on the subject?" If the married couple became one person, "why should woman always remain on the losing side? Turn the tables. Let the identity and interest of the husband be merged in the wife. Think you she would act less generously towards him, than he towards her?"[6]

Mothers educated their children; if they themselves lacked education, then not just the children but the entire nation would suffer. Why should a mother be deprived of her home, her property, and her children if her husband died, while he kept all if she did? Why should the theft of a pair of boots bring a jail term, when a husband who beat his wife received only a reprimand? Countering the common objection that if women were to vote, this act would "expose" them "to the contact of rough, rude, drinking, swearing, fighting men at the ballot-box," Rose argued that women's presence could only improve both the voting process and society as a whole:

> How much more beneficial would be woman's influence, if, as the equal with man, she should take her stand by his side . . . in the Legislative halls, in the Senate chamber, in the Judge's chair, in the jury box, in the Forum, in the Laboratory of the arts and sciences, and wherever duty would call her for the benefit of herself, her country, her race. For at every step, she would carry with her a humanizing influence.[7]

In the final section of her lecture, Rose insisted that if women were given equal opportunities, their intellectual and artistic achievements would rival those of men. Turning to man's physical strength, she joked that if that were the only criterion, "the inmates of the forest are his superior." Asserting that proper exercise would produce healthy women, she deplored the strictures that limited middle- and upper-class girls. "A robust development in a girl is unfashionable, a healthy, sound, voice is vulgar, a ruddy glow on the cheek is coarse; and when vitality is so strong within her as to show itself in spite of bolts and bars, then she has to undergo a bleaching process, eat lemons, drink vinegar, and keep in the shade." Such practices led to "that nervous sensibility which sees a ghost in every passing shadow, that beautiful diffidence which dares not take a step without the protecting arm of a man to support her tender frame, and that shrinking mock-modesty that faints at the mention of a leg of a table."[8]

The solution? Education—through "this and many more Conventions." Men must be made to realize that their subordination of women led to the misery of both sexes, since "nature has too closely united them to permit one to oppress the other with impunity." Rose rejected dividing humanity into villainous men and victimized women. The female sex needed to end its complicity in its own degradation. "Man may remove her legal shackles, and recognize her as his equal . . . but the law cannot compel her to cultivate her mind and take an independent stand as a free being." Rose concluded by urging women to ignore "the taunts, ridicule, and stigmas cast upon us," to "cast off that mountain weight, that intimidating cowardly question . . . `What will people say?'" The result would be a new era, "the grandest step forward in the onward progress," leading to woman's occupying that "high and lofty position, for which nature has so eminently fitted her, in the destinies of humanity."[9]

The success of this speech, coupled with her energy and dedication, catapulted Rose to the inner circles of the new women's rights movement. This movement circulated a printed version of her lecture widely. Rose spoke at scores of US venues throughout the 1850s, ranging from Maine to Virginia and from the East Coast to Michigan. She became a chief organizer of the yearly Woman's Rights Conventions that met until the Civil War and she carried their message to Europe on an extended tour in 1856. "Mrs. Rose is the queen of the company," the *Albany Transcript* asserted about her role at an 1854 convention in the New York capital. "She has as great a power to chain an audience as any of our best male speakers." More famous than either Elizabeth Cady Stanton or Susan B. Anthony in the mid-nineteenth century, Rose received heartfelt praise from Anthony, who became a good friend. "They who sat with her in bygone days on the platform will remember her matchless powers as a speaker," Anthony reminisced near the end of Rose's life,

> and how safe we all felt when she had the floor that neither in manner, sentiment, argument, nor repartee would she in any way compromise the dignity of the occasion. She had the advantage of rare grace and beauty, which in a measure heightened the effect of all she said. She had a rich, musical voice and a ready flow of choice language. In style she was clear, logical, and impassioned.[10]

In order to participate in conventions advocating their rights, women had to break with everything they had been taught. Raised to be modest, domestic, unassertive creatures, accepting their own subordination and deferring to men, they needed to reject the roles their mothers embodied, the roles their religions preached to them, the roles their reading and education glorified.

"A virtuous woman is little lower than the angels," the French philosopher Rousseau rhapsodized in his immensely influential novel *Emile,*

> I would a thousand times rather have a home-loving girl, simply brought up, than a learned lady. . . . A female wit is a scourge to her husband, her children, her friends, her servants, to everybody. From the lofty height of her genius, she scorns every womanly duty, and she is always trying to make a man of herself.[11]

Early feminists questioned this division of life into "separate spheres," which allotted women home and the family while giving the rest of the world to men. They challenged their period's assumption that they lost their femininity if they spoke in public, wanted to vote, or yearned for higher education. "The reformation we propose, in its utmost scope, is radical and universal," Paulina Wright Davis asserted in her Opening Address to the Worcester Convention of 1850. "It is not the mere perfecting of a progress already in motion, a detail of some established plan, but it is an epochal movement— the emancipation of half the world, and a conforming re-organization of all social, political, and industrial interests and institutions."[12]

To arrive at this perspective, to become a "woman's rights woman," required an immense imaginative and moral journey. No participant in the 1851 convention traveled further in this regard than Ernestine Rose. She was the only foreigner in this group of native-born Americans. Unlike them, she had lived in numerous countries—Poland, Prussia, France, and England—before coming to the United States in 1836. Among these religious Protestants, she was the only atheist; as an adult she believed in no religion and took an active part in free-thought organizations. She had been brought up as the daughter of a rabbi in the small Polish city of Piótrkow Trybunalski, where she was born in 1810. Instead of leading the traditional life expected of her, she defied her father's attempt to marry her off, abandoned her religion, and left Poland. Her lengthy travels brought her to different cultures where she absorbed new concepts and values. In Berlin, she encountered the Enlightenment ideals of reason, progress, and equality that remained guideposts throughout her career. In Paris, she witnessed the Revolution of 1830, which overthrew an attempt to restore divine right monarchy and absolute church power. This strengthened her belief in non-monarchical, republican government and the dangers of religious rule.

In London, where she lived for five years while she was in her twenties, she found the philosophy that illumined her life: the teachings of the radical industrialist Robert Owen. Owen believed in social rather than individual responsibility for evil and crime, attempted to engineer improved societies, supported democratic socialism, and championed women's equality. In his movement she met the man who shared her beliefs and became her devoted and beloved husband. Together, she and William Rose immigrated to the United States of America, which they considered the best society on earth. They lived there from 1836 to 1869.

In the states, William financially and emotionally supported Ernestine's unusual career as an activist and public speaker. (The couple also did not hire a servant in order to free more money for her travels.) She fought ardently for three causes: free thought, anti-slavery, and women's rights. "To enlighten and to free all slaves—that has been the object of Mrs. Rose's life and labors," a female journalist wrote in 1876, "slaves of race, slaves of faith, slaves of sex" and "to each she preached from the same text, 'Knowledge—Liberty.'"[13] Rose consistently maintained that her basic creed was "emancipation" and that freedom from religion, from female subordination, and from any kind of slavery constituted a single great demand for human rights. Her unification of these three causes did not succeed, but she continued to champion them throughout her life. As a successful lecturer and activist, Ernestine Rose argued for and lived out her ideals, both in America and then in England, to which she and William returned in 1869.

In the United States, she became central to the women's movement of the 1850s, serving on important committees, giving keynote speeches at conventions, and advocating equal rights throughout the Northeast and Midwest. She also lectured frequently for abolition. From the late 1840s through the years following the Civil War, she claimed equal rights for all blacks, both female and male, and battled for integration as well as equality. Her labors for free thought, although less well known, were equally impassioned. From her arrival in New York City until her last days in London, she forcefully spoke and wrote about the evils of religion, which she always called "superstition." Living in an era in which many governments ruled by "divine right," she maintained that all religions, including the popular new belief in spiritualism, represented an outgrown stage of human development. Feeding on ignorance, religions perpetuated both oppression and bigotry. The only book she wrote was her 1861 *Defence of Atheism.* Her outspoken endorsements of free thought handicapped her in this period of devout belief. "There can be little doubt that if Mrs. Rose had . . . denied her honest, earnest conventions in regard to theological matters," the journalist wrote, "she would today occupy a far higher position in public favor than she does. Her name . . . would not have been omitted in the list of those 'eminent women' who have distinguished themselves on the lecture platform, in their chivalric crusade against all forms of slavery."[14]

As a "foreigner," which she was often called, Ernestine Rose brought a unique background and perspective to her three related causes. Her overseas travels and views illuminated the transatlantic conversations about women's rights, religion, slavery, and democracy that shaped American growth. In the US women's movement, she contributed her internationalism to its efforts for equal rights, always maintaining that "we are not contending here for the rights of New England, nor of old England, but of the world."[15] Her years in England convinced her that the vote was all-important, while her Owenism taught her that prostitution and unhappy marriages could be eliminated by providing women with decent, well-paying jobs and equitable divorce and child custody laws. The sole female orator for atheism throughout her years in the United States, she provided American free thought—a cause often stigmatized as "infidelism"—with the presence of a respectable, married, female advocate who had connections to Western European non-believers. Believing that the most crucial justification for slavery came from the Bible verses so many southerners cited, most US freethinkers did not support abolitionism. To them, it followed that ending religion had to come before ending slavery. In contrast, Rose insisted that freethinkers must support "Universal Mental Liberty," and so, abolitionism. She became equally active in British free thought after she moved to England, giving her last powerful speeches at the 1878 London Conference of Liberal Thinkers.

In the US anti-slavery movement, she joined with the most committed, again bringing a unique perspective to the cause. Because of her Owenite socialism, she denounced wage slavery and poverty as well as race-based and chattel slavery. She supported not only abolitionism but also integration, complete equality, and if necessary, disunion from the slaveholding southern states. She always held that "a Union of freedom and slavery cannot exist any more than fire and water." After the Civil War, when many pushed for "the black man's vote," she consistently championed equality for black women and democracy for all. "We have proclaimed to the world universal suffrage, but it is universal suffrage with a vengeance attached to it—universal suffrage excluding the negro and the woman, who are by far the largest majority in this country," she declared in 1867. "White men are the minority in this nation. White women, black men, and black women compose the large majority."[16]

The fact that such an assertion is still pertinent today makes Rose seem amazingly contemporary. But in the nineteenth century, her radical views isolated her into becoming "a minority of one," as she often stated. Used to being the only atheist in feminism and anti-slavery and the only woman within the activist free-thought movement, she reacted by always needing to be correct, a defense against the stigmatization and criticism she invariably received. This righteousness easily became self-righteousness, Rose's chief fault. She condescended to those who disagreed with her, like a Wisconsin woman at an 1863 convention who argued—correctly—that a resolution advocating rights for women would diminish support for black emancipation. "It is exceedingly amusing to hear persons talk about throwing out Woman's Rights, when, if it had not been for Woman's Rights, that lady would not have had the courage to stand here and say what she did," Rose replied. "It will be exceedingly inconsistent if, because some women out in the West are opposed to the Women's Rights movement—though at the same time they take advantage of it—that therefore we shall throw it out of this resolution." At a Boston anti-slavery convention the previous year, Rose harshly denounced Abraham Lincoln as "dishonest," which caused her abolitionist audience to hiss her. She responded by saying that the hissing was a sign that "I have said the best thing in the Convention" and proof she was correct. When she left on a trip to Europe in 1856, she justified her sense of superiority by writing, "If, in expressing my opinions, I have been severe alike on friend and foe, it is because in principle I know no compromise, I expect no reward, I fear no opposition—but with an earnest desire my aim has been steadily directed onward and upward."[17]

And yet, self-righteousness aside, how refreshing she remains! She had an excellent sense of humor, which she often turned against herself. When an evangelical anti-slavery colleague said she hoped to meet her in heaven, Rose answered, "Then you will say to me, 'I told you so,' and I shall reply, 'How very stupid I was!' " She ridiculed an English member of Parliament who declared he could not support women's voting because he needed his wife to provide "the perfect, soothing, gentle peace which a mind sullied by politics cannot feel" by jesting that "his happiness must be balanced on the very verge of a precipice, when the simple act of depositing a vote by the hand of a woman, would overthrow and destroy it forever." Sarcastically rebutting a clergyman who insisted that women should remain in the domestic sphere, providing "ornamentation," she wrote, "New Jersey is said to be out of the world; but where, Oh! Where has Dr. J. T. resided? For if he had ever lived within sound, sight, or smell of a human habitation, he would have found out before 1869 that . . . poor woman like poor man has always been 'doomed to labor,' only she has not yet been doomed to be paid for it as well as he."[18]

Ernestine Rose wrote very little that was personal. In addition to her speeches and letters, three lengthy articles written by nineteenth-century journalists who interviewed her provide the most information about her. The first was Lemuel E. Barnard's "Ernestine L. Rose." He met Rose in 1855

in his home city of Cleveland and published his portrait of her the following year. His piece was widely disseminated by being reprinted in volume I
of Elizabeth Cady Stanton's, Susan B. Anthony's, and Matilda Joslyn Gage's
History of Woman Suffrage in 1881. The second article was French feminist Jenny P. d'Héricourt's "Madame Rose," published in September 1856.
D'Héricourt met Rose in Paris during her travels in Europe that year. I wrote
about d'Héricourt and Rose in my previous book, *Joyous Greetings: The First
International Women's Movement, 1830–1860*. Ernestine Rose played a major
role in this movement and what I learned convinced me that I had to find out
more about this fascinating woman. The third contemporary interview was
done in 1868 by the writer Sara Underwood in New York City. She later published a chapter on Rose in her 1876 anthology *Heroines of Free Thought*, placing Rose in a cluster of eleven French and English women, among them Mary
Wollstonecraft, George Sand, and George Eliot.[19] The other major sources for
Rose's life are the two atheist newspapers she avidly read, which printed both
her letters and articles about her: the *Boston Investigator*, published weekly
from 1831 to 1895 in eight four-columned pages crowded with tiny print, and
the equally jam-packed pages of its English counterpart, the weekly *National
Reformer*, in print from 1860 to 1893. Here, in *The Rabbi's Atheist Daughter*, I
have included every scrap of personal history about her I have found.

I

Self-Creation

THE BABY GIRL who grew up to become Ernestine Rose was born into three oppressive situations. First, she belonged, as she said later, to "the down-trodden and persecuted people called the Jews, 'a child of Israel.'" Second, she was also "a daughter of poor, crushed Poland," the nation that had been so "partitioned" among Austria, Prussia, and Russia before she was born that it ceased to exist as a separate state. Finally, both Polish and Jewish cultures devalued women, considering them to be less important than men and, ideally, subordinated to them. And yet this remarkable young person found the strength to rebel against these adverse circumstances. In part, her singular ability to reject oppression stemmed from some advantages in her upbringing. But it also came from the core of her personality—her unusual ability to re-create herself in opposition to conditions she deplored.[1]

As Jews, she and her family were part of a permanent sub-group within Christian Europe, which continuously treated them as separate and unequal beings. Virtually all Jews were Orthodox then, and since her father was also a rabbi, life within her household would have been especially observant of Jewish law and practice. The food her family ate, the clothes they wore, the language they spoke, the sabbath they honored, as well as all the prayers, rituals, and holidays they celebrated differed from those of the Polish Catholic community that surrounded them. When this family's only child was born on January 13, 1810, her being female rendered her mother ritually impure for twice as long as a newborn son. If her parents gave her Hebrew first names, they have been lost, as have the given names of both her father and mother. Polish history since 1800 has been so turbulent that many records no longer exist.[2] Rose consistently told her biographers that she had been named "Ernestine Louise Susmond Potowsky."[3] (Since she changed her last name when she married, I refer to her as "Rose" after 1836, and "Potowska" before.)

"Ernestyna" is a Polish name and she seems to have been called this during her early teenage years. "Louise" was a popular German name in this period, used to honor Queen Louise of Prussia, who shortly before Ernestine's birth had pleaded for her nation with its conqueror, Napoleon. "Susmond," a Germanic surname, may have been Ernestine's mother's maiden name. In the United States, Polish names are ungendered and always used in the masculine form, like "Potowsky" or "Potowski." But in Poland, last names are gendered and Ernestine and her mother would have been called "Potowska." As a married woman, Ernestine Rose completely dropped her maiden last names and used the middle initial "L." for Louise.

Rose never revealed much about her private life, but she did consistently relate a few anecdotes about her childhood. The earliest took place when she was five. Her parents sent her to a local school, most likely a Jewish *heder*. There ten to forty students in a class, with girls and boys routinely mingled together in the early grades, would have learned rudimentary Hebrew from a male teacher. These schools taught by rote learning and practiced harsh discipline. Ernestine's first rebellion occurred there.[4] She refused to return to class because she had been punished for doing something no one told her was wrong. With this act, she demonstrated the sense of justice that became so important a part of her character. "I was a rebel at the age of five," she later proudly declared about this incident, adding that "submission to wrong was wrong in itself and opposition to wrong was right in itself." Her father then allowed her to study at home with him.[5]

Like many feminists, Rose barely mentioned her mother in her public accounts of her childhood. In contrast, her father loomed large. One of the chief rabbis of the city, he "was respected for his knowledge, his virtue, and a bit for his wealth," she later asserted. As a rabbi, he functioned as a religious teacher authorized to make decisions on issues of Jewish law. Custom held that girls would learn to read Yiddish, a Judeo-German language written in Hebrew characters, with perhaps a short time at school to master phonetic Hebrew so they could understand Bible verses, prayers, and blessings. Boys, on the other hand, studied Hebrew intensively so that they could read and study Torah—the first five books of the Bible. Tradition forbade such study for girls, since it held that their limited mental capacity would only "pervert" the texts' meaning. This difference divided Jewish men and women into two unequal groups. "There was a clear hierarchy, and the male sphere was higher and more prestigious," writes a Jewish historian. "Women were prevented from entering the men's arena by being deprived of formal traditional Jewish education; men had no temptation to go into the women's sphere because it was culturally degraded. . . . Knowing Hebrew was essential to maleness; allowing females to know it would let them have access to maleness and threaten male identity and the gender hierarchy."[6]

But Rabbi Potowsky treated his only child like a surrogate son, teaching Ernestine Hebrew in depth and having her intensively study Torah. When Ernestine interrogated her reading and asked questions, as Jewish boys were supposed to do, her father declared that "little girls must not ask questions." This "made her at an early day an advocate of religious freedom and woman's rights," she later told an interviewer, "as she could not see, on the one hand, why subjects of vital interest should be held too sacred for investigation, nor, on the other, why a 'little girl' should not have the same right to ask questions as a little boy."[7] She must also have been aware of the traditional Jewish morning prayer, in which a woman thanks God for having made her according to his will, while a man thanks God for "not having made me a woman." As an adult, Ernestine Rose condemned other gender disparities in her upbringing, like limited education. Without equal opportunities to study, women's minds become "cramped and stifled" because they cannot "expand under bolts and bars." "And yet," she added, "amid all blighting, crushing circumstances— confined within the narrowest possible limits, trampled upon by prejudice and injustice, from her education and position forced to occupy herself almost exclusively with the most trivial affairs—in spite of all these difficulties, her intellect is as good as his." She also deplored preventing girls from exercising because it was not "fashionable" or "feminine." "The boy may run, the girl must creep," she added, blaming such restrictions for her "feeble health" as an adult. She also criticized having her ears pierced, calling it a "barbarous, irrational practice" that caused her "pain and suffering" from infection "for months."[8]

The bulk of her reminiscences, however, focused on religious battles with her rabbi father. He fasted twice a week, a stringent practice that left him weak and dispirited. When Ernestine asked why he did this, Rabbi Potowsky answered, "Because God wants it." "If God wants to make you ill and punish you," she replied, "it is not good, and since it's not good, I don't like it!" Her questioning expanded to include almost all the Bible verses she studied.

"It is necessary to believe, because God has spoken," her father said.

"But what proves that it is God?" . . .

"Tradition proves it, my daughter."

"But father, isn't what you call tradition what you have seen and heard from men? Are we supposed to believe in what we can't see and hear, especially when we can't understand it?"

"Shocked and alarmed, her father ended the discussion," Rose reported, "telling her that a young girl did not need to understand, nor reason about her faith, but only to believe and obey."[9]

Ernestine's doubts increased. As a young girl she challenged her religion's strict insistence that no work be done on the Sabbath by combing her hair then. Her father severely criticized her for doing this: under current practice hair could be combed just to smooth it—if any strands came out, it was considered work and so, condemned. At twelve, Ernestine decided to test God's approval of such strictures. Her community mandated keeping the Sabbath holy, even "to the breaking of a piece of straw." Taking a stalk in her hands one Saturday, she told God she did not want to disobey him—"I would rather die"—but she could not believe that this rule came from him. If it did, would he send her a sign? When nothing happened, she broke the straw and "with the same act broke with the God of Moses and began her break with any personal God."[10]

With this defiance, she also broke with her father, whom she said she "worshipped" and had "made into her God." Because of her "remarkable affection" for him and her "great delight in his company," she seems to have gone through the motions of practicing traditional Judaism for another two years. But when she turned fourteen, "she renounced her belief in the Bible and the religion of her father, which brought down upon her great trouble and persecution alike from her Jewish friends and from Christians." As late as 1960, elderly residents of her city insisted that she had been called "Ernestyna Heretyczka"—"Ernestine the Heretic." For her own part, Ernestine Rose commented in 1852 that

> she was the same as every other human being born into a sect. She had cut herself loose from it, and she knew what it cost her, and having bought that little freedom, for what was dearer to her than life itself, she prized it too highly to ever put herself in the same shackles again. . . . The moment a man has an intellectual life enough to strike out [on] a new idea, he is branded as a heretic. [11]

For the rest of her life Ernestine Rose rejected any religious belief and identified as an atheist. For her, it was all or nothing. She went from being an observant Orthodox Jew to repudiating every precept she had been taught. Later, she argued that this break characterized all Jews who questioned their religion. "The Christian can change, and change, and change again, and still remain a Christian," she wrote, referring to those people who rotated between different Catholic and Protestant denominations. But "the Jew can only make one change. There is but one step between his religion and Atheism. . . . [I]f the Jew takes one step in advance, he is out of darkness into the broad light of day." This assertion probably reflected the absence of any modernization or "Reform" option within Polish Judaism, which remained a bastion of traditional orthodoxy in this period.[12]

Ernestine's loss of faith led to a painful struggle with her father, who "tormented" his daughter, both because of "the tenderness which he had for her and his interest in her salvation. The battle between these two beings who cherished each other was as unproductive as it was long and cruel." Ernestine's defection from Judaism coincided with her puberty. Her community expected all to marry, ideally the girls at sixteen and the boys at eighteen. Parents normally arranged their children's unions, since it was assumed that teenagers could not choose wisely for themselves. Rose told her interviewers that her father betrothed her to a man of his own choosing when she was fifteen and a half, to bring her back "to the bosom of the synagogue." Her mother had recently died and left Ernestine a large inheritance. The engagement contract mandated that if Ernestine did not go through with the marriage, her fiancé would keep most of her legacy.[13]

"Jewish daughters were not bold enough to wrench free from the restraint of unbending customs that in reality enslaved them," wrote a Polish Jewish feminist two generations younger than Ernestine. "A girl did not even have the audacity to oppose the match that her father made for her." But Ernestine Potowska did. This engagement roused her sense of injustice. Believing that marriage should be between two equals and that she could not "marry a master without finer feelings whom she did not love," she begged her fiancé to release her, weeping and throwing herself at his feet. She told him that she did not and could not love him. He replied that since she was both beautiful and rich, he would not break the engagement, reminding her that if she did not go through with it, he would keep a large portion of her inheritance. He then brought a suit to possess her property at a district court in the city of Kalisz. Ernestine decided to go to this court to plead her own case.[14]

Where did she find the backbone to take such an unprecedented step? Part of her strength came from her previous experience of defying her father's paternal and rabbinic authority. Part came from her own bravery. But part also came from the heritage of the city where she grew up, Piótrkow Trybunalski, the site of the Polish Royal Tribunal—its Supreme Court—from the late sixteenth to the late eighteenth centuries. This name is never abbreviated and the city prides itself on being "the cradle of Polish democracy and parliamentarianism." Ernestine Rose believed deeply in justice and the power of law throughout her entire life. Some of this conviction came from her Polish home city.

There Ernestine experienced both hope for reform and discrimination. Conditions for Jews in Poland during her years in Piótrkow Trybunalski worsened, but bore little resemblence to the extreme antisemitism that drove so many to the United States in the late nineteenth and early twentieth centuries. Jews had flocked to Poland in earlier times because they considered it a haven from persecution; by 1800 the largest Jewish community in the world lived there, primarily in cities and towns. The restricted ghetto of the Polish shtetl belongs to a later era. When Ernestine was born, Jews constituted almost 50 percent of her city's population of 4,000 and had many interactions with their Christian neighbors.[15]

Like the rest of Poland, Piótrkow Trybunalski suffered the dismemberment of the nation. In 1793, the city came under Prussian rule, which made little difference to its inhabitants. For the next twenty-odd years, the entire European continent experienced the ideological wars of the French Revolution and the Napoleonic Era. These struggles particularly affected Eastern Europe's Jewish communities as they learned of French reforms. Revolutionary France had overthrown its ancien régime of separate, unequal, medieval "estates" in favor of a modern nation-state peopled by citizens with equal rights. The new system embodied the ideals of Enlightenment philosophy, which questioned traditional arrangements and assumed that progressive change was both possible and desirable. Why should kings have absolute power? Why should there be a state-supported church? Was religion the only true way of understanding the world, or should science and reason replace it? If so, why should peasants and Jews remain under legal and religious liabilities? Shouldn't they be liberated from oppression, or, in the terminology of the day, "emancipated"? Throughout her life, Ernestine Rose remained a child of the Enlightenment, believing in its ideals and philosophy, first encountered in her youth. "I remember I was but a little child, hardly able to understand the import of words, that I had already listened to them who pronounced it the Republic of the United States of America," she recalled in midlife, "and even then, though unable to appreciate the import, the nobility of it, yet somehow or other it touched a vibrating chord in my heart, and I thought, if I live to grow up a woman, O how I should like to see *a Republic*!"—that is, a government without a monarch. Those who interviewed her during her lifetime asserted that the concept of "emancipation" underlay Rose's lifelong beliefs.[16]

In 1791, France emancipated its Jews by abolishing all laws that made them separate and unequal. In 1807, it briefly applied this to all of Poland. However, Piótrkow Trybunalski's Jewish population, despite free interactions with Christians, still suffered from antisemitism. A large painting depicting a "blood libel"—Jews supposedly murdering a Christian child to use its blood in a religious ritual—hung on the outer wall of one of the city's main churches. In 1815, at the Congress of Vienna concluding the wars, Poland was given to the czar of Russia as his personal kingdom. From then on, conditions worsened for Polish Jews. In 1822, when Ernestine was twelve, Piótrkow Trybunalski ordered that its Jews be expelled—a standard gambit that could be overturned by paying a fine. Three years later, a large fire devastated the Jewish section of the city. Ernestine Rose later denounced "Russian tyranny in her own country, Poland," recalling that the government seized some land belonging to her family "without a farthing of compensation!" But the situation of Jews in Piótrkow Trybunalski remained relatively favorable. "The history of Piótrkow Trybunalski consists in the perpetual struggle of the Christians and Jews," a Polish historian wrote in 1850. "In spite of numerous restrictions they managed to squeeze into the town. The more severe the authorities were, the more resourceful they were. Now they triumph: they constitute half of the population."[17]

In this period, Jews often used Polish courts, as Ernestine decided to do. She could not have successfully presented her case to a rabbinic council, which naturally would have sided with her father and fiancé. By going to a Polish law court, she joined a number of other Jewish women who appeared there as both plaintiffs and defendants. Showing remarkable initiative, Ernestine hired a sleigh and driver to take her the sixty-five miles from Piótrkow Trybunalski to the district capital of Kalisz. She had just turned seventeen and the weather that winter was extremely harsh. In the course of the trip, the sleigh broke down. The driver wanted to wait until the following morning to fix it, but Ernestine persuaded him to go for help that night, since her case began the next day. He left and she waited alone, "wrapped in furs . . . from 11:30 at night until 4 in the morning on an immense plain of snow, listening to the howls of packs of starving wolves."

Arriving at the court in time, Ernestine presented her case personally, as lawyers were rarely used in these proceedings. She successfully argued that she should retrieve her inheritance "by proving to the judges that she should not lose her property because of an engagement she did not want."[18] The court records for this case have been lost, as have so many other Polish documents.[19] Yet Rose's account rings true, in tune with her other actions, values, and beliefs. This triumph became the foundation story of her self-created adult identity as an advocate for personal independence and women's equal rights. Throughout her life, she referred back to her impressive victory as proof of what women could accomplish. "I have known a case in a foreign land under despotic rule, pleaded by a woman," she told a Cleveland Woman's Rights Convention in 1853;

> this was the case of a girl hardly seventeen, who had to go to law to rescue her property staked on such a [marriage] contract, which she could not and would not fulfill; and against all the laws of the land, she gained that cause. How came she to get it? Because she pleaded it, and called down the Justice of Heaven against the laws.

"Laws" in this instance almost certainly refers to the Jewish laws of the Bible as well as secular law. But "the Justice of Heaven" seems an odd phrase for a committed atheist to use. Rose revered justice all her life, with a passion she almost certainly first absorbed in Piótrkow Trybunalski. "I have faith, unbounded, unshaken faith in the principles of right, justice, and humanity," she declared in 1861. She probably invoked heaven to give greater weight to her argument before her Christian women's rights audience. Rose also maintained that "above all things" women "want to be able to plead our own cause before the courts of justice; we want to be in the jury-box, to judge our own sisters; we want to be in the judge's chair." If her health were better, she argued in midlife, "I should study law—not to make the 'worse a better cause,' but for the purpose of maintaining justice—justice to man as well as to woman."[20]

Back in the winter of 1827, however, Ernestine faced a difficult new situation after her courtroom triumph. She had stayed in Kalisz "somewhat longer than she expected and on her return found that her father had solaced himself in his loneliness during her absence by taking to himself a wife, a young girl" the same age as Ernestine. She later said only that she "could not harmonize" with her new stepmother, but this brief phrase almost certainly contained a welter of difficult emotions: shock, anger, jealousy, and sorrow. Not wanting "to force her father to take the side of one or the other in the disputes and conflicts that she foresaw," Ernestine decided to leave home. Her father's house had "become distasteful and unpleasant to her," she explained. "She longed also for a wider field of action. She had youth, good health, and an abundance of energetic daring. She determined to seek her fortune in the great world." Leaving much of her inheritance with her father and taking only enough to support herself "honorably," she left her birth family, the Jewish community, and her native land. Continuing her process of self-determination, she decided to go to the capital of the Kingdom of Prussia, Berlin.[21]

She deliberately chose Berlin, nearly 300 miles from Piótrkow Trybunalski, when she could have opted for Warsaw, only ninety miles away. The capital of Poland, Warsaw had 150,000 inhabitants, a sizable Jewish community, and enough culture and charm to be called "The Paris of the East." Two import-ant factors shaped her decision. First, Poland remained a conquered nation, under the "iron yoke" of Russian "despotism," as Rose later wrote. Referring throughout her life to "my own poor native land," Rose countered a charge that she had "fled" from there. "It is true I came from Poland," she wrote in 1854, "but it is false that I was compelled to fly from my country, except by the compulsion or dictates of the same spirit . . . that induced so many of my noble countrymen. . . . I left my country, not flying, but deliberately." In leav-ing Poland, Ernestine Potowska briefly preceded such famous political exiles as the musician Frederick Chopin and the poet Adam Mickiewicz.[22]

Her second chief reason for not going to Warsaw may have been the nature of its Jewish community, which by the late 1820s had embraced Hasidism, a deeply religious movement that prized ecstatic faith, charismatic leaders, and mystical spirituality. Like many other eastern European Jews who wanted a more secular or modern milieu, Potowska headed west to Berlin. The Berlin Jewish community had become known for its universalist Enlightenment val-ues. It prized secular education, and many of its members discarded Jewish traditions, from speaking Yiddish to dressing distinctively to keeping kosher. Berlin Jews were no longer confined to a ghetto but mixed socially with Christians and lived among them in the old city center. Much of this "Jewish Enlightenment" originated with "the Berlin Socrates," the philosopher Moses Mendelssohn, who championed a "rational" or reformed version of Judaism, urged Jews to join German society, and initiated a radically new form of social life by mingling Jews and Christians at his Open Houses. Traditional Jews warned their children not to marry "Berliners" or "heretics" (*apikorsim*) — the two terms had become almost synonymous. Ernestine Rose, on the other hand, later praised Mendelssohn as a "liberal, intelligent, and well-behaved" example of how Jews had successfully modernized. Berlin Jewry provided her with the community in Europe whose beliefs were most congenial to her own.[23]

Deciding to go to Berlin was one thing; getting there was far more diffi-cult. In this pre-railroad era, the wealthy rode in their own carriages while the poor walked along the highways. For a middle-class traveler like Potowska, postal coaches provided the only option, but these "boneshakers," which crammed six to eight passengers into their dark, stuffy interiors, were known for their lack of comfort and speed. Most of the roads on this almost 300-mile journey were unpaved and dirty, filled with potholes and ruts, and coaches moved at only three miles per hour.[24]

Potowska also faced the special perils of traveling as a young woman alone. When the German philosopher Wilhelm von Humboldt sent his daughters to Rome at that time, he insisted they wear male clothing so that they would not be sexually molested. A German guidebook of 1811, which presumed all travelers to be male, advised passengers to carry their own pistol, lock, and bedding with them, to guard against their fellow voyagers, predatory inn-keepers, and vermin. Female Jewish merchants rarely went on business trips because of these dangers, leaving journeys to their male relatives. But travel by single young women was not unheard of in these years. Potowska almost certainly knew Gotthold von Lessing's extremely popular play of 1767, *Minna von Barnhelm*, in which the spunky, independent heroine successfully goes alone to Berlin to find her missing fiancé. In addition to this fictional exam-ple, respectable women traveling alone appear in memoirs as well. In 1820, the English economist Thomas Hodgskin reported that in small German inns, a number of beds would be placed in the same room. "On more than one occa-sion," he wrote, "I have seen decent female travellers sleep in the same room with gentlemen and from their never remarking that the practice was curious or offensive, it may be inferred that it is general."[25]

The word "decent" was key. Most governments tried to keep prostitutes out of their districts. Potowska never mentioned that this was an issue for her. As a young woman traveling by herself, she would have had to master the appropriate demeanor both to repel advances and appear respectable. Travel documents presented more of a problem. An 1817 law gave Prussian border guards the authority to issue entry documents. Those riding in postal coaches and non-citizen Jews needed passports to travel within the Kingdom of Prussia. Potowska reported no difficulty in either crossing the border or traveling through Prussia.[26] Settling in Berlin, however, proved far more chal-lenging, and Rose spent quite a bit of time telling her interviewers how she achieved this.

Fearing an influx of Eastern European Jewish peddlers and merchants, Prussian cities forbade "Israelites" to remain there for more than three days. To stay longer, Jews had to have a German citizen post three monetary bonds for them or obtain royal permission to stay. Ernestine Potowska refused to have bonds posted for her. "Either I am or am not capable of doing evil," she told a Berlin police chief. "If I am, the punishment should fall on my head and not that of anyone else; if not, I do not need bonds." The police magistrate sent her to a government minister, who "could not break the law on her behalf." The minister directed her to see the king, Friedrich Wilhelm III.[27]

Rose then recounted her interview with the Prussian monarch. "Convinced that the law was absurd and thinking that the best way to solve the problem was for the young girl to be baptized, he graciously offered to be her godfather," he said. Although records documenting this meeting have been lost, Friedrich Wilhelm's suggestion squares with his practice and beliefs during these years. An affable and friendly ruler, he held brief meetings with petitioners. His youngest daughter was only two years older than Ernestine and perhaps this explains his paternal approach to the seventeen-year-old traveler. In this period, Friedrich Wilhelm III attempted to convert Jews to Christianity. In addition to founding a Berlin branch of the London Society for Promoting Christianity among the Jews a few years earlier, he often served as godfather at Jewish baptisms, presenting the new converts with gifts.[28]

Rose replied to his suggestion that she convert by saying, "I thank you, Your Majesty, but I have not abandoned the trunk in order to attach myself to the branches: if my reason prevents me from being Jewish, it cannot permit me to be Christian." The perfect aptness of this remark smacks of "*l'esprit d'escalier,*" the brilliant remark thought of when going down the staircase after an event is over. But this quick-witted rabbi's daughter had been well-trained in intellectual repartee and indeed may have actually said this. The king then gave her permission to reside in Berlin as long as she wished.[29]

Ernestine Potowska lived in Berlin for the next two years, from 1827 to 1829. She revealed less about this stay than she did about her interview with the king, reflecting an inexplicable lifelong reluctance to write about Germany and the Germans. When she returned to Europe in 1856, she remained in Berlin for six weeks and barely mentioned it.[30] But her early years in this vibrant, growing metropolis proved important for her intellectual development.

The first national capital Potowska ever experienced, Berlin contained 220,000 inhabitants of whom about 5,000 were Jews. She lived "alone, in a modest, little room," supporting herself on "the money she had brought with her." She most likely rented a chamber in one of the numerous three- to four-story apartment buildings that thronged Berlin's side streets. Each housed several families, jumbling Jews together with Christians. She probably lived on one of the cheaper upper stories; more well-off families resided on the first or second floors. Like all large cities, Berlin contained extremes of poverty and wealth, encompassing both "miserable alleys" and "ramshackle houses" as well as "beautiful, wide streets" in the prosperous areas. Its fine monuments—the palace, the university, the library, the opera house, the tree-lined boulevard known as Unter den Linden—clustered in the city's center. Unlike Piótrkow Trybunalski, Berlin displayed the trappings of modernity: the beginnings of industry and manufacturing, numerous shops, and the first gas streetlamps east of Paris.[31]

In Berlin, Ernestine Potowska mastered German. She had to have spoken some German to be able to converse with the king, but during this period she became expert enough to teach the language a few years later. While spoken German is easy for Yiddish speakers to understand, Potowska also learned to read it. During her time in Berlin, she studied "not dead books, but living ones, with great curiosity." "Dead books" referred to the Bible she had pored over at home. Reading "living books," presumably in German, connected her to the Berlin Jewish community, for whom learning through the written word became a passion. Lending libraries, book groups, and reading rooms proliferated in these years, making access to expensive volumes possible. All this constituted the modern "reading revolution." Previously, readers had been like Potowska in Poland, working "laboriously through . . . the Bible, over and over again." Now they read all kinds of literature, for education and amusement as well as religious reasons. Reading became secularized and more critical.[32]

In Berlin, Potowska "began to question" social arrangements "just as she had questioned Bible verses as a child." In the process, she built her intellectual foundation, based on Enlightenment principles. "The only answer she came up with" as to why "vices of all sorts" and "public and private miseries" existed "was that all evil comes from two causes: ignorance supported by revelation and inequality supported by egoism and ignorance." These precepts consti-tute core axioms of Enlightenment thought, which condemned revealed reli-gion as superstition and held that progressive education and reform could eliminate social ills and unhappiness. Potowska absorbed these values during her years in Berlin, where Enlightenment ideals became especially important to the Jewish community, since they supported its equality and emancipation from ancient restrictions. She continued to believe in reason, progress, critical thinking, and secularism throughout her life. "Emancipation from every kind of bondage is my principle," she frequently declared; "I go for the recognition of human rights, without distinction of sect, party, sex, or color."[33]

In addition to forging her basic philosophy in Berlin, Potowska found a new way to support herself. She created "a paper to perfume apartments." Residents kept windows and doors closed all winter for warmth and needed to dispel the resulting unpleasant odors. The young entrepreneur sold her room deodorizer throughout the next decade: an 1838 piece in a New York newspaper advertised that she manufactured and merchandised "Cologne and other German waters" to bring pleasant scents to lodgings. This product afforded her, a young, single woman, a decent and inventive way to make a living. After describing this product, Potowska abruptly concludes her German reminiscences, saying only that since "she had nothing more to learn in Berlin," she decided to leave.[34]

Almost certainly she went next to Paris. At this point, her various interviews, given decades after the fact, become confusing. One says that she first sailed to England, got shipwrecked, and then returned to Paris during the Revolution of July 1830 because "she believed that something could be done in France for the emancipation of women." But the July Revolution lasted only three days and raised no issues about women, so this account seems unlikely. A second interview declares that she went to The Hague, where she met with the King of Holland and convinced him to undo a woman's imprisonment. Unsupported by any documents, which tend to exist in the Netherlands, this anecdote also seems improbable. The third account does not mention her going to France at all. But in 1856, when Ernestine Rose visited Paris again, she wrote that "I have been fifteen months in Paris before" and gave details of her experiences there during the Revolution of 1830. She probably traveled directly from Berlin to Paris sometime in 1829.[35]

Potowska's trip to Paris, far longer than that from Piótrkow Trybunalski to Berlin, would have been much easier because better roads and superior coaches existed between Germany and France. More than twice as large as Berlin, Paris had almost 600,000 inhabitants then. Its Jewish community, smaller than that of the Prussian city, was growing and rapidly becoming less traditional. The capital of the most developed nation on the continent of Europe, Paris remained vital to Western culture, art, diplomacy, and politics. Its city center included the Palais Royal, the Place du Carrousel, where dissidents had been guillotined during the 1789 Revolution, and the immense, prestigious Louvre Museum. "The Louvre, if not the most beautiful building in the world, is certainly one of the most beautiful in that small portion of it that I have had the pleasure to see," Rose wrote on her 1856 European tour, adding that "the material of Paris, beautiful as it is" does not "so much interest me as the social, the moral, the progressive Paris."[36]

In her letters on Paris, Rose rhapsodized about the French. "I thought perhaps I was too young then to judge of such matters," she wrote, recalling her earlier stay there, "but I found my ideas of the people were correct." . . .

They combine the finest elements in human nature. The Frenchman is
frivolous on trifles, but he is the philosopher on any subject of importance. The mass of the people work hard and live still harder, but they
have the arts, the sciences, the beautiful, the elevating. No country so
abounds in these elements, and no people on earth enjoy them as much
as the French. . . . In the theatres, gardens, walks, museums, concerts,
balls, they mix together, treat each other with becoming respect and
fraternal civility.

A great deal of Rose's affection for the French and Paris stemmed from her
belief that the city embodied progressive ideals: "To me it speaks the language
of universal brotherhood; it seems the capital of the world, the representative
of mankind; its inmost heart vibrates for all times, nations, and grades. . . .
[E]veryone finds his own element, and a sympathizing c[h]ord, which runs
through whole humanity." Her emotional tone came in part from having
witnessed the revolution that prevented the return of absolute monarchy to
France.[37]

After the final defeat of Napoleon in 1815, the victorious European monarchs, including the Russian czar, restored the Bourbon dynasty overthrown
by the French Revolution. The king regained almost complete power—a
legislature existed but was severely weakened. The white royal flag, with its
gold *fleurs-de-lis*, replaced the revolutionary blue, white, and red *tricolore*.
When the ultra-conservative Charles X ascended the throne in 1824, he
tried to restore both the supreme power of the Catholic Church and absolute monarchy based on divine right. Mandating the death penalty for various
acts of sacrilege, he began ruling by decree in early July 1830, dissolving the
legislature and suspending freedom of the press. These acts sparked "*les trois
Glorieuses*," the three "glorious" days of revolution witnessed by the twenty-
year-old Ernestine Potowska. Street fighting erupted in the center of the city,
as Parisians erected barricades, raised the revolutionary banner, and sacked
various royal buildings. "The Louvre was attacked by the people . . . and
defended at the time by the Swiss Guards," Rose recalled. "I remember to have
seen that whole building, after that revolution, without one pane of glass in
it." Its collection remained undamaged, however.[38]

As the royal army began to retreat and desert, the king and his son
abdicated. Power shifted to the city of Paris, and the seventy-two-year-old
Marquis de Lafayette took charge. A hero of both the American and French
revolutions, Lafayette had gone into exile during Napoleon's rule. In 1830,
he was invited to become dictator but instead brokered a transfer of power

to the king's more liberal cousin, Louis Philippe d'Orléans. The two men appeared on the balcony of the Hôtel de Ville in front of an immense crowd that included Potowska. They embraced while each held up a large *tricolore*. Lafayette called Orléans "the best of republicans" and Orléans promised to support "a popular throne surrounded by republican institutions." The crowd responded with cheers of "Long live the Republic!" and "Long live Lafayette!" "In 1830 I saw Gen. Lafayette present Louis Philippe from . . . one of the central windows of the Hôtel de Ville," Rose remembered, telling an interviewer that at the time she remarked to a friend that Louis Philippe, "as well as Charles X, will one day have good reason to wish himself safely off the throne of France." Louis Philippe was overthrown during the Revolution of 1848. A few years later, Ernestine Rose wrote that "nations learn but very slowly, and the French" have "paid very dearly for allowing themselves to be deceived after 1830 by the recommendation of Lafayette."[39] She always preferred republics over monarchies, however much they limited royal power or how liberal they appeared.

The French Revolution of July 1830 sparked the November Uprising in Poland, in part because the Russians planned to use the Polish army to try to overthrow the new French government. As Poles battled the Russian Empire, Ernestine Potowska decided to return to her native land to take part in the insurrection. A number of Polish women fought then; the most famous was Countess Emilia Plater, who organized a partisan unit of close to a thousand troops. She cut her hair short, wore a man's uniform, and led her soldiers to a short-lived victory. Potowska herself did not succeed in reaching the battlefield. Traveling over 250 miles eastward to the German city of Koblenz, she was halted by Austrian troops supporting the conservative opposition to the Polish rebellion. If "she did not want to perish in an Austrian blockhouse," she later declared, she had to turn back.[40]

She did not return to France. She visited there many more times, but despite her love of the French, she never lived there again—and never explained why. Instead, she promised the Austrian authorities that she would go to London.

No matter where she lived, however, she remained a Polish exile for the rest of her life. In 1850, when she had been in the United States for fourteen years, she still referred to Poland as "my poor unhappy country, which has been prostrated, but I hope not lost." Whether known as Ernestyna Potowska or Ernestine Rose, she continued to yearn for a successful Polish rebellion that did not come, although failed uprisings occurred again in 1848 and 1863. She never returned to Poland, either on her 1856 trip to Europe or on later visits to the continent, probably because of her discouragement over Poland's continuing bondage to Russia. But she had escaped the disadvantage of having been born in "poor, crushed Poland."[41]

Through her own efforts to challenge and defy existing conditions, she also freed herself from religion. As a committed atheist, she incurred far more prejudice than she did as a Jew, but she never regretted leaving "superstition" behind. In addition, she spent her life combating the injustice of women's subordination and lack of equal rights. Unwilling to acquiesce to oppression and discrimination, she truly re-created herself from the person society intended her to be. Ernestine Potowska then made her next home in London, where she lived for five years. There "she found friends . . . who were as radical and liberty-loving as herself," many of whom worked for women's equality. She discovered a congenial belief system, taught by Robert Owen, who became her new, surrogate father/educator. And she met the man for whom she changed her name, her beloved and devoted husband, William Rose.[42]

2

The New Moral World

IN 1831 THE intrepid twenty-one-year-old Ernestine Potowska sailed alone to England to continue "her studies on men and laws."[1] As she traveled westward, she not only stayed in increasingly larger cities, from Berlin to Paris to London, but she also experienced increasingly liberal societies. Political life in Eastern and Central Europe remained frozen under absolute regimes, which outlawed political organizing and labor unions, censored speech and the press, and used their armies to crush uprisings and block change throughout the continent. France repelled a renewal of absolute monarchy while she was there, but England had limited its monarchy for over a century. By the time Potowska arrived, British ultraconservatism of the 1820s had thawed. Parliament had legalized trade unions, lowered taxes on newspapers and journals, and "emancipated" Roman Catholics so that they could vote and run for office. All English Jews were citizens, unlike in the rest of Europe except for France. Allowing more men voting rights became the dominant political issue of the day. The possibility of reform, both conceiving of progressive change and making it a reality, was in the air. In London especially, a wide variety of reformers—radical aristocrats, Quaker philanthropists, socialist artisans, working-class democrats, and Unitarian ministers as well as utilitarian philosphers who advocated "the greatest happiness of the greatest number"— explored how to improve society.

Potowska's entry to England would have been easy, since the nation did not require passports then and welcomed political refugees from all over Europe. In moving to London, she became part of a city of immigrants—more than one-third of its inhabitants had not been born there. Irish, German, Italian, French, and Jewish groups created their own neighborhood communities. On her arrival, Potowska joined about 500 other Poles fleeing Russian repression as well as a small but steady stream of Jewish immigrants from Central and Eastern Europe seeking a better life among London's 20,000 Jews. But whether she contacted her fellow immigrants or lived among them remains unknown.[2]

With more than 1,655,000 inhabitants, London was by far the largest city in the Western world, over twice as populous as Paris, more than five times larger than Berlin. "What an enormous city London is!" Potowska's contemporary, the French feminist Flora Tristan, wrote when she visited there, cataloging "the ships of every size and denomination, too numerous to count, which fill every inch of the river, . . . the docks, the huge wharves and warehouses, . . . the monumental chimneys belching their black smoke to the heavens." Great Britain pioneered the Industrial Revolution and led the world in shipping goods, many of them produced in its new factories. Contemporaries acknowledged it as the most advanced commercial nation on the planet. "London is the real capital of the world," a German visitor proclaimed in 1835, "not Paris. . . . Paris is more pre-eminently the Town, Germany the Country, but London alone is entitled to talk of being the World. . . . [T]he *quantity*, which surpasses that of all other cities in Europe, or indeed in the world, is itself in the highest degree remarkable and imposing."[3]

This new economic system increased wealth for a few manufacturers and impoverished many who toiled in their establishments. Ernestine Rose and others continually emphasized London's extreme contrasts between rich and poor. "What can I say on this subject . . . so teeming with glory and degradation, splendor and wretchedness, the highest cultivation and refinement, and the almost barbarian ignorance and rudeness, the immense wealth with all its pride, and the lowest depth of poverty with all its abjectness?" she wrote when she returned in 1856. Shortly after she first arrived in the city twenty-five years earlier, a London correspondent to a US newspaper highlighted these same disparities. A visitor "will see here in England . . . a long street of magnificent palaces . . . coaches-and-four graced with coronets and golden and crimson liveries rolling in lordly state along its centre . . . and the way side crowded with beggars so thick and so importunate, that the pedestrian at times can scarcely tread his way through the heart-sickening maze."[4] When she came to live in London and needed to earn a living, Potowska herself experienced these extremes of wealth and poverty firsthand.

Unable to speak English on her arrival, she carried a dictionary with her. She visited a series of pharmacies to persuade their managers to sell her perfumed room deodorizers on consignment. Although she later became eloquent in English and spoke the language for the rest of her life, she never lost her accent. "I am a foreigner," she declared to an 1869 convention in

New York City when she had lived there for over thirty years; "I had great difficulty in acquiring the English language, and I shall never acquire it." Still, at
twenty-one in London, Potowska parlayed her linguistic skills to supplement
her income. She rapidly mastered enough English to be able to give lessons
in German and Hebrew. These, plus her sales of perfumed paper, allowed her
to live modestly—"from hand to mouth," as she later put it.[5] She and others
deplored the weather in London, especially when comparing it to Paris or
Berlin. "The thick fog which generally prevails is thoroughly impregnated
with water and this, blended with the air, is chilling and penetrating to a
degree, of which we, in Berlin, have no idea," a German visitor complained
in 1835. Increasing use of coal in this period intensified London's "pea-soup"
fogs, further dirtying its buildings and darkening its air. Ernestine Potowska
never detailed her work experiences there, but this account by another female
immigrant twenty years later might have captured some of her daily life:

> What it means, especially when it's rainy and foggy, when you can
> hardly see a step ahead, and you are always surrounded by a thick, yel-
> lowish, damp, fetid atmosphere, through which the sun shines like a
> paper lantern . . . where it is often so dark inside at mid-day that you
> have to light lamps in order to work—what it means on such a day to
> go from one lesson to another, from warm rooms into the damp cold,
> to wait on street corners for the omnibuses, to be packed in wet and
> dripping with other wet and dripping creatures, and often to be satis-
> fied with only a meager lunch hastily taken in a bakery between two
> lessons until late afternoon—you can only know this if you have gone
> through it yourself.[6]

Potowska's language pupils included four daughters of the aristocratic
Grosvenor family. Richard, Earl Grosvenor, later the second Marquess of
Westminster, and his wife, a duke's daughter, possessed tremendous wealth
and belonged to the highest echelons of British nobility. Grosvenor, a liberal
member of Parliament during these years, and his wife had eleven children
when Potowska went to work for them. How she came to be employed by
this family remains unknown, but she would have taught the Ladies Evelyn,
Elizabeth, Mary, and Eleanor, who ranged in age from six to twelve in 1832.
The family planned to tour Germany and Italy a few years later, which might
explain the German lessons. Lord Grosvenor was very religious and may have
wanted his daughters to learn Hebrew so they could read the Hebrew Bible
in its original language.[7]

Potowska's instruction took place in Grosvenor House, one of London's grandest mansions, located in the exclusive Mayfair district near Hyde Park. The contrast between this palatial home and her own "modest existence" could hardly have been greater. Architects and craftsmen renovated Grosvenor House during her time there, adding a new east wing, an extensive carriage drive, and expanded private stables. A newly enlarged picture gallery displayed four Rubens paintings; other old masters hung throughout the building, which also featured a large, ceremonial central staircase and cut-glass gas chandeliers. Despite his wealth, Lord Grosvenor was a liberal interested in reform. Ernestine Potowska may have made her other contacts with London reformers through her connection with this family.[8]

She later told an interviewer that at this time she "became acquainted . . . with many prominent members of the Society of Friends, among them Joseph Gurney and his sister Elizabeth Fry." By then, a number of English Quaker families had become socially accepted and immensely wealthy: The Gurneys dominated banking. Both brother and sister became ministers and embraced philanthropy and improving society. Joseph Gurney supported early childhood education, opened soup kitchens for the poor, and backed his sister's efforts to improve prison life. He participated in political reform circles, concentrating on the abolition of slavery, both in the British Empire (slavery no longer existed in England) and the United States. An extremely religious man, he opposed women's rights because of New Testament pronouncements that women should be subordinated to men. "I do not approve of ladies speaking in public," he declared in 1839, "even in the anti-slavery cause, except under the immediate influence of the Holy Spirit. Then and then only, all is safe."[9]

Elizabeth Fry had to battle such strictures to work outside her home to improve society. "It is only within a short time that the prejudice against women appearing alone in public has begun to pass away," a Dutch feminist wrote almost fifty years later. "How was this change brought about? By women simply doing, while strictly adhering to propriety and decorum, what society had been pleased to call improper." Fry focused on Newgate, the women's prison in London. Before her efforts there, visitors came to gawk at cells crowded with filthy, half-naked, drunken women cursing and begging for pennies. Fry reformed their situation, bringing in clothing, cleaning supplies, food, and water. She organized a prison school, teaching inmates to read, knit, and sew. The goods they made in their new workshop were sold at a prison store; the women received the profits. Treating the prisoners as fellow Christians, Fry mandated twice-daily Bible readings and allowed no gambling, card-playing, quarreling, or "immoral conversations."[10]

Fry's efforts succeeded and inspired others to reform society. "Having heard from various quarters what highly beneficial effects had been produced by Mrs. Fry," the industrialist Robert Owen came to see for himself in 1817:

> In passing from room to room we were met in every instance (there was not one exception) with kind looks and the most evident feelings of affection in every prisoner towards Mrs. Fry. . . . She spoke in manner and voice the language of confidence, kindness, and commiseration to each; and she was replied to in such accordant feelings as are, and ever will be, produced in human beings, whenever they shall be spoken to and treated thus rationally.[11]

Ernestine Potowska visited Newgate with Elizabeth Fry. The older woman's determination to make her own way against social opposition, her passion to improve existing conditions, and her ability to bring about positive change may have inspired Potowska to work for reform herself. But she was repelled by Fry's religiosity. Visiting a Prison Reform Society in New York a few years later, she rejected the group's Bible readings and prayers. Let those who want to "pray and read at home," she later declared, "but the moment we cross the threshold . . . to do something for the relief of the poor convict, from that moment the time is not ours, even to pray, but to work." Instead of taking the ardently Christian Elizabeth Fry as her model, Potowska instead "warmly espoused" the principles of Robert Owen, "which she has faithfully advocated ever since."[12]

By the time Ernestine Potowska met Robert Owen in 1832, he was one of the most famous men in the Western world. His early life constituted a great success story of the Industrial Revolution. Born into a lower-middle-class Welsh family in 1771, he went to work full-time in a clothing store when he was ten years old. By twenty, he successfully managed a spinning mill employing 500 people. At twenty-nine, in 1800, he became head of the largest textile plant in Great Britain, supervising 2,000 workers at the isolated factory town of New Lanark, Scotland.

New Lanark's brutality, typical of British manufacturing establishments then, appalled Owen. His poorly paid labor force included almost 500 pauper apprentices, sent out for employment from age five. Both children and adults worked fourteen-hour days tending fast-moving, repetitive machinery in unhealthy conditions. Foremen routinely beat, whipped, cursed, and fired workers—more could always be found to replace them. Living in squalid houses, having no sanitation or schools, forced to shop at expensive company stores, adult workers retaliated by being "idle, intemperate, dishonest," Owen later wrote. His solution to these problems was both unique and amazingly effective. Reversing his era's truism that poverty resulted from workers' bad behavior, Owen decided that preventing poverty would transform the way workers acted: "I had to change these evil conditions for good ones."[13]

To this end, Owen immediately stopped bringing impoverished orphans to New Lanark and refused to employ any child under ten. He built decent houses to attract new families to the town, upgraded the village shops so they sold quality items at low prices, and made liquor difficult to buy. He erected new mills, replaced old machinery, and continued paying wages during a long trade stoppage in 1806. He introduced an individual monitoring system, which he personally supervised, to replace threats, beatings, and firings. Winning over his labor force, he reaped soaring profits. Thousands visited New Lanark to observe Owen's spectacular success. This factory is "conducted in a manner superior to any other . . . ever witnessed, dispensing more happiness than perhaps any other institution in the kingdom where so many poor persons are employed," the Leeds Guardians of the Poor reported in 1819. "They appear like one regulated family, united by ties of the strongest affection." When Ernestine Rose later paid tribute to Robert Owen, she focused on the importance and effectiveness of his benevolence. He worked "to infuse the benign spirit of charity and kindness into every heart," she declared at a celebration of his eighty-third birthday in 1853, "to teach mankind that the law of kindness is the most effective law in the well training of man; that if we want to have man rational, consistent, virtuous, and happy, we must remove the causes that have a tendency to make him irrational, inconsistent, vicious, and consequently miserable."[14]

Owen concentrated on the children, believing that by providing them with an improved environment, he could reshape their lives for the better. He opened new schools for all village children a year or older and replaced the then popular model of strict discipline and rote learning with humane treatment, innovative teaching methods, and group activities. "The first instruction which I gave" the new teachers, he wrote later, "was that they were on no account ever to beat any one of the children, or to threaten them in any manner of word or action, or to use abusive terms; but were always to speak to them with a pleasant countenance and in a kind manner and tone of voice." Paintings, maps, and local produce sparked class discussions; singing, dancing, and gymnastics enlivened the day. Owen virtually invented modern early childhood education, with impressively positive results; observers marveled at his schools' success. "I visited our infant-school almost daily for years; and I have never, either before or since, seen such a collection of bright, clean, good-tempered, happy little faces," wrote his son, Robert Dale Owen, who did not hesitate to criticize other aspects of his father's life. Potowska came to share Owen's conviction about the importance of education: one of the first meetings she attended in New York City concerned improving public schools.[15]

In 1815, Owen attempted to reform the nation the way he had New Lanark. He campaigned for labor laws preventing children under ten from working in factories and limiting the workday for those under eighteen to ten and a half hours. He met with universal opposition. His parliamentary bill received no votes at all and Owen concluded that "in this and all other cases between the tyranny of the masters and the sufferings of their white slaves, the error is in reality in the system of society, which created the necessity for tyrants and slaves, neither of which could exist in a true and rational state of society." This experience radicalized him. For the rest of his long life, Owen maintained, as Rose later declared, that "the character of man was made *for* him and not *by* him." To this end, he attempted to restructure society by reproducing the community he created at New Lanark. People should live in groups of about 1,500, manufacturing and farming in common, under the supervision of qualified leaders like himself. He believed that the success of these communes would inspire others to copy them and eventually they would expand throughout the world.[16]

Owenite communes then began to form in both Britain and the United States. Later, Ernestine and William Rose flirted twice with living in one of these experimental communities but decided against it each time. Meanwhile, Robert Owen toured the United States from 1824 to 1829, intermittently overseeing the villages founded on his principles, none of which lasted long. On July 4, 1826, the fiftieth anniversary of the US Declaration of Independence, he issued his own provocative Declaration of Mental Independence. He proclaimed man to be "a slave to a TRINITY of the most monstrous evils," defined as private property, religion, and contemporary marriages, founded on property and religion.[17]

Robert Owen's conviction that character was formed "for him" by society directly opposed his culture's Christian belief in "original sin," which held that people were innately evil, were individually responsible for their own bad behavior, and should be punished accordingly. He came to believe that all religions contained "gross errors" that have made man "a weak, imbecile animal; a furious bigot and fanatic; or a miserable hypocrite." "I am not of your religion," he concluded, "nor of any religion yet taught in the world! To me they all appear united with much—yes, with very much error!"[18] When Potowska met Owen a few years later, this rejection of religion provided an important bond between them. Although he became a deist and sought to create a "rational religion," while she remained a committed atheist, she admired his rejection of "the fashionable superstition called religion" throughout her life.

Owen's rejection of private property came from his conviction that individual ownership led to pernicious extremes of wealth and poverty. He believed that workers should prevent "the products of their toil from going out of the circle of the productive classes into that of the unproductive classes." His rejection of marriage as it then existed followed from the rigid policies of the state-supported Church of England. Until 1837, marriages of all Christians, from Catholics to non-Anglican Protestants, had to be performed in the Church of England to be legal. Divorce was virtually nonexistent, as each one took a separate and expensive Act of Parliament. Owen opposed these "marriages of the priesthood" for leading to both domestic misery and prostitution. Instead, he advocated "marriages of nature," which would be based on attraction and could be ended if both parties agreed and provided for their children.[19]

These beliefs shocked and outraged most of Owen's contemporaries. Lucretia and James Mott were nearly expelled from their Philadelphia Quaker meeting just for supporting the right to listen to the "Infidel Owenites"; others called Owen's followers "whoremongers," immoral libertines, and free lovers. Owen's lifelong fidelity to his wife and benevolent personality largely protected him from such criticism. Hearing him speak in America, the writer Frances Trollope recalled that his "gentle tone . . . his kind smile—the mild expression of his eyes—in short, his whole manner, disarmed zeal, and produced a degree of tolerance that those who did not hear would hardly believe possible." Ernestine Rose consistently praised his vision. "We have been told that Robert Owen was a dreamer—and what glorious dreams he dreamt!" she proclaimed at his centenary celebration in 1871.

> It has been said that he was a fanatic! Who ever did anything good without being a fanatic? That he was an enthusiast! Who ever accomplished anything great without enthusiasm? It is said that he did not succeed. But where he did not succeed in the past, he will in the future. He shook the foundation of the old system, and left it to time to do the rest.[20]

Before she met Owen, he had become the leader of an important new working-class movement. Reform of the House of Commons—transferring unpopulated voting districts controlled by a single landowner to new, growing cities, reducing property requirements for voting so that more men became eligible—agitated the nation from the time of Owen's return from the United States in 1829 onward. As the House of Lords, which had equal power with Commons then, continuously rejected all measures for improvement, riots broke out in many English cities. When "the Great Reform Act" finally passed in 1832, it enfranchised one out of five adult men, hardly any of them from the working class. It also deliberately excluded all women, adding the word "male" to voting qualifications for the first time in English history. In later years, Ernestine Rose often argued that winning the vote was all-important. "The ballot-box is the focus of all other rights, it is the pivot upon which all others hang," she frequently asserted. Her lifelong dedication to enfranchisement almost certainly stemmed from her experience of these years of tumult in England over the suffrage issue.[21]

Meanwhile, a growing radical working-class movement, which created its own artisanal trade groups and cooperative associations, heralded Robert Owen as its natural leader. "Loud applause" followed his declaration at the second meeting of its Co-operative Congress in 1831 that "We have now before us a plan for improving society ... [and] we are now in a position to command it from the hands of Government; and why? Because they do not know how to relieve the community from a state of wretchedness and poverty, and we will show them the means of creating a Paradise." Members scoffed at others' disapproval. "I have been called an infidel," one stated, "but if Co-operation is infidelity, I don't believe there is such a thing as infidelity in the world." Co-operators also sought to enlist women to their cause. "I rejoice to see so many females present, for in Co-operation *they* have everything to gain," a male delegate proclaimed.[22]

Ernestine Potowska met Robert Owen in 1832, at the height of this political activism. Owen was sixty-one, almost forty years older than Potowska, but he still possessed amazing energy. Under his leadership, Owenite groups grew rapidly at this time. The Co-operative Congresses met twice yearly in various English cities with Owen presiding, while more than 200 Owenite unions created bazaars where co-operators could sell articles they made in exchange for "Labour Notes." Owen's National Equitable Labour Exchange, established in London in 1832, soon became the largest and best known of these markets. That same year, Owen also began to publish a weekly newspaper, *The Crisis, or the Change from Error and Misery, to Truth and Happiness*, given the name

of the US radical Thomas Paine's book calling for an American revolution
in homage. Costing only a penny and circulating widely, *The Crisis* provided
Owen and the Owenites with a popular forum through which to promulgate
their plans for reforming society. In 1833, a national trade union movement
coalesced under Owen's auspices. Within a few months it claimed half a million members and became the Grand National Consolidated Trades Union,
an umbrella organization of workers.

Meeting Owen during these tumultuous years, Potowska seems to have
been immediately attracted to this "celebrated communist," as one of her
interviewers wrote—the words "communist" and "socialist" were often used
interchangeably in this period. "It has been my great happiness to know
Robert Owen for over twenty-five years," she declared;

> I have known him under difficulties and great trials; under a variety of
> circumstances which would have tried the patience and perseverance,
> energy and good feeling, of ninety-nine out of a hundred ordinary
> men. But he was the same at all times—the great apostle of human-
> ity; the man of one idea, and that idea the happiness of the human
> race. . . . He bestowed charity and kindness on all sides. He softened
> harsh judgments.[23]

Many commented that Owen saw the world paternally, often treating other adults like children. This trait appealed to Potowska, who had
recently lost the company and approval of her own father. She addressed
Robert Owen as "my dear and respected Father" and called herself his
"Daughter." Like Rabbi Potowsky, Owen had absolute faith in his belief system and wanted to pass it on to younger followers. Unlike her father, Owen
preached views she could wholeheartedly embrace, from belief in reform to
scorn for religion. Owen's son wrote that his father was "a most affection-
ate, even indulgent, parent," but that he wanted "a believer in his specific
plans for regenerating the world—or to use his own favorite phrase, his 'disciple.'" Ernestine Potowska "became a disciple of the good philanthropist"
and embraced his ideals for the rest of her life. For his part, Owen rapidly
welcomed Potowska to his movement. He lost two daughters and his wife
during these years, and the young Polish radical may have provided a welcome female presence.[24]

Potowska and Owen both based their goals and methods on the
Enlightenment; both prized reason. Both believed if they presented rational
arguments, they would soon convince others. Both assumed that religion

would disappear shortly and be replaced with humane values informed by social science. "The old erroneous idea of the depravity of human nature is daily giving way to philosophical inquiries into the nature of the causes that produce depravity, vice, and misery," Ernestine Rose declared in 1853, "and just in proportion as this truth is perceived, and the corresponding remedies applied, so is moral reform successful." Both believed that what Owen called "The New Moral World" would soon arrive. "The religion of the New Moral World consists in the unceasing practice of promoting the happiness of every man, woman, and child . . . without regard to their class, sect, party, or color," Owen wrote. In this new state of society

> there will be no worship—no forms and ceremonies—no temples—no prayers—no gloom—no mortification of the flesh or spirit—no anger on account of religious differences—no persecutions. But friendship, and kindness, and charity for the Jew and Gentile.[25]

In addition to ratifying Potowska's previous convictions, Owenism also introduced her to new concepts and experiences. Owen's Grand National Consolidated Trades Union (GNCTU) championed socialism in its labor exchanges and cooperative groups, presenting an alternative to capitalism. Union members would buy and sell only to each other and refuse to supply the government, army, or police. Owen pledged to "support the Union to the utmost of my power" and argued, as he had about his communes, that "its example will be speedily followed by all nations."[26] But this optimistic vision collapsed abruptly as the British government moved vigorously to quash the GNCTU, exiling six members to harsh Australian prison camps just for taking the oath to join it. Although petitions and marches resulted, the union possessed few funds and it collapsed as swiftly as it had formed. By the end of 1834, the Owenite movement had shrunk dramatically. Owen replaced the GNCTU with a second short-lived group. He closed *The Crisis* and began publishing *The New Moral World*, another low-priced weekly. He then created the Association of All Classes of All Nations, with himself as "Social Father" and only a few hundred official members. Present at its founding, Potowska played a prominent role in this small organization, which sought to effect "an entire change in the character and condition of mankind, by establishing . . . the religion of charity for . . . all individuals, without distinction of sex, class, sect, party, country, or colour, combined with a . . . system of united property." The most expansive part of this successor group was its name. But Potowska cited its doctrines all her life.[27]

Owenism's most important contribution to Ernestine Potowska's development lay in its attempts to do away with the "distinction of sex." From its inception, the movement encouraged women to join. "It has hitherto ... been the object of certain persons to keep females in the back-ground, but such is not the case with the members of our body," a male Owenite proudly declared at the 1832 Co-operative Congress in London. "Some call women cyphers, but a cypher with the addition of one, as you all know, makes ten— and it would take hundreds of London men to make one good co-operative woman." Owenites drank a toast to women's emancipation at each Co-operative Congress and made efforts "to ensure that female voices would be heard." In 1833, a visiting socialist Frenchman reported seeing many women at all Owenite meetings, adding "I have seldom seen faces so animated as theirs, they felt their equality with men." Most Owenite branches offered special "female classes" for their women members and charged them only a penny to attend lectures while the men paid three pence. Women "are not recognized as human beings, except in a company of Co-operators," a male Owenite asserted.[28]

With some exaggeration, this assertion reflected contemporary reality. Outside of these radical circles, most early Victorians believed men and women to be each others' opposites. By the 1830s, the relatively new ideal of domesticity for women, who were supposed to limit themselves to their homes, families, and churches, had taken hold. "The 'rights of women,' what are they?" went a widely reprinted poem of the era,

> *The right to labor and to pray;*
> --
> *The path of meekness and of love,*
> *The path of faith that leads above;*
> *The path of patience under wrong,*
> *The path in which the weak grow strong:*
> *Such women's rights, and GOD will bless,*
> *And crown their champions with success.*

This division into "separate spheres" for males and females would be "highly congenial to the feelings and habits of Englishmen," argued a public letter of 1825, "as conducive to domestic comfort and kindly affections as tending to establish the authority of fathers, and as making each man responsible for the comfort, respectability, and the education of his family." While some women felt safe and protected within this framework, others were cowed. "Like a bird whose wings have been early clipped . . . she [woman] has imbibed an indistinct feeling of awe and dread—an inward acknowledgment of *man's* superiority," a female Owenite wrote. This ideal of womanly dependence originated in the middle class but spread rapidly to other groups. Connecting female domesticity to respectability, it presented an appealing way to "Live Happy Together," as a contemporary English song put it:

> *Woman was formed to please man*
> *And man to love and protect them,*
> *And shield them from the frowns of the world,*
> *Through the smooth paths of life to direct them.*[29]

In contrast, Owenites sought to attract women to their movement with the goal of liberating them from such debilitating beliefs. When a male speaker at a Co-operative Congress declared that Owenites "claimed for woman full, free, and equal enjoyment of all those privileges which belonged to her as a human being," a woman agreed wholeheartedly, saying she had found "none to sympathize with her" until "a new sun broke upon her, and that was Robert Owen." The only solution to women's oppression, she continued, was "the remedy of Socialism." Thousands of women joined the GNCTU, which included a woman on its governing board. "Nothing short of a total revolution . . . will be productive of the great change so loudly called for by her [women's] miserable state," a female Owenite wrote to *The New Moral World*. "Indeed, I am confident that if women really understood the principles and practice of Socialism, there would not be one who would not become a devoted Socialist." Later, Ernestine Rose asserted that she had "no doubt that he [Owen] would have advocated the Woman's Rights Bill had he lived."[30]

Owenite journals frequently published pieces by women, almost all of which expressed feminist ideas. "In China, they cramp the feet of the ladies, by bandaging them from childhood," the female "E. N." wrote in 1832; "in England they do the same, by means of the iron fetters of custom and etiquette." The following year, *The Crisis* printed a translation of a French feminist "Call to Women," which urged them to organize into "*one solid union*. Let us no longer form two camps—that of the women of the people and that of the women of the privileged class. Let our *common interest* unite us to obtain this great end" defined as "*liberty* and *equality* . . . the free and equal chance of developing *all our faculties*."[31]

Ernestine Potowska almost certainly read both *The Crisis* and *The New Moral World*, which helped develop her feminist perspective. Several articles seem to have influenced her later behavior. In 1833, a female writer asserted that "women have been too long considered as playthings or as slaves" and denounced the "mock chivalry" which held that "no man could ever contradict a lady." Four years later, Potowska, by then Ernestine Rose, met the identical situation in New York, where a man who publicly opposed her said he had been taught "never to fight with a lady." She faced him "with a look that seemed to pierce the soul and to say in terms stronger than language can use, 'While I pity your degeneration and ignorance, I am not intimidated by your brutality,'" a sympathetic observer reported. An 1835 piece extolling Elizabeth Fry's work may have encouraged Potowska to visit Newgate prison. This same article went on to argue that women should become members of Parliament, an argument Rose later transposed to the US Congress:

> If nature has endowed her with eloquence, and study possessed her with knowledge to serve the cause of her country, should she be declared incompetent because she were wrapped in a silken shawl instead of a senator's robe? Because she spoke with a voice of silver instead of brass?

Another article maintained, "While human society is compounded of the two sexes, so also should be human legislation," a proposition Rose often asserted in later decades. On a more personal level, this same feminist writer questioned why "grey hairs bring no honour to women? I may say, why do they bring *dishonour*? For an *old woman* is the *ne plus ultra* of contempt?" She answered her own question: "Because women are taught to think the carriage of the head of more consequence than its contents." This might have contributed to Ernestine Rose never dyeing her own hair, which won a French feminist's admiration in 1856.[32]

Owenism did not just provide Potowska with feminist readings; it also introduced her to the radical feminist practice of women speaking in public. A number of women lectured regularly to Owenite audiences. "She felt it her duty to address and excite her own sex," *The Crisis* wrote about the Irish feminist Anna Wheeler; "she said that . . . female exertion was now wanting. She enlarged very eloquently on this subject and met with great approbation." Outside of Owenite circles, however, female lecturing received almost universal condemnation throughout the Western world. An English newspaper denigrated a female Owenite orator as "a weak and misguided woman who degrades the very name and form of woman." Female speakers were routinely stigmatized as "witches," "she-devils," and "whores," and a standard tactic of the opposition in both Great Britain and the United States was for men to shout out Bible verses mandating women's silence during female lectures. American anti-slavery women's speeches in these years provoked a torrent of abuse. New England ministers issued a public letter declaring that such actions would cause women to "not only cease to bear fruit, but to fall in shame and dishonor into the dust," while the prestigious *American Quarterly Review* thanked Heaven it knew of no woman who would "get up at a public meeting and make a . . . speech."[33]

In contrast, Owenism encouraged women to lecture and Ernestine Potowska gave her first public talks in this friendly milieu. "In the old days, when Robert Owen was filling all England with his socialist ideas," a friend of hers wrote later,

> a young and remarkably beautiful girl, just from Poland, was intro-
> duced to him. Discovering that she was a precocious Radical, and pos-
> sessed of considerable ability, he invited her to speak in his huge hall,
> on an occasion when several thousands of people had gathered there.
> Notwithstanding her slight knowledge of the English language, the
> good looks and enthusiasm of the girl made a good impression on the
> audience. She was thenceforth encouraged to appear in public again.

Ernestine Potowska began to take "part in the weekly meetings" on Sundays where Owen "discussed his doctrine." She helped organize these gatherings of "1500 to 1800 people" where they could listen to speeches about Owenite principles. Potowska often spoke at these events, championing Owen's doctrine and debating "many times with Protestant ministers." She also confided to an interviewer that she lectured only after she "had washed and put away with her own hands all the dishes used to make and serve tea" at these meetings. Even within Co-operation, women remained responsible for housework. But the movement still treated them more equally than anywhere else in England.[34]

Owenism gave Potowska a social life. Sunday gatherings provided a pleas-ant alternative to either going to church or drinking in a pub. Members not only met and had tea, they also usually held a dance party. Dancing—which Potowska enjoyed all her life—also occurred on some nights during the week and at the Co-operative Congresses. "At the conclusion of the lecture the com-pany formed themselves into groups for dancing," went one report, "in the long corridor, 'the gay Quadrille' was performed, while in the saloon the waltz was the prevailing dance . . . and during the evening several songs were sung to musical accompaniments." The Owenites also offered numerous evening classes, providing basic instruction in many subjects. They opened bookstores, cooperative groceries, and Halls of Science. In addition, the group developed secular alternatives for holidays, weddings, and funerals. Part of their goal was to create fellowship as well as to provide education and entertainment.[35]

At some point during these years, Ernestine Potowska met William Rose, a fellow Owenite. He was born in England in 1813, making him three years younger than she was, but hardly any documentation about his life exists. In this period, British censuses only recorded the numbers of people born, not where they came from nor who their parents were. He had the unusual middle name of "Ella," but there is no information about its origin. He was not Jewish; although "Rose" became a relatively common Jewish name in twentieth-century England, in the nineteenth century it denoted a Christian. Like Potowska, he was a freethinker and did not believe in God. They both enjoyed singing as well as dancing and sang solos at events. William had probably apprenticed as a silversmith; he later made an elaborate silver pitcher for Robert Owen's son and worked all his adult life as a jeweler. He did not receive much schooling. His only surviving letter is poorly written, with weak grammar and phonetic spelling: "wat" for "what," "effectsionately" for "affectionately." But he adored "My Dear Ernestine," as he called her twice in this brief note to Owen. He consistently supported all her endeavors, both emotionally and financially. For her part, Ernestine Rose hardly ever referred to her personal life, but she did tell an interviewer that she had "a husband whom she loves tenderly and is tenderly loved by." In her only public mention of her marriage, made at an 1858 convention, she declared that "my husband is a law-unto-himself" in being happy to have her do as she wished. She quickly added that his individuality did not mean there should be no laws limiting other husbands' behavior.[36]

The couple married in 1836. They probably knew that when Owen's son, Robert Dale Owen, married Mary Robinson a few years earlier, he had publicly repudiated "the unjust rights, which, in virtue of this ceremony, an iniquitous law tacitly gives me over the person of another." But Dale Owen had married in New York City, where civil ceremonies existed. Since that was not a possibility in London, the freethinking couple chose a different method. They hired a notary public who came to Ernestine's rented room and witnessed a statement attesting to their mutual vows. Although this document did not strictly have the force of law, it did register their union.[37]

Shortly thereafter, the Roses decided to emigrate to the United States with an Owenite colony of thirty-six people. Although none of these communes survived for more than a few years, they continued to be founded into the

1840s. Owen's journals published enthusiastic support for these outposts. "We're like a hive of busy bees," went a verse invoking a common image for the co-operators:

> *Who want an opportunity*
> *To place ourselves and all mankind*
> *In a bless'd community.*
>
> *Before we heard of Owen's plan*
> *Of serving one another*
> *We tried to outwit everyone*
> *And all kind feelings smother.*[38]

Ernestine Rose "was full of faith in the ideas of Robert Owen" and "resolved to act on them" by joining this new US commune. Both Owen himself and many Owenites traveled frequently back and forth across the ocean in these years, helping to create a transatlantic radical community. These connections made leaving England for the United States relatively easy. Co-operative journals on both sides of the Atlantic championed the United States of America as a better place to build a new society. "Land of the West! we fly to thee," went a song published in a US Owenite newspaper:

> Sick of the old world's sophistry;
>   Haste then along the dark blue sea,
>
>   *Ebor Nova [New York]*
>
> Home of the brave, soil of the free!
>   Huzza! she rises o'er the sea —
>
>   *Ebor Nova.*

Later, in New York, Ernestine Rose explained that "I chose to make this country my home, in preference to any other, because if you carried out the theories you profess, it would indeed be the noblest country on earth." Referring to other Poles like Kosciusko, who fought for the American Revolution, she added that just as "my countrymen so nobly aided in the physical struggle for Freedom and Independence, I felt, and still feel it equally my duty to use my humble abilities to the utmost in my power, to aid in the great moral struggle for human rights and human freedom."[39]

The exact settlement the Roses planned to be part of cannot be identified. During the spring of 1836, a few months before they left England, *The*

New Moral World published excerpts from a guide on *Practical Emigration to the United States*. This treatise strongly recommended that "foreigners" not waste their capital wandering "about from state to state in search of lands, suitable to their idea of settlement," but instead dwell "prosperously and happily within the precincts of civilized life, where alone, from previous habits, customs, religion, and associations, they were fitted to reside." A few weeks later, the journal wrote, "We have great hope that the detachment of Sisters and Brothers who have emigrated to America, to put our principles into practice, will be attended with great and good results, and prove the utility of our Association." However, during the weeks spent crossing the Atlantic, Ernestine Rose realized that "every kind of life demands preparation, especially that of communal life. She became convinced that her companions were far from being prepared." This is all she wrote about the voyage. So instead of continuing westward with this group, the Roses left them in New York City. Arriving on the auspicious date of Robert Owen's birthday, May 14, 1836, they decided to make their home there. They stayed for the next thirty-three years.[40]

3

A Radical in New York City

ERNESTINE AND WILLIAM Rose arrived in New York with both a desire for more freedom and the comfort of knowing that a group of Owenites had formed there. A few years earlier, the *Times* in England predicted that the American metropolis would soon become "the London of the New World." In 1836, however, the contrasts between the city the Roses left and the one they settled in remained striking. London had more than 1.5 million inhabitants, New York fewer than 300,000. London stretched for miles in all directions; New York extended only from Manhattan's Battery at the south end of the island north to Washington Square.[1] London ruled not only the United Kingdom of Great Britain, Scotland, and Ireland but also a growing overseas empire; New York was not even capital of the Empire State, much less the nation. But the city "swarmed intense," as an 1836 guidebook declared, with more than 3,000 new buildings erected in the previous eighteen months.[2]

By the 1830s, New York had become the United States' largest and busiest urban center, surpassing its rivals, Boston, Philadelphia, and Baltimore. Now the "Empire City" dominated many fields: commerce, finance, entertainment, communications, and transport. It assumed a central role in American life. It "is the capital of our country," the artist and inventor Samuel F. B. Morse asserted in 1831. "We always found something new to see and to admire" in New York, the English traveler Frances Trollope declared, making it highly "desireable as a residence." New York was a city of immigrants, and coming from England, the Roses joined the largest group to arrive: 75 percent of those entering the United States then came from Great Britain, about 40 percent of them from Ireland.[3]

Shortly after landing, the couple leased their first New York City apartment, at 484 Grand Street. By the late nineteenth century, this address lay in the middle of New York's teeming Lower East Side, home to tens of thousands of Jewish immigrants from Eastern Europe. But in 1836, the Jewish population of the city numbered only about 4,000, less than 2 percent of the whole. Mild but pervasive antisemitism existed: the economic crash of 1837 prompted a widely disseminated cartoon featuring a pawnshop run by "Shylock Graspall." On Grand Street, the Roses would have encountered an immensely diverse population: immigration made New York's citizenry far more varied than London's. "The inhabitants of New York . . . derive their origin from every part of the world," the 1836 guidebook explained, reproducing the stereotypes of the day:

> They exhibit a sort of human patchwork. . . . Here is the shrewd Yankee; the cool and twice-thinking Scotchman; the warm and never-thinking Irishman; the mercurial and light-hearted Frenchman; the grave Spaniard; the romantic German; the thoughtless African; in short, the natives, and the descendants of the natives, of every nation, and kindred, and tongue on the face of the earth.[4]

The first New York event after their arrival that impressed itself on Ernestine Rose was Independence Day. "I doubt whether I should ever forget . . . the first Fourth of July that I spent here," she recalled. "Why, everything in nature appeared to change and become superior. The sun shone brighter; the trees looked more beautiful; the grass looked greener; the birds sang sweeter . . . for I viewed them all through the beautiful rainbow colors of human freedom." The Roses probably attended the celebration in Washington Square Park, "where the 4th of July is principally glorified," the guidebook advised. "There floats the American banner, with its thirteen stripes and twenty-six stars, on a staff one hundred feet high. . . . [M]en and women, girls and boys stand the whole day through, in crowds, to behold the troops of the military and listen to the sharp voice of the musketry, and the deep tone of the cannon." Festivities always included a reading of the entire Declaration of Independence as well.[5]

In July, the Roses almost certainly suffered from the city's "fierce summer," as Trollope called it. They probably arrived with woolen garments better suited to the English climate. Clothing remained scarce and expensive then, geared to year-round wear, since most people could afford only a few outfits. Cotton cloth still cost more than wool; only the wealthy purchased silk. Like other respectable women, Ernestine Rose wore the confining dark-colored dresses of this period, with their high necks, long tight sleeves, small waists requiring corset stays, voluminous skirts, and layers of petticoats. Custom required all adult women to cover their heads with a cotton or linen "day cap," often ruffled and tied under the chin, topped with a summer or winter bonnet when the wearer left her home. But Rose defied protocol by going bareheaded, at least indoors. One of the first newspaper accounts of her, from December 1837, describes her at a large meeting as "a young, beautiful, and interesting Lady with uncovered head, and fine flowing locks."[6]

That newspaper, *The Beacon*, was the publication of New York's Anglo-American Owenite community of freethinkers. Owenism had always been a transatlantic movement and many East Coast cities, but especially New York, became havens for British radicals fleeing their nation's conservative persecutions of the 1820s. "It is owing to the debased English migration that such abominable stuff is circulated thro' presses devoted to decry Christianity & loosen the bonds of Society and government," a Gotham merchant complained about them.[7] The Roses soon made contact with this radical group, who formed the flourishing society of "Moral Philanthropists," a name identifying them as non-religious lovers of humanity. Meeting in the newly built, prestigious Tammany Hall, home of the Democratic Party, they drew "overflowing houses" interested in their debates on religion and society. The 1836 New York guidebook enumerated 150 houses of worship in the city before adding that "besides these religious societies, there is a congregation of Atheists who meet regularly on Sundays.... The Atheist sneers at the Christian; while the Christian, on the contrary, descends from his dignity to blast the Atheist." In addition to publishing the weekly *Beacon*, this group maintained libraries and bookstores dedicated to free-thought writings, as well as sponsoring lectures, debates, and dinners. They welcomed the Roses into their circle.[8]

Within a few months of her arrival in New York, Ernestine Rose plunged into political action for women. Befriended by the older men who formed the core of the Moral Philanthropist society, she followed the lead of one of them, Judge Thomas Herttell, a well-known champion of free thought. The sixty-five-year-old Herttell had sought for years, unsuccessfully, to remove New York State's religious laws, which excluded all non-Protestants from government service or being witnesses in lawsuits, mandated beginning legislative sessions with prayer, and compelled a religious sabbath. A week after the Roses arrived in New York, Herttell introduced a proposal to the Albany state legislature giving married women the right to own property. Current Anglo-American laws made a husband "upon marriage entitled to all the goods and chattels of the wife," as well as her wages, inheritances, and custody of any children. A wife had no corresponding share in her husband's possessions. Despite her accented English and unfamiliarity with the city's streets, the twenty-six-year old Ernestine Rose went door-to-door through lower Manhattan to gather names on a petition supporting Herttell's bill. "After a good deal of trouble I obtained five signatures," she recalled. "Some of the ladies said the gentlemen would laugh at them; others, that they had rights enough; and the men said the women had too many rights already." Rose remained immensely proud of this activism and referred to it repeatedly as the beginning of an American women's movement.[9]

Property ownership might seem like an odd cause for an Owenite socialist to embrace, but it went to the heart of Rose's belief in justice and equality under law. As a newlywed who earned income from selling perfumed products and who might still have had some of her mother's legacy, she may well have wanted to protect her own property rights—even from William, who she might not yet have realized was "a law unto himself." At the same time that she worked for married women's property rights, she also spoke frequently in favor of a "community of property." Most socialists living in capitalist societies have had to hold money-making jobs. However, although many New York freethinkers supported Owen's socialism, a sizable number did not. Barely a year after she arrived in the United States, Rose began debating the paid Moral Philanthropist lecturer Benjamin Offen, on whether private or communal property was more conducive "to the happiness of mankind." Offen, from the same generation as Herttell, opposed socialism and advocated free thought so singlemindedly that an associate compared listening to him to "dining *daily* on mutton." He and Rose debated at Tammany Hall for thirteen weeks, from June to October 1837. Although they agreed on Owen's maxim that the "accidental circumstances" of birth determined people's religion and character, they differed on property ownership. Offen argued that "Mr. Owen's system is not adapted to promote happiness." Rose rebutted that "society may be improved by the few enlightened, and then rendered happy by a community of property,—which would destroy all that baseness on which much of trade and private property is based."[10]

The Beacon's first mention of Ernestine Rose did not use her name, instead calling her "a Polish lady, of great literary attainments, and warmly attached to Robt. Owen's system." "Polish" in these years denoted romantic heroism to Americans. "This distinguished and talented lady is a worthy descendant of that noble race whose country gave birth to the brave and generous Koskiusko," the atheist *Boston Investigator* wrote a few years later about Rose. "*He* drew his sword [to support the American Revolution], and flew to the rescue of political freedom. *She*, with tongue and pen is doing good service in the cause of mental freedom. *Her* name will be equally cherished by all philanthropists." Despite the "Polish lady's manner of delivery, the number of facts introduced, and the many important isolated truths, which she stated," Rose had difficulty convincing her New York audience of "the evils of private property." Even though she supported socialism intellectually and morally, both she and William lived by private enterprise. He worked as a jeweler, she sold Cologne water out of the same shop, on Frankfort Street near the city's center. They lived above the store and had moved there when their first one-year lease expired.[11]

Knowledge about their wares comes from a unique article in the free-thought *Beacon* newspaper, edited by Gilbert Vale. Vale, like Offen, had come from England to New York, where he taught navigation and mathematics before helping found the Moral Philanthropist society. He edited *The Beacon* from 1837 to 1846 and showered Ernestine Rose with praise throughout his years there. He mentioned "the Polish Lady" at least seven times in 1837, publicized her speeches, and lauded her "great literary attainments," her "enlightened" views and "liberal" sentiments, and called her "young, beautiful, and interesting." In March 1838, he used her last name for the first time, printing a piece on "Mrs. Rose and Cologne Water." This prodded readers to patronize the Roses' store and buy her products. Praising Rose as "an interesting Polish lady of education and great accomplishments . . . already partially known . . . from the part she had taken in some liberal public meetings," he touted her "genuine" cologne as "infinitely superior to what is sold in New York." "She therefore boldly challenges comparison, and invites inspection, and thus takes a useful and honorable position, which deserves to be crowned with success," he added, before giving the store's address and reporting that "Mr. Rose . . . repairs jewelry, watches, ornaments, and trifles, which nobody else thinks of. . . . Our fancy friends should call and see."[12]

Although *The Beacon* published many paid advertisements, this was the only piece specifically recommending a business printed in the newspaper's nine-year history. Part of Vale's motive may have been the financial hardship the Roses probably suffered after the economic crash of 1837, since William Rose, an accomplished silversmith, now resorted to repairing "trifles." But why did Gilbert Vale so favor Ernestine Rose, giving her free publicity and praising her with such warmth?

As an attractive, respectable, youthful married woman who spoke in public, Rose was unique in free-thought circles. Vale touted her as a worthy exemplar of his movement. Like most male freethinkers, Vale believed American women to be more "bound" by "the chains of superstition" than

men, more "attracted to the priests, by whom they are controlled, and sometimes abused." Both Frances Trollope and Alexis de Tocqueville confirmed
this view, Trollope writing that she "never saw or read of any country where
religion had so strong a hold upon the women."[13] There had been one other
prominent female freethinker who lectured in the United States: Frances
Wright from Scotland. But by the time Ernestine Rose came on the scene,
"Fanny" Wright was notorious as an immoral, scandalous figure, denounced
as "the Red Harlot of Infidelity" and "a crazy, atheistical woman."[14]

An orphaned heiress fifteen years older than Rose, Wright became an
Owenite in 1824. She founded her own interracial commune in Nashoba,
Tennessee, which soon failed. She then worked with Robert Dale Owen,
Owen's son, publishing the *Free Enquirer* newspaper, lecturing frequently,
and moving to New York in 1829. She turned a former church into an Owenite
Hall of Science that seated 1,200 and spoke there weekly for more than a year.
Initially Wright met with tremendous success. Her coherent Owenist philos-
ophy, which explained the oppression of workers, women, and society in general by blaming religion, capitalism, and ignorance, inspired the short-lived
Workingmen's Party in New York City. But in 1830, Wright abruptly left the
United States. Pregnant out of wedlock, she lived privately in Paris after mar-
rying her child's father, Phiquepal d'Arusmont, and ended her Owenite connections. When she returned to New York in May of 1836, just as the Roses
arrived in the city, she resumed lecturing but had lost her old power. She was
chased from the stage by men throwing stink bombs, hammering the floor
with their canes, and shouting curses at her.

Gilbert Vale almost certainly wanted to spare Ernestine Rose such attacks
by calling her "a Polish lady" and not using even her last name until 1838. But
attacks on any female freethinker who attempted to speak in public occurred
anyway. In December 1837, Rose left the friendly precincts of Tammany
Hall and attended a large meeting in the evangelical Broadway Tabernacle
on improving primary public school education. Discussion soon focused on
whether the New Testament should remain part of the curriculum. A minister fulminated against "infidels" who wanted to remove religion from the
schools, denouncing them as "abominable" and "blasphemous" opponents
who "were industriously disseminating the horrible opinions that in proportion as we renounced God, despised virtue, trampled on morals, and violated
all the finer sensibilities of our race, so were we free." Ernestine Rose, bareheaded, stood to reply. Saying that "it was very painful to her, being a woman
and a foreigner, to intrude upon the audience," she asserted that a "desire to
propagate knowledge and truth without mystery, mixture of error, or the fear

of man" induced her to ask the minister a question about "his remarks on infidelity." She was instantly shouted down. Three women screamed "Infidel, Infidel," "Tammany Hall," and "put her out," while men hissed and hooted. The minister quieted the crowd and Rose asked if he would debate her. He replied that he "had always been taught, never to fight with a lady." He was applauded; Rose continued to receive "hisses and groans."[15]

Male freethinkers also met with extreme disapproval in this period. Abner Kneeland, editor of the atheist *Boston Investigator*, was convicted of blasphemy in 1838 and sent to prison for making an equivocal statement about God's existence. (Rose denounced his imprisonment at Tammany Hall.) Freethinkers were routinely called "infidels" and harshly condemned. "If the principles of Infidelity continue to prevail, as they did now, we must perish and should deserve it," the minister who opposed Rose declared. Believers charged infidels with all sorts of immorality and vice, arguing that without religion, the innate "depravity of human nature" would lead to "floods of dissipation." An 1824 denunciation of "Characteristics of Modern Infidelity" in a Christian newspaper claimed that "The bloated countenances of the victims of intemperance and crime, which crowd the halls of Free Inquiry, give us an index . . . of the kind of instruction to which they listen. . . . There will be found the drunkard, the gambler, the libertine, herded together in a fellowship of iniquity." Accused of all sorts of sins, infidels were also blamed for everything Christians objected to in the modern world, beginning with the French Revolution. "They are atheists, socialists, communists, red Republicans, Jacobins on one side," went a blast from 1838, "and the friends of order and regulated freedom on the other. In one word, the world is the battle-ground, Christianity and Atheism the combatants, and the progress of humanity the stake." A Massachusetts newspaper labeled the entire city of New York as a place "where infidelity openly stalks abroad, boasting of its power and of its deluded and accumulating numbers."[16]

Female freethinkers received even harsher criticism, since in their case sexual immorality became added to the charges against them. "Infidel" literally meant "unfaithful," signifying someone who did not believe in Christianity. But the word also carried the additional meaning of sexual promiscuity when applied to married persons, especially women. Female virtue had always been closely connected to sexual chastity and fidelity; in the early nineteenth century, this connection strengthened. Western culture viewed women primarily through a sexual lens. Routinely called "the sex" or "the fair sex" in this period, they were assumed to have a great deal of erotic power over men. This argument became a standard justification for keeping them out of political life. "The Fair Sex—Excluded by necessity from participation in our labours, since the presence of women would make us slaves, and convert the temple of wisdom to that of love," a US politician toasted in 1825. "The hearts of your readers will shudder," the *Christian Advocate and Journal* wrote about an 1828 New York freethinker meeting, "when they learn that fifty or sixty ladies have so far divested themselves of the fear of God, the respect for their characters, and that jewel which alone ornaments their sex [modesty], as to attend these lectures, where they are taught . . . to ridicule the Bible, that 'they may learn chastity from Lot's daughters.'" Lot's daughters got their father drunk and had sex with him—a reference familiar to Bible readers. Such extremism in describing women simply sitting in a freethinker audience typified the hysteria of this era, which equated women's lack of religious belief with sexual infidelity and moral corruption. "When a female undertakes to ridicule religion," a contemporary wrote, "it is one of those marks of depravity that carries with it the most unnatural and odious idea in nature."[17]

Neither Ernestine Rose's probity nor Gilbert Vale's protection prevented others from attacking her morals and conflating her with Frances Wright. "A new Fanny Wright has sprung up in New York," the *Connecticut Courant* reported with gleeful inaccuracy; "Mrs. Rose, a Polish woman, divorced from her husband, doubtless with sufficient reason, is lecturing Sunday evenings at Tammany Hall. She is opposed to marriage, and all such monopolies, and carries leveling doctrines to their utmost extent."[18] Such charges contributed to Rose's decision not to raise the issue of marriage until much later in her career.

Ernestine Rose and Frances Wright d'Arusmont met in 1839, when they spoke at a benefit for Benjamin Offen, who had fallen on hard times. The two women had a complex relationship. Rose would have naturally admired a freethinking Owenite woman who lectured publicly, but Rose's heroes, the Owens, had been deeply offended by Wright d'Arusmont. She helped edit the *Boston Investigator* in 1837–38 and in its pages accused Robert Dale Owen of defrauding her. He replied that this ended "what once was friendship" between them because of "the deep injustice she has done me." In 1844, Robert Owen and Frances Wright d'Arusmont found themselves on shipboard together en route to America. "I regreted to hear that Madm. D'Arousmond came on the same Boat that you was [*sic* throughout]. I know it must have been unplasent to you, she has an invateret spite amounting almost to vengence against you and your family," Rose wrote Owen, in her poor English spelling. "I think she is a woman of a good deal of book-learning but of *very* smale mind," Rose concluded. In later life, however, Ernestine Rose paid tribute to her predecessor and acknowledged her influence. "Frances Wright was the first woman in this country who lectured and wrote on the equality of the sexes," Rose declared in 1860.

> It was a Herculean task, the ground was wholly unprepared, all the ele-
> ments were antagonistic, and consequently she received the reward of
> all noble reformers in the avant-guard of a good cause—slander, abuse,
> and persecution—yet her agitation shook the time-hardened crust of
> conservatism and prepared the soil for the plough. . . . In 1837, another
> woman [Ernestine Rose, speaking modestly in the third person] took
> up the work where she left off.[19]

Rose's early debates with Benjamin Offen seem to have created a bond between them. In addition to speaking at his 1839 benefit, she collected dona-
tions for him when he required more help from 1843 to 1845. She and William delivered these funds to the elderly freethinker so that he could continue his lecture tours. Offen had originated the central annual event in US radical circles in these years: the commemoration of Thomas Paine's birthday on January 29. Honored surreptitiously by London dissidents, this celebration had been transplanted by Offen to the United States in 1825. By then, evangelical Christian revivalism was replacing eighteenth-century Enlightenment Deism and free thought, which came to be seen as old-fashioned as well as "ungodly." Paine's *Common Sense* and his role in sparking the American Revolution had been largely ignored because of his later *Age of Reason*, in which he opposed all organized religions, but especially what he labeled "the Christian Mythology." "All national institutions of churches, whether Jewish, Christian or Turkish, appear to me no other than human inventions, set up to terrify and enslave mankind, and monopolize power and profit," Paine declared in this 1794 treatise. "It took a brave man before the Civil War to confess he had read the *Age of Reason*," Mark Twain remembered. The opinions that led believers to denigrate Paine endeared him to the Roses. In addi-
tion, Paine had been a hero to their "father," Robert Owen, who named his newspaper *The Crisis* in homage to Paine's pamphlet of the same name and who shared Paine's Deism and Enlightenment ideals. Thomas Paine joined Owen in the Roses' pantheon of heroic radicals. Throughout her long life, Ernestine Rose lauded Paine, although she wished he had been born at a warmer time of the year.[20]

The yearly celebrations of Paine's birthday on January 29 led Ernestine Rose to influence the New York radical movement rather than just participate in its events. She came to the fore as a pioneer for women's equality over

the Paine activities. In 1839, William Rose was invited to "the dinner in the afternoon, to which ladies were not admitted" while his wife was asked to join "the ball in the evening." Both Roses declined to participate at all, Ernestine remarking that "I thought Paine's *Rights of Man* did not exclude women." She added that if the hosts prevented women from dining, then they "may as well have the ball without them." Meanwhile, she would work to "inspire" the other women "to have sufficient self-respect" not to attend as well. The Roses then organized an alternate Paine celebration that included women equally. This successful event led the other group to discard their "'old English' exclusive style," and in 1840 "a large hall was taken, and we had a very fine party of men and women, young and old," Rose remembered.[21]

Ernestine Rose first became central to the New York Paine celebrations in 1840 and remained integral to them until they ended twenty-one years later with the Civil War. She helped set a new tone for her first dinner, "which discarded that stiffness and reserve too prevalent in many of the fashionable meetings for amusement," the *Boston Investigator* reported. Rose assisted the evening's president and then gave the first speech (which was not recorded) "in a ready, extemporaneous and eloquent manner." She went on to sing a song and offer three standard free-thought toasts: to "the march of improvement," Robert Owen, and "reformers." William Rose also sang and proposed three more original toasts, the first a qualified salute to the United States: "Our country—While we give it our patriotic support, let it not be at the sacrifice of that philanthropy and justice due to all mankind as brethren." The second was for "freedom to the slave," the third to Paine:

> *The philosophic Thomas Paine,*
> *Who wrote his "Common Sense" so plain,*
> *His "Crisis" in a trying time,*
> *His "Rights of Man" 'gainst royal crime,*
> *His "Age of Reason" 'gainst the priest,*
> *Has thus Columbia's sons released.*[22]

Although Ernestine Rose spoke at this Paine dinner, she lectured very infrequently from 1839 to 1843, much less often than in the previous two years. Nor did she join a US branch of Owen's Association of All Classes of All Nations (AACAN) organized by her friend Lewis Masquerier in 1840. The most likely reason for this hiatus from public activities was childbirth. Although Rose remained extremely reticent about her private life, she later assured an American interviewer that she did not lecture "to the neglect of her home duties, but only as she found the time to spare from her household and maternal cares, Mr. Rose aiding and encouraging her by every means in his power." She confided more to her French interviewer, saying that she gave birth to "two children, whom she cherished, nursed with her own milk, and had the sorrow of losing at a very young age." Public records for these babies and their deaths do not exist, but in this period, births occurred at home and registration often depended on individual choice. Although Rose never publicly mentioned her children again, she spoke movingly in 1852 about such losses:

> When our little ones are removed by death from our care and affection, we feel most keenly our ignorance, and long to know more about the laws of health. Woman might be physician to her self and her children. But the medical schools are closed against her; she is denied the advantages granted to men, for obtaining the knowledge of these things, more necessary if possible to her than to the other sex.

In addition, Rose wrote Robert Owen in 1844 that her health had been "very bad." "I had several quite severe attacks of depression of mind," she informed her "dear Father," "Mr. Rose wishes me to go to Washington, he and our friends think that the change of climate, scenery and society will be beneficial to me."[23]

The Roses made a number of good friends within the US radical community. She became especially close to J.[osiah] P.[aine] Mendum, publisher of the atheist weekly newspaper the *Boston Investigator*. Ernestine Rose introduced him to her "intimate friend," Elizabeth Munn, whom she taught "to believe in the principles of Free Thought, and also in the large sphere of womanly activity." The couple married in the Roses' apartment in 1847 and named their son Ernest after her. The Roses also socialized often with James Thompson, who helped organize the Paine banquets and founded the New York Chess Club in 1839. When he died in 1870, Ernestine Rose wrote that "he was our oldest and most intimate friend in New York." She was also close to Dr. William Wright, a fellow freethinker. They agreed that whoever lived longer would attend the other's funeral to make sure that no clergyman interfered with the secular ceremony. Others can no longer be traced, like the person who later wrote that "Mrs. Rose informed me that there was a sociable held at her house once a week, at which quite a number of young people attended, and gave me an invitation to come to the next meeting. I did."[24]

In addition to mentioning friends in her 1844 letter to Robert Owen, Rose discussed "the community of Skaneateles," an Owenite venture the Roses supported and hoped to join. Established near the town of the same name in the Finger Lakes region of central New York State, the settlement had been founded in 1843 by John A. Collins, a leading anti-slavery agent who converted to Owenism. Ernestine Rose addressed this new commune in its first year, urging "all here present who feel with me" that "the noble spirit of universal philanthropy is here to destroy the narrow-minded selfishness" to "come forward with the money" to support the project. As in many communes, money caused divisions from the start, since Collins wanted the property to be collectively owned, while Rose and others preferred investors to hold the land themselves. Rose prevailed and Skaneateles succeeded for about two years.[25]

Around ninety members lived on the 300-acre property, the men farming, running a sawmill, and building an aqueduct; the women raising the community's children, sewing clothes, and cooking. Collins issued "Articles of Belief and Disbelief" mandating not only the familiar Owenite goals of no religion, no government, and "new moral marriage," which allowed for separations and new unions when the spouses "can no longer contribute to each other's happiness," but also vegetarianism. Meat-eating, "together with the use of all narcotics and stimulants," should be "renounced as soon as possible." Ernestine Rose defended Skaneateles in speeches at least six times in Boston during the spring of 1844. She also visited the community that September and lectured, taking "a log for her stand" and "dwelling particularly on the advantage of always keeping the great object for which we came together, before us," the group's newspaper, *The Communitist*, reported.[26]

Trouble soon tore the commune apart, however. The diet caused problems, with one group subsisting only on "boiled wheat, rice and Graham mush, without seasonings of any kind," while criticizing the others for eating "dead creatures." Also, some members had affairs, "which caused considerable gossiping." Rose and others blamed John Collins. He "is not the man for so great an undertaking," she wrote Owen in December 1844. "Some of the other members do not understand the first rudiments of the social science and the rest are moral cowards though good men and thus become tools of the more designing." Ernestine and William Rose never went to live at Skaneateles and the community formally ended in January 1846. It was the last Owenite commune in the United States.[27]

Rose's trip to Boston in the spring of 1844, when she was thirty-four, prompted the first detailed description of her appearance and elocution, showing that by then she had become an accomplished lecturer. The *Boston Investigator* praised her "extraordinary powers to enchain the minds of an audience" and wrote that

> her personal appearance wins the attention and respect of her hearers, the moment she rises. Her head is marked with traits of high intellectual dignity. The lines of her countenance express gravity and deep thought, mingled with much gentleness, and the beautifully expanded forehead towers above them, a fit abode for the lofty intellect dwelling therein. Her eye is large and beaming, and, in moments of inspiration, dilates with wonderful lustre. Her voice is very pleasant—full, rich, and varied; and her gestures singularly graceful, expressive, and appropriate.[28]

From then on, Ernestine Rose devoted herself to public speaking, initially for the free-thought movement.

That movement, however, had fallen on hard times. Flourishing in the mid-1830s, when the Roses arrived in New York, the Moral Philanthropists suffered financially during the economic crash of 1837. A few years later they could no longer afford to rent Tammany Hall and moved their meetings to smaller and smaller venues. Their free-thought bookstore closed in 1839 as business declined and their newspaper, *The Beacon*, faltered, becoming a monthly in 1844 before folding in 1846. The national Moral and Philosophical Society failed in 1841. The New York Owenites spent "their time more in discussing theories and abstract principles, than in using the means at their command to reduce them to practice," a visitor complained. Similar problems also prevailed in Britain. Robert Owen's extravagance had caused the collapse of his commune, Queenswood, and led to a revolt against him in 1844. Owen then visited the United States, which prompted the Roses to help organize a national convention of freethinkers in New York to celebrate his presence and try to revive the movement.[29]

The Infidel Convention, as it was advertised, opened at the Coliseum on Broadway with 500 freethinkers in attendance on May 4, 1845. With the group's typically provocative defiance of Christian practice, the meeting assembled on a Sunday morning. The seventy-four-year-old Robert Owen, eternally optimistic, gave the first address, asserting that "if this Convention should now plant itself upon the true ground of *universal charity* and human brotherhood, it would carry the whole world along with it." Ernestine Rose, equally positive, followed Owen. "She could not but hope for a brighter day, when she saw a body of free men and women, thus assembling in a public meeting and carrying with them so intelligent and enthusiastic an audience as the present," a newspaper reported. "What had been stated by Mr. Owen needed nothing added thereto. . . . Enough was said to produce a new state of society—enough—more than enough had been said by him to produce universal reform—more, indeed than could be found in the united libraries of the whole world."[30]

The convention then announced the names of 176 delegates from fourteen states, the District of Columbia, and Europe. In addition to Ernestine Rose, five other women represented their states, but none besides her spoke or served on committees. The group discussed grandiose ways to expand the influence of free thought, from building new libraries to hiring more lecturers, but without additional funding such plans remained pipe dreams. Both Owen and Rose spoke again that first evening, Owen reasserting that knowledge and charity could change the world. Rose expanded her previous argument for education into a specific endorsement of socialism, maintaining that "so long as the precept exists, Everyone for himself, and some supernatural power for us all," the world would remain in a sorry state. "Those who create the most, get the least; those who build the largest castles, often have not where to lay their heads: and then we say that man is bad by nature, because if he has not a crumb to eat, he will take some from his neighbor," she concluded. Samuel Ludvigh, editor of *Die Fackel* (The Torch), a German-language free-thought newspaper published in New York, spoke for the next hour in German. He represented a growing immigrant presence in the city. Just as British radicals had fled to New York in the 1820s because of their government's persecution, so too Germans arrived in the 1840s, providing the city with a new wave of radical reformers and freethinkers.[31]

The next day, the convention ratified its elaborate constitution but spent the bulk of its time debating whether it should include the word "infidel" in its title. After hours of discussion, during which she had not spoken, Ernestine Rose argued that the group should adopt the epithet:

> It seems that the name given us in derision, is, after all, the best, if only for this reason, to show the world that even nicknames can be lived down, or made respectable and fashionable. . . . We are not unfaithful to our principles. . . . She did not wish to wear the name; but if given to us, let us adopt it, and make our enemies ashamed of the hour they ever applied it to us.

"Infidel" presented the same quandary to nineteenth-century freethinkers that the word "queer" did to late-twentieth-century gay men and lesbians: should the community embrace an initially insulting name?[32] The final title the freethinkers chose, "The Infidel Society for the Promotion of Mental Liberty," did not resolve the conflict. A number of members, including Gilbert Vale, defected, and wrangles over the issue tore the society apart. A convention the following year drew only thirty-four members and the final one, in 1847, demonstrated that the Infidel Society had melted away. "The third convention?—It was a shadow of the first," wrote Ludvigh in *Die Fackel*. "The gathering was very small and the valuable words of the speaker Mme. Rose spoken in the empty spaces of the hall. No spark of enthusiasm—the solemnity was like that after a lost battle. No Germans to be seen, and sadly I sat there, a silent observer of the event."[33]

Ernestine Rose remained committed to free thought for the rest of her life. In the 1840s, she continued to weave the subject into her speeches on other topics, no matter how controversial it proved. At the end of a three-hour lecture to the New England Social Reform Society in 1844, she told women "never to enter a *church* again. Countenance them not. They oppress you. They prevent progression. They are opposed to reason." Even this liberal audience had trouble with such sentiments, but Rose stood firm:

> This appeal burst upon a listening throng like a thunderbolt and they were instantly lashed into the wildest excitement of fury and applause.... [T]he speaker was assailed with a shower of hisses. Mrs. R. [*sic*] waited calmly until the tumult had subsided, when she again repeated the injunction, and again the tumult rose still higher; and the repetition and uproar went on until the excited multitude, unable longer to keep up the din, were compelled, through exhaustion, to hear the daring heresy in silence.[34]

Ernestine Rose also continued to love Robert Owen. Owen's optimism, which seemed ridiculous to many, rested on his hard-won and unshakable conviction that his dissident views about the world were correct. People would be better off if religion did not handicap them, if they had decent schools and jobs, if society's wealth were more evenly distributed. On his deathbed, in 1858 at the age of eighty-seven, a minister asked him if he regretted wasting his life in fruitless efforts. Owen replied, "My life was not useless; I gave important truths to the world, and it was only for want of understanding that they were disregarded. I have been ahead of my time."[35]

Rose did not blindly agree with Owen on everything. When he became a devotee of spiritualism in the 1850s, she commented that although "I never hear the name of Robert Owen, but I feel rising within me a sentiment amounting almost to reverence for that noble man," she would only follow him on matters of fact, not his views of a supposed afterlife. "If Robert Owen should tell me that he saw a mouse pull a three-decker [building] through the streets of New York, I would say, 'I cannot believe it.' "[36] After the failure of Skaneateles, Rose no longer shared Owen's conviction that a model community could change the rest of society. But she remained convinced that the world was wrong in many ways and that those who saw the truth needed to champion and work for their beliefs in the face of ridicule, hostility, and skepticism.

This passion grounded her work for the causes that next consumed her energies: the emancipation of women and anti-slavery. "Politically, Mrs. Rose is a radical; that is to say she believes that all members of the human race should enjoy complete freedom, consequently. . . . [S]he uses all her reason and energy to combat black slavery and women's subordination," her French interviewer concluded in 1856. From the early 1840s, Rose began to speak out in favor of women's freedom and equality. In her 1843 speech at Skaneateles, she "made a spirited appeal to the women, respecting their degradation and rights. It was a most effective appeal, and met its response in the tears of the whole audience." The text of that speech has disappeared. Only a few months later, however, near the end of Rose's lengthy 1844 talk to the New England Social Reform Society, she made a passionate entreaty to "her sisters":

> What rights have women? Are they not the merest slaves on earth? What of freedom have they? In government they are not known, but to be punished for breaking laws in which they have no voice in the making. All avenues to enterprise and honor are closed against them. If poor, they must drudge for a mere pittance—If of the wealthy classes, they must be dressed dolls of fashion—parlor puppets—female things. . . . My sisters, speak for yourselves. Tyrants never will willingly relinquish their grasp.[37]

As a "woman's rights woman," Ernestine Rose achieved her greatest success, becoming a leader in the new movement for female emancipation. Her earlier battles for free thought and socialism prepared her for the intense struggle to create a movement for women's freedom and equality.

4

Building a Women's Movement

WHEN ERNESTINE ROSE described how she and others had formed a women's rights movement, she began with having been shouted down at an 1837 meeting on public schools, even though "any man could have said what she said." The realization that society treated women differently from men for identical actions often began the process for a woman of becoming a feminist, or a "woman's rights woman," as feminists were called then. Despite opposition, "that voice has never ceased, and the voice of that woman"—Rose herself—"had been echoed and echoed until it found a voice in this community. She claimed for women all the rights that men claimed." In this uncharacteristically poetic description, Rose sketched the process of first working individually for women's rights and then linking up with "this community"—others who shared the same convictions—to form a movement. First, she began to make demands for women's rights in her free-thought and anti-slavery speeches. Then, instead of continuing to work as a lone individual, she joined with others in lobbying and lecturing. These connections led to her active participation in the first National Woman's Rights Convention in 1850. From then on Ernestine Rose became integral to this new movement, helping it to coalesce and then flourish in the 1850s. "These are not the demands of the moment or the few," she asserted in 1854; "they are the demands of the age; of the second half of the nineteenth century."[1]

Ernestine Rose's path to women's rights, however, differed from those of many of her co-workers. Because of her commitment to free thought, she made extensive speaking tours from the mid-1840s on, gaining experience in addressing audiences that were often initially hostile. Wherever Rose "announced her lectures," her women's rights colleague Paulina Wright Davis wrote later, "they were the subject of ridicule. The audacity of a woman attempting to treat such subjects astonished men and excited curiosity. They

went to hear, and, if not convinced, they admired her clear, strong intellect, respected her logic, and many were her enthusiastic converts." During
these tours, Rose made new contacts with supporters, who often hosted her.
In September 1845, she became severely ill in Buffalo with "ague," a form of
malaria she caught while lecturing that summer in Indiana. Suffering from
"brain fever," "delirium," and general weakness, she recuperated for several
weeks at the Howlands', "an excellent Quaker family, who spare neither attention nor expense to save her life and make her comfortable." Both William
Rose and her friend, "Mrs. S_____ from Syracuse," traveled there to help
nurse her. Despite later recurrences during the next few years, brought on by
"over-exertion or excitement," Rose persevered, lecturing extensively when
"free of the ague." She and others often justified these trips as being "for the
recovery of her health," a remedy used in this era far more by men. Women
were supposed to rest instead.[2] In March 1846, Rose journeyed even farther
west and twice addressed the state House of Representatives in Michigan.
Although her topics were "The Science of Government" and "Antagonisms
in Society," she infused these speeches, like her others in this period, with
women's rights demands. "The agitation on the question of woman suffrage
began in this state with the advent of Ernestine L. Rose" in 1846, a Michigan
feminist wrote later.[3]

A few months after going to Michigan, Rose traveled to Washington,
DC, where she met Anne Royall, a legendary character who published *The
Huntress*, a free-thought newspaper. Royall had the distinction of being the
only American woman ever tried and convicted as "a common scold," the
almost obsolete medieval crime of "kindling strife" with one's neighbors,
which only females could commit. (The 1829 lawsuit, brought by clergymen,
occasioned the building of a "ducking stool," but the punishment was trans-
muted into a $10 fine.) A freethinker like Rose, Royall lobbied Congress for
decades in favor of the separation of church and state, taking "Good works
instead of long prayers" as her motto. But she was too individualistic and
peculiar an ally for Rose to make into either a model or a friend. However,
when Rose returned to Washington in 1854 with Susan B. Anthony, they visited this eighty-five-year-old "Living Curiosity." Royall "lives in a small house,
has two little boys whom she is educating," Anthony wrote in her diary:

> She is the most filthy speciman of humanity I ever beheld, her fingers
> look like birds claws, in color & attenuity, they shone as if glazed.
>   A great black New Foundland dog, old Cat & kittens sat at her
> feet—& Mrs. R. says eight years ago she had in addition to these

2 Guinea hens & two little pigs running about the floor—she was writing her editorial for this weeks paper. Said I to her what a wonderful woman you are, she answered me, "I know it."[4]

In 1847, the year after she met Royall, Ernestine Rose went to Columbia and Charleston, South Carolina. Her reasons for going south remain unknown, but this trip sparked her first anti-slavery lecture. "After being there a little time, her soul was stirred by what she saw going on," a friend recounted:

> So she advertised that she would publicly lecture the Charlestonians. The novelty of a woman appearing in public attracted a large audience, who were amazed and overwhelmed to hear her rate them about slavery. . . . It was due partly to her sex, and partly to the paralysis caused by her audacity, that she was not torn to pieces; as it was, it required considerable influence to get her safely out of the city.[5]

Rose expanded this account in an 1853 speech to a New York anti-slavery audience. She said that she told a Carolina lawyer who wanted the southern states to secede that the region could never be independent since the North provided it with food, clothing, and education. When another male southerner asked her what she thought of South Carolina, she answered that the state was "a century, at least, behind," since "the only civilization," which she defined as "industry and the mechanical arts," was performed by slaves. The Carolinian told her "to thank her stars for being a woman" because if she were a man, she would be given "a coat of tar and feathers." Rose replied that she "always thanked her stars for being a woman" and that she "was an Abolitionist in the fullest sense of the word," adding that white southerners were "so exceedingly lazy and inactive . . . that it would be an act of charity to give you something to do, were it even to give me a coat of tar and feathers. To say that he was enraged would express no idea whatsoever." Rose concluded this 1853 speech by raising the issue of women's rights. "The slaves of the South are not the only people that are in bondage. All women are excluded from the enjoyment of that liberty which your Declaration of Independence asserts to be the inalienable right of all." She ended with the familiar Owenite precept that "emancipation from every kind of bondage is my principle. I go for the recognition of human rights, without distinction of sect, party, sex, or color."[6]

In 1837, a year after the Roses arrived in New York, the Anti-Slavery Convention of American Women met in the city. The first political gathering of women in the nation, this integrated group had to combat both racism and sexism—most white Americans believed in black inferiority and in leaving the public realm to men. A few years later, in 1840, the chief US anti-slavery organization divided over women's participation, with the far larger group opposing it. Although seven previously chosen female delegates, led by the Quaker activist Lucretia Mott, crossed the Atlantic to represent the United States at the World Anti-Slavery Convention in London, they were not allowed to take their seats. Excluded from leading anti-slavery societies and even barred from presenting petitions to the US Congress, many female anti-slavery workers ceased campaigning during these years, just when Ernestine Rose entered the fray.[7]

Most US abolitionists found the strength to combat anti-black laws and prejudice through radical Christianity, which denounced slavery as a cardinal sin, as William Lloyd Garrison, leader of the pro-woman anti-slavery group, had done. Garrison's uncompromising ideals included avoiding all violence and leaving one's church if it countenanced slavery or segregated its black congregants into a "Negro pew," as most of them did then. From 1844 on, he also denounced the US Constitution and publicly burned it at least once for endorsing southern slavery. He advocated "disunion" from the slaveholding states and refused to vote, since elections tacitly condoned the institution of slavery enshrined in the US Constitution. Believing that women should have the same rights as men, he held that they should be able to vote. He also hoped that they would choose not to do it, like him. Garrison wholeheartedly supported women's rights, creating a "Ladies Department" to publish their writings in his newspaper, *The Liberator*, sitting in the balcony with the rejected female delegates at the London convention, and inviting Ernestine Rose to lecture in an 1844 series he produced in Boston. Garrison and Rose became friendly allies in the 1850s.[8]

Female abolitionists were especially inspired by radical interpretations of Christianity. They saw slavery as a "giant sin" and opposition to it as "the cause of God." Abby Kelley Foster, whom Rose later joined on an anti-slavery lecture tour, declared, "I can say from my heart of hearts, abolitionism is Christianity applied to slavery: here is the rock upon which our cause rests, and 'the gates of hell shall not prevail against it.'" Working for anti-slavery led many of these women to conclude that "the rights of the slave & woman blend like the colors of a rainbow," or as Abby Kelley put it, "In striving to strike his [the slave's] irons off, we found most surely that we were manacled *ourselves*." Most early US feminists came to support women's rights because of the discrimination they experienced from male allies who opposed their full participation within the abolitionist movement.[9]

Ernestine Rose, in contrast, came to woman's rights and anti-slavery in a completely different way, through Owenism. "Not being a native of this country, I have probably had some different ideas with regard to the working of slavery from what many abolitionists have. I do not belong to any abolition Society," she told her 1853 audience. Socialist Owenites like Rose condemned the "wage slavery" of early industrialism as much as the "chattel slavery" of the US South. Owenism taught her to "go for emancipation of all kinds—white and black, man and woman. Humanity's children are . . . all one and the same family, inheriting the same earth; therefore there should be no slaves of any kind among them."[10]

Most American Owenites, however, believed it was more important to combat Christianity than southern slavery, since they held that biblical justifications of slavery provided the chief support for the South's "peculiar institution." John Collins, the founder of Skaneateles, left anti-slavery to become an Owenite for just this reason. In addition, many Owenites shared most white Americans' bias against blacks. "Although according to our principles, no . . . *colour* can be excluded from our society," Rose's Owenite friend Lewis Masquerier wrote, "the prejudice of colour is yet so great that some of our members cannot bear to sit down with them." Ernestine Rose did not share this racism, nor did she share the religious beliefs that led most female abolitionists to work against slavery. Garrison recalled that "during the whole history of the movement, with the single exception of that noble woman, Ernestine L. Rose, I do not remember a single prominent speaker on our platform who could truthfully have been called an infidel. Not that we should have failed to welcome their aid, but that like so many Christians of the period they were hostile or indifferent."[11]

Although Rose remained the only atheist within radical abolitionism, she met activists there who shared many of her values. Originally prejudiced against Rose because of her atheism, Julia Wilbur, a white Quaker, came to praise her as "a lovely and noble woman . . . a glorious woman" because "in speaking of the *wrongs of woman* she did not forget the poor outcast from society, the *prostitute* wh. other Lecturers have scarcely, if ever, alluded to." The white Rochester reformer Amy Post asked her black abolitionist friend in New York, William Nell, to send her Rose's lithographic portrait. Most of these radical allies came from white Quaker and black evangelical communities. Like Rose, they worked for more than one reform movement. Like her, they advocated human rights for everyone, everywhere, and wanted to end all discrimination based on race, color, class, or sex.[12]

In the summer of 1849, Rose joined with three of these radical abolitionists—the Philadelphia Quaker Lucretia Mott and Stephen and

Abby Kelley Foster from Worcester—for an anti-slavery speaking tour through upstate New York. Mott developed an independent Christian vision that relied on "Truth for authority, not authority for truth." This enabled her to reject standard biblical interpretations, as well as most clerical and political authorities. Frequently lecturing against slavery, Mott struggled with the Society of Friends, which alternated between treating her as a respected leader and a dangerous dissident, too enmeshed in "worldly" issues like abolition. Although Mott asserted that she was a "heretic" who gloried "in radicalism and ultraism," she remained a believer who thought "free-thinking to be a religious duty" mandated by Jesus Christ. "Free-thinking" for Mott meant "independent-minded," while for Rose it denoted having no religious beliefs whatsoever. Despite these distinctions, Mott and Rose admired each other, often shared woman's rights platforms, and occasionally visited each other. "She is one of our best," Mott later wrote about Rose, while in her turn, Rose praised Mott as standing "forward nobly and gloriously."[13]

Rose had less contact with the Fosters. Abby Kelley began lecturing against slavery in 1838 and encountered even greater hostility than that which greeted Ernestine Rose. Audiences opposed to both abolition and woman's rights hurled "unsavory eggs, the contents of stables and out-houses" at her and screamed epithets like "Jezebel," "fornicator," and "nigger." She married her fellow abolitionist Stephen Foster in 1845. He had especial contempt for churches that did not condemn slavery and developed the tactic of attending them, denouncing their sermons and then going limp when dragged out and arrested. Abby Kelley Foster remembered "standing against the whole world on the woman question." Not having experienced discrimination within anti-slavery and ignorant of free-thought practice, she maintained that abolition provided the only movement that "received women on equal terms with men. No other women were on the public platform."[14]

This quartet toured from May to August 1849. Differences soon developed. *The New York Anti-Slavery Standard* reported on an interchange in Milton, New York. In her speech, Mrs. Rose, "the eloquent Pole," showed that she has "a vein of kindness and charity running through her every look, thought and word. . . . She views humanity as one great unity." Consequently, "all mankind are her brothers, and the meanest does not escape her attention." In contrast, Stephen Foster was more "combative," using "satire" with "an edge of surpassing keenness" to make his points. He stated "his dissent from the notion" that "'more flies can be caught with molasses than vinegar.'" After he finished, Rose "felt called upon to reply to some of Mr. Foster's remarks. . . . Her exposition of the law of kindness was beautifully grand, and grandly sublime," the newspaper commented, and the audience "hung upon the eloquence of her lips" in "silent stillness and breathless suspense." Rose's rejection of Stephen Foster's militant approach alienated Abby Kelley Foster. Ernestine Rose "made very acceptable speeches but they were not so useful as remarks from a person who sympathizes fully with us would have been," she wrote a fellow abolitionist. In contrast, Lucretia Mott did "great service" and performed "invaluable" work.[15]

Like a number of other abolitionist lecturers, the Fosters were paid for each speech they gave. Rose remained unpaid, funding her own tours, but she continued to lecture for anti-slavery, or attempted to do so. The *New York Herald* fomented a successful campaign against the May 1850 annual meeting of the Antislavery Association in the city, urging its readers to prevent "black and white brethren and sisters" from "fraternizing, slobbering over each other, speaking, praying, singing, blaspheming, and cursing the Constitution of our glorious Union." When the abolitionists tried to speak, the mob shouted them down "with hisses, catcalls, and a general charivari" as the mayor and police stood by. When Rose began lecturing, a man shouted ironically, "Women's rights, boys!" Laughter ensued as she tried to talk about similar suppressions of free speech in Ireland. The mob's leader declared that he respected "ladies" but doubted "very much whether women who cohabit and mix with the woolly-headed negro, are entitled to any respect from a white man." Rose kept patiently repeating "Are you done?" but after fifteen minutes of continuous jeers had to leave the stage without giving her speech.[16]

This melée introduced her to Frederick Douglass, the era's leading black abolitionist. By the time they met at this gathering, Douglass had gained fame for his slave narrative, his oratory, and his outspoken anti-slavery newspaper. He and Rose lectured together many times throughout the years, both against slavery and for woman's rights. They each used the slogan "Agitate, agitate!" in their speeches. No mention of Douglass by Rose survives, but he thanked both her and William Rose for being among those "who met me as a brother, and by their kind consideration did much to make endurable the rebuffs I encountered elsewhere." When Ernestine Rose died, he paid tribute to her as being one of "the best of mankind [who] can afford to support unpopular opinions" and among "the glorious constellation" of those who "cheer us on in the good work of lifting women in the fullest sense to the dignity of American liberty and American citizenship." He also acknowledged that Rose was one of the early feminists who convinced him to support married women's property rights. Rose also frequently shared the platform with black female abolitionists like Sojourner Truth and Frances Ellen Watkins Harper, but neither she nor they left comments about each other.[17]

While Ernestine Rose lectured for anti-slavery, she also continued her work to compel New York State to grant married women their right to own property. She addressed the legislature five times during the 1840s on this subject. Lack of these rights made married women legally "dead" and put them in the same category as infants, convicted felons, slaves, and the insane. Property rights challenged the legal fiction that husband and wife constituted "one person" with identical interests. In April of 1848, New York finally gave wives a limited victory: women married after 1848 could retain property but not their earnings. "This was not much, to be sure," Rose later commented, "for at best it was only for the favored few, and not for the suffering many. But it was a beginning, and an important step, for it proved that a law had to be altered, and some others might need it just as much."[18]

Working for married women's property rights introduced Ernestine Rose to Paulina Wright Davis, an important colleague in the future women's movement. While Rose walked door to door with her petition in lower Manhattan, Paulina Wright "sent a petition of similar import with thirty names" from Utica, New York. "Neither of these petitions made much impression or received much attention," she wrote later. Rose and Wright met around 1840 as they lobbied representatives in Albany. At that time, Wright also worked for abolition, and two years later, she and her husband left their church to protest its pro-slavery views. She wanted to speak publicly for her causes, but unlike William Rose, her husband objected. "After some unhappy hours," she decided not to "lecture on antislavery or women's rights so long as my husband feels as he does about it. I could joyfully bear all the trials and reproach that would follow but it is my duty to seek the *happiness* of my *husband*," she wrote Abby Kelley. Wright's husband died in 1845 and left her independently wealthy. She then moved to New York, studied medicine, and began lecturing to all-female audiences on anatomy and health throughout the Northeast. In 1849, she married Thomas Davis, a Rhode Island anti-slavery politician who supported both her public speaking and her dedication to woman's rights.[19]

Paulina Wright Davis and Ernestine Rose became close allies within the women's rights movement. Although Davis occasionally considered Rose to be too "ultra" because of her free-thought views, she paid tribute to her in her 1870 *History* of the movement, calling her "a beautiful and highly cultivated Polish lady" who at the 1851 Convention "made an address of an hour in length, which has never been surpassed."[20]

"By chance in Albany in 1844," while lobbying for married women's property rights, Paulina Wright and Ernestine Rose met another future leader of the women's movement, Elizabeth Cady Stanton. The three advocates addressed New York State legislative committees as well as circulating petitions. Stanton and Rose became allies in the women's rights movement during the 1860s.[21]

Stanton had first gone to London in 1840 on her honeymoon with Henry Stanton, an abolitionist politician who attended the anti-slavery convention that refused to seat Lucretia Mott and the other female delegates. Elizabeth Cady Stanton later wrote that this event radicalized her. Before meeting Mott, she "had never heard a woman" lecture, but when Mott did so, she "found in this new friend a woman emancipated from all faith in man-made creeds. . . . It seemed to me like meeting a being from some larger planet, to find a woman who dared to question the opinions of Popes, Kings, Synods, Parliaments." Despite Stanton's admiration for Mott, the two women did not meet again for any length of time until 1848. During the 1840s, Stanton lived privately, moving three times and giving birth to the first three of her seven children.[22]

In July of 1848, Lucretia Mott traveled to upstate New York, where she and Stanton reconnected. Their reunion, the passage of the state's Married Women's Property Act, and the recent creation of two local groups supporting equal rights for women—the abolitionist Liberty Party and the dissident Quaker Congregational Friends—moved them to action. Stanton, Mott, Mott's sister, and two Quaker friends rapidly organized the first women's rights convention, held in Stanton's village of Seneca Falls. Following her lead, the organizers used the Declaration of Independence as their template, substituting women for the rebellious American colonists and men for the tyrant-king George III. "We hold these truths to be self-evident," they wrote, "that all men and women are created equal." With Lucretia's husband, James Mott, presiding, the meeting charged men with denying women the rights they claimed for themselves, from no taxation without representation, to access to higher education and decent jobs, to the suffrage itself. The group reconvened two weeks later in the city of Rochester, where they repeated and strengthened their claims.[23]

Ernestine Rose attended neither the Seneca Falls nor the Rochester meeting. Both conventions were advertised only in local upstate New York newspapers, were called on very short notice, and drew audiences who lived in the immediate area. Roughly 300 people gathered for each event and about 100 of them signed the resulting Declarations. As the first-ever women's rights convention, Seneca Falls received a great deal of publicity. Frederick

Douglass, the convention's only African American participant, praised it in his *North Star* newspaper; New York City's *Herald* gave it a condescending write-up, calling the women's use of the Declaration of Independence "amusing." As its influence grew beyond its local origins, Seneca Falls transformed public sentiments in favor of female equality into an expanding movement for change. After 1848, women's rights groups met throughout the Northeast, culminating in the first National Woman's Rights Convention in Worcester in 1850. From then on, these national conventions met annually (except for 1857) until the Civil War. [24]

At the 1853 national in Cleveland, Ernestine Rose paid tribute to the Seneca Falls Declaration. It is "no less great, noble, and important, than the first honorable declaration of Independence," she asserted, adding that "this declaration of women's independence is even more far-sighted and sublime. For . . . it was never before dreamed that woman would be included in it." The creative imagination displayed at Seneca Falls helped bring a national women's movement into being.[25]

Before that movement coalesced, however, Ernestine Rose lectured for free thought as well as anti-slavery. Free thought continued to decline. Its founders were dying off and only half as many supporters attended the annual Thomas Paine dinners as had a decade earlier. From 1848 on, Rose delivered the keynote address at these celebrations, usually adding women's rights claims to her speeches. In 1848, she replied to a toast to "Woman" by saying she was "happy . . . to see so many Ladies present" since women in particular benefited from "the works and exertions of Thomas Paine." "Superstition keeps women ignorant, dependent, and enslaved beings," she continued, "Knowledge will make them free. The churches have been built upon their necks; and it is only by throwing them off, that they will be able to stand up in the full majesty of their being, and assert their rights and equality with man." The next year, Rose recited a poem predicting women's progress (and also added it to at least one public letter):

> *When as the equal to man each woman will think,*
> *And burst all the fetters that bind her,*
> *At the fountain of knowledge she freely will drink*
> *And be what fair Nature designed her.*
> *Then, Science will shine like the bright orb of day,*
> *Diffusing its influence o'er all,*
> *And those who now turn from her teaching away*
> *Will be proud to attend to her call.*

While women now attended the Paine dinners, almost always with their husbands, Ernestine Rose remained the only female speaker who replied to men's toasts (although other women occasionally made them), gave lectures, or presided over the festivities. Her male colleagues complimented her by emphasizing her femininity and often punning on her last name. "Mrs. Rose—She was the Morning Glory of Poland; the Lily of England; and she *is* the Rose of America," went a typical tribute. Freethinking men's toasts about women in general either praised female company: "Their agreeable society is the height of domestic felicity" or disparaged their religiosity: "Women ... when they are emancipated from Clerical Influence the true millennium is at hand."[26]

In addition to infusing them with women's rights demands, Ernestine Rose also began commenting on international events in her Paine speeches. She deplored Irish oppression and applauded the European Revolutions of 1848–49, which sparked nationalist rebellions and replaced some monarchs with democratic governments. The United States had been the first nation to recognize these new republics, and Rose gave full credit to Thomas Paine for ensuring that "among the many nations of earth we are as yet the only one that enjoys the blessings of comparative liberty and independence." By 1850, however, those European revolutions had been suppressed by reactionary forces—a defeat that echoed throughout the Paine evening's proceedings. The *Boston Investigator* told its readers that the coffee and tea provided after dinner "disappeared just as surely as Hungary has disappeared before Haynau" (the Austrian general who brutally put down the Hungarian uprising) and praised the United States, "to which the oppressed of all nations are hastening."

Rose built on that theme. Introduced as a Polish native who inherited the spirit of Kosciusko, she began by hoping that her "poor, unhappy country ... will yet rise, like a Phoenix out of her ashes." After praising Thomas Paine, she asserted that "Paine, Lafayette, Kosciusko, and many other noble minds who enlisted in the cause of right over might were foreigners; and ... this country owes a debt of gratitude which it is now time to pay." In part, Rose was rebutting the nativist sentiments of the New York–based American Party—nicknamed the "Know-Nothings"—which urged limits on immigration, a twenty-one-year residency before citizenship could be applied for, and restriction of political offices to the native-born. She then urged Congress to grant asylum and give land to contemporary European "martyrs of freedom," like the Pole Jósef Bem, the Hungarian Lajos Kossuth, and the Italian Guiseppe Mazzini, all of whom had rebelled unsuccessfully against the Austrian Empire.[27]

Ernestine Rose turned next to her "Polish countrywoman . . . now in this city," Apollonia Jagiello, who provided a heroic example "where woman has burst her fetters, and stood up in defense of Humanity." Jagiello had fought in the unsuccessful 1846 Polish uprising against Russia and in the 1848 Polish and Hungarian Revolutions before emigrating to America. Although Rose deplored both violence and war, she argued that Jagiello proved that "woman is wanting neither in strength of mind, courage, nor perseverence, and if her capacities and powers were to decide her sphere of action (and nothing else ought to do it), methinks not a few of our legislators, would . . . have to change places with woman." As a "foreigner," Rose necessarily developed an international perspective. She brought this point of view to the first National Woman's Rights meeting in 1850, where she asserted, "This Convention was not for the women of New England, nor of Old England, but for the world."[28]

That convention arose from a June anti-slavery meeting in Boston. With Paulina Wright Davis presiding and "a large number in attendance," but not Ernestine Rose, William Lloyd Garrison presented the case for a separate women's movement. Just like slaves, he argued, women deserved equal rights, including the right to vote. Just like slaves, women might initially demur and deny they were oppressed, but they would soon realize that there was no "good reason why woman should not have her political rights in this country." The meeting ended with Davis appointing an all-female Committee of Arrangements, who agreed to convene in the major city of Worcester that October. The resulting "Call" to the Convention asked women and men to "meet each other in free conference" to discuss "Woman's Rights, Duties, and Relations," specifically

> Her Education, Literary, Scientific, and Artistic;
> Her Avocations, Industrial, Commercial, and Professional;
> Her Interests, Pecuniary, Civil, and Political; in a word
> Her Rights as an Individual, and her Functions as a Citizen.

It concluded by urging those interested to "give the protection of your name and the benefits of your efforts" to achieve "the success of this high and holy movement."[29]

Although her associates Paulina Wright Davis, Abby Kelley Foster, William Lloyd Garrison, Lucretia Mott, and Elizabeth Cady Stanton were among the eighty-nine signers of this invitation, Ernestine Rose's name was not on it. She almost certainly had not been asked to participate because of her outspoken and unpopular opposition to religion. The "Call" to the

Worcester Convention contained many religious references, in addition to designating the movement as "holy." It associated women's rights with "the world's redemption," maintaining that "the inspiration of the Almighty" led "Womanhood . . . to assert its divinely chartered rights," and declaring that "the Providence of God" vindicated the Convention's aims "to separate the light from darkness." During the Convention, every speaker and correspondent except Ernestine Rose used Christianity to justify their demands. Davis's Opening Address interwove radical claims for women's rights with words like "salvation," "martyrdom," "angels," and "Divine Providence." She applied Jesus's words about the Romans to men: " 'They know not what they do,' is the apology that crucified womankind must concede in justice and pity to the wrongdoers." As another female speaker argued, "Only where Christianity has dawned and *right* not *might* been the rule, has woman had anything like her true position." A third, the female doctor Harriot Hunt, declared that she had only been able to do her work because of her "state of religious trust and a dependence upon the Lord as the source of all life." Elizabeth Cady Stanton, who did not attend, sent a letter declaring "I believe in Christ" before writing that "God intended" man and woman to be "always together, in counsel, government, and every department of industry."[30]

Given her atheism, Ernestine Rose's restraint at the Convention over such religiosity was remarkable. She never argued there that women's subordination was due to religion, never called religion "superstition," never attacked any religious belief, never denigrated biblical authority. She continued this policy at subsequent women's rights meetings, expressing her atheism only in free-thought forums, like the Paine dinners or the 1853 Hartford Bible Convention. Realizing that in the women's rights community she had finally "found a voice" that "echoed" her own, Rose accommodated her co-workers in order to serve the cause that she declared "has so long lain at my heart."[31] By muting her free-thought beliefs, she made possible her participation in this movement that often invoked Christianity to justify its feminism.

In this way Rose was able to play a major role at the first Worcester Convention (she gave her "speech which has never been surpassed" the following year). Early in the proceedings, she was elected to the powerful Business Committee. Throughout the Convention, this committee led the way, presenting resolutions often more far-reaching than those suggested in speeches. Committee deliberations remained secret, so Rose's role in discussions cannot be known, but all the measures squared with her belief in favor of complete equality between "white and black, man and woman." She introduced the first resolution, a task for an experienced and reliable speaker.

Wearing a russet gown with her "black hair let down in ringlets over her eyes," Rose moved that since "the very contracted sphere of action prescribed for woman . . . is highly injurious to her physical, mental, and moral development," the Convention should work "for her political, legal, and social equality with man." The *New-York Tribune* reported that Rose spoke "with great eloquence on the subject of the resolution." Arguing that women were currently "transferred" from being "the property" of their parents to the property of their husbands, she asserted that if women had rights and a decent education, "marriage would be the union of two hearts from real affections . . . instead of being as it now too frequently is, an artificial bond producing more misery than happiness."

She then turned to the recently passed Fugitive Slave Act, which mandated that runaway blacks be arrested in the North and returned to the South, a measure detested by this anti-slavery audience because it tried to force northern complicity in these actions. "But it was no more unjust than some of the laws are towards women," Rose maintained. "If a woman is compelled by the tyranny and ill treatment of her husband, to leave him and seek refuge among her friends, the law will deliver her up into his hands. He may compel her return." Rose concluded by saying that "she did not propose to examine the laws that bear so unequally upon woman. What she claimed was that the laws should be made equally for both." "Hers was the speech of the afternoon," a Boston newspaper commented.[32]

Rose spoke again that evening, declaring that this convention was "for the world." After admitting that unfortunately the greatest opposition she had encountered "came from her own sex, who had the false idea that they were naturally inferior to men," she declared that "that great error would have to be attacked boldly." Rose then evoked the American past, contending that the lack of attention paid to women's history contributed to her sex's mistaken sense of inferiority. "Much has been said of the Pilgrim fathers, but what had been said of the Pilgrim mothers?" she asked. "Had they not suffered as their husbands had done?" Turning then to her European past, which she confused with American history, she accused "those very pilgrim fathers" of burning "the daughters of the pilgrim mothers" at the stake as witches, "thus showing the prejudice against the sex was present even in those boasted times." Rose concluded by arguing that "society would never strike its natural tone until woman's equality with man . . . was recognized." "Loud applause followed Mrs. R's speech," the Boston *Daily Mail* reported.[33]

On the Convention's second day, the Business Committee recommended a series of "next-steps"—resolutions working for women's equality in education, employment, government, and morals. The final resolution sought to extend women's rights to "the million and a half of slave women of the South, the most grossly wronged and foully outraged of all women. . . . [W]e will bear in our heart of hearts the memory of the trampled womanhood of the plantation, and omit no effort to raise it to a share in the rights we claim for ourselves." Although this measure prompted later discussion over tying women's rights too tightly to anti-slavery, it passed without debate at the Convention. "Mrs. Rose" then addressed the group "in a short but animated speech showing that women were inventive, and that the reason they have not produced high inventions is that they have been continually employed with trifling duties, as drudge in the kitchen, or a puppet-show in the parlor."

The final session was especially well attended. "Every spot in the large room was filled with persons standing in a solid phalanx," the *New-York Tribune* reported, "There must have been over a thousand people present through nearly all the meetings. . . . Many have gone away, not being able to find admission." The Convention's last act was to establish six standing committees—Ernestine Rose was designated "Chairman" of the one on Civil and Political Functions. In conclusion, Davis thanked those speakers "less well known to the public" than leading anti-slavery advocates like Garrison or Mott. Among them was Rose, who "gave utterance to her clear strong thoughts in her own peculiarly graceful style of eloquence."[34]

This was a tactful way of referring to Rose's accent, which contemporaries always noticed. "There too was the Polish woman Ernestine L. Rose, ardent, eloquent, intellectual," Harriot Hunt recalled. "Her foreign accent added interest to the truths she uttered." Newspapers covering the Convention all mentioned Rose's distinctive manner of speech, emphasizing her foreignness although they often misplaced her origin. The *Tribune* wrote that "her French accent and extemporaneous manner added quite a charm to her animated and forcible style," while the *Daily Mail* asserted that "her sonorous German style of expression, and the use of certain idiomatic phrases, more than her accent, showed this lady to be a native of the land of Goethe."[35]

This 1850 Convention generated a women's rights movement. It received a great deal of publicity, both positive and negative, but all agreed that an important new force had been unleashed. The *New York Herald* published a lengthy lead editorial, charging that the Convention was founded on "abolition, socialism, amalgamation [interracial sex], and infidelity." Garrison's *The Liberator*, in contrast, wrote that "in point of numbers, spirit, and ability" it was "the noblest series of meetings that we ever attended," crowded with "intelligent, orderly, and interested" people. He added that "the speaking was uniformly the best we ever heard from such a large number of speakers." He mentioned a few of them by name, including Ernestine Rose.[36]

Although only 300 women and men signed up as members, close to 1,000 "Friends of Woman's Rights" attended the Worcester meeting. Participants came not just from New England and the Mid-Atlantic but from as far away as Ohio, Iowa, and even California. Although they were not present, both Dr. Elizabeth Blackwell of London and Maria Waring of Dublin received places on the Committee of Industrial Avocations, signifying the movement's international scope. National Woman's Rights Conventions followed each year for the next decade, except in 1857. They convened in Syracuse and Cleveland, Philadelphia and New York, drawing audiences of thousands. State and local conventions also proliferated. Women's rights women and their supporters petitioned legislatures and politicians; published in newspapers and magazines, some of which they founded; spoke at public meetings and private gatherings. Although Ernestine Rose remained the only foreigner among her American-born coworkers and the only freethinker within this all-Protestant group, most of them came to accept her. In the mid-1850s, Susan B. Anthony remembered, "one of our noblest men said to me, 'You would better never hold another convention than allow Ernestine L. Rose on your platform'; because that eloquent woman, who ever stood for justice and freedom, did not believe in the plenary inspiration of the Bible. Did we banish Mrs. Rose? No, indeed!"[37]

Instead, by the Second National meeting in Worcester, 1851, Rose had become integral to the movement. Now placed on the Central Committee, she gave the Convention's main address, the one discussed in my introduction. Proclaiming that "Humanity has no sex," Rose challenged unequal laws, customs, and practices, maintaining that all would benefit from female equality. Convinced that now was the time to achieve "this great reform," Rose argued that an unprecedented era had begun. "A new sign has appeared in our social zodiac," she declared to her audience of over a thousand,

> prophetic of the most important changes, pregnant with the most beneficial results, that have ever taken place in the annals of human history. We have before us a novel spectacle, an hitherto unheard-of undertaking, in comparison to which all others fall into insignificance, the grandest step in the onward progress of humanity. One half the race stands up against the injustice and oppression of the other, and demands the recognition of its existence, and of its rights.

Arguing that the movement needed "many more Conventions, to protest against the wrong and claim our rights," she ended by using a carefully worded metaphor calculated to appeal to her religious audience without violating her own free-thought principles: "We must remember that we have a crusade before us, far holier and more righteous than led warriors to Palestine—a crusade, not to deprive any one of his rights, but to claim our own. And as our cause is a nobler one, so also should be the means to achieve it. We therefore must put on the armor of charity, carry before us the banner of truth, and defend ourselves with the shield of right against the invaders of our liberty."[38] The 1851 Convention in Worcester ushered in a period of intense activism for early feminism. At the center of it was Ernestine Rose.

1 The only surviving photograph of Ernestine Rose, taken in 1856. Her pose deliberately mimics that of her predecessor, Frances Wright, shown in Figure 6. Schlesinger Library, Radcliffe Institute, Harvard University.

2 1856 lithograph of Ernestine Rose by Leopold Grozelier. Library of Congress LC-USZ62-52045.

3 Engraving of Ernestine Rose from a daguerreotype, in a collection of Portraits of American Abolitionists. Massachusetts Historical Society, 81.565.

4 The Piótrkow Trybunalski Synagogue of Rose's day in a modern photograph. Wikipedia.

5 Portrait of Robert Owen in 1834, at the time when Ernestine Rose met him. W. H. Brooke, National Portrait Gallery, London, 943.

6 Portrait of Frances Wright, Rose's predecessor. Frontispiece of *History of Woman Suffrage*, vol. 1, 1881.

7 *Boston Investigator* masthead, 1875, showing Paine Hall, which was completed that year. The mottos "Devoted to the Development and Promotion of Universal Mental Liberty" and "Truth, Perseverance, Union, Justice—The Means. Happiness the End. Hear All Sides, Then Decide" had been on the masthead for decades. The books at the base of the building are by Hume, Hobbs, Jefferson, Kneeland, Paine, and Voltaire. From 19th Century US Newspapers database.

8 Portrait of Lucretia Mott in 1858 when she and Rose worked together for women's rights. Friends Historical Library, Swarthmore College.

9 Portrait of Paulina Wright Davis in the 1850s when she and Rose worked together for women's rights. Library of Congress, LC-USZ62-37939.

10 French feminist Jenny P. d'Héricourt, around the time she interviewed Rose in Paris in 1856. Bibliothèque nationale de France, 78A 40464.

11 Elizabeth Cady Stanton and Susan B. Anthony around 1870. Stanton routinely wore this cross around her neck in these years. Smithsonian Institution, Washington, DC S/NPG.77.48.

12 Lucy Stone in 1848, with short hair and wearing the bloomer outfit. Library of Congress, LC-USZ62-77001.

13 Horace Seaver, editor of the *Boston Investigator*, around the time of his 1864 battle over Judaism with Rose. Library of Congress, BL2775.54.

14 J[osiah] P[aine] Mendum, publisher of the *Boston Investigator* and Rose's friend. From Samuel Putnam, *400 Years of Free Thought* (New York: Truth Seeker Co., 1894).

A PETITION

FOR

UNIVERSAL SUFFRAGE.

- - -

To the Senate and House of Representatives:

The undersigned, Women of the United States, respectfully ask an amendment of the Constitution that shall prohibit the several States from disfranchising any of their citizens on the ground of sex.

In making our demand for Suffrage, we would call your attention to the fact that we represent fifteen million people—one half the entire population of the country—intelligent, virtuous, native-born American citizens; and yet stand outside the pale of political recognition.

The Constitution classes us as "free people," and counts us *whole* persons in the basis of representation; and yet are we governed without our consent, compelled to pay taxes without appeal, and punished for violations of law without choice of judge or juror.

The experience of all ages, the Declarations of the Fathers, the Statute Laws of our own day, and the fearful revolution through which we have just passed, all prove the uncertain tenure of life, liberty and property so long as the ballot—the only weapon of self-protection—is not in the hand of every citizen.

Therefore, as you are now amending the Constitution, and, in harmony with advancing civilization, placing new safeguards round the individual rights of four millions of emancipated slaves, we ask that you extend the right of Suffrage to Woman—the only remaining class of disfranchised citizens—and thus fulfil your Constitutional obligation "to Guarantee to every State in the Union a Republican form of Government."

As all partial application of Republican principles must ever breed a complicated legislation as well as a discontented people, we would pray your Honorable Body, in order to simplify the machinery of government and ensure domestic tranquillity, that you legislate hereafter for persons, citizens, tax-payers, and not for class or caste.

For justice and equality your petitioners will ever pray.

NAMES.	RESIDENCE.
Elizabeth Stanton	New York
Susan B. Anthony	Rochester — N.Y.
Antoinette Brown Blackwell	New York
Lucy Stone	Newark N. Jersey
Joanna S. Morse	48 Livingston. Brooklyn
Ernestine L. Rose	New York
Harriet E. Eaton	6. West 14th street N.Y.
Catharine C. Wilkeson	83 Clinton Place New York
Elizabeth R. Tilton	48 Livingston St. Brooklyn
Mary Trowler Gilbert	293 W. 19th St New York
Mary E. Gilbert	New York
M. Griffith	New York.

15 *A Petition for Universal Suffrage*, January 29, 1866. Ernestine Rose signed in large letters, using especially black ink. National Archives, RG.233, 39th Cong., 1st sess., House 39A-H14.9.

16 "The Champions of Woman's Suffrage," from *Harper's Bazar* [*sic.*], June 12, 1869: 38. New York Public Library.

MRS. FAWCETT   MRS. MARK PATTISON   MRS. ERNESTINE ROSE MISS LYDIA E. BECKER   MISS RHODA GARRETT

WOMEN'S RIGHTS—A MEETING AT THE HANOVER SQUARE ROOMS

17 "Women's Rights—A Meeting at the Hanover Square Rooms." "Mrs. Ernestine Rose" is seated third from the left in the front row. In addition to her name, those of the English feminists Mrs. [Millicent Garrett] Fawcett, Mrs. Mark Pattison, Miss Lydia E. Becker, and Miss Rhoda Garrett are given. *The Graphic* (London), vol. 5, May 25, 1872. New York Public Library.

18 Photograph of Charles Bradlaugh, around the time he and Rose met in London in 1870. © National Portrait Gallery, London.

19 Photograph of Alice Bradlaugh when Ernestine Rose knew her in the 1880s. From Arthur Bonner and Charles Bradlaugh Bonner, *Hypatia Bradlaugh Bonner: The Story of Her Life* (London: Watts 1942): 40.

20 Photograph of Hypatia Bradlaugh Bonner in 1890, two years before Rose's death. From Arthur Bonner and Charles Bradlaugh Bonner, *Hypatia Bradlaugh Bonner: The Story of Her Life* (London: Watts 1942): 40.

21 George Jacob Holyoake, Rose's fellow Owenite and friend, in old age, when he and Rose were neighbors for a few months of the year in Brighton. National Portrait Gallery, London.

22 Susan B. Anthony in her office in 1900, with Rose's lithograph on the wall above her head. Sophia Smith Collection, Smith College.

5

"Agitate, Agitate!"

IN 1860, WIVES in New York State finally achieved complete ownership of their property within marriage. "How has all this been achieved?" Ernestine Rose asked rhetorically, "The answer is, by agitation—conventions and public lectures to enlighten woman on the laws which oppressed her—to enlighten men on the injustice he perpetrated against her. . . . By forming public opinion in favor of our claims. . . . Agitate! agitate! Ought to be the motto of every reformer," she concluded. "Agitation is the opposite of stagnation—the one is life, the other death."[1] Throughout the 1850s, Rose had worked constantly for the women's movement, organizing and attending national and local conventions, giving lectures both in New York City and on numerous tours, writing letters and circulating petitions. In 1856, she announced that she had already traveled to twenty-three of the existing thirty-one states—through many of them multiple times. She avoided only the Deep South, where she would not have been allowed to lecture, and the Far West, which was too difficult to reach in these years before the transcontinental railroad. She was "always on the go," an interviewer wrote, "leaving the train to speak two or three hours from a stage, getting back on a rail car only to do the same in other places."[2]

During one of her busiest years, 1855, Ernestine Rose began in January by lecturing at ten different Woman's Rights gatherings throughout western New York State, a tour organized by the new "Napoleon" of the women's movement, Susan B. Anthony. Rose returned to New York City for the Thomas Paine dinner on January 29, where she delivered the main speech, as she did throughout the decade. In early February, she gave a lecture at Taunton, Massachusetts, on women's rights and in mid-month addressed a committee of the New York State Assembly in Albany to present petitions for laws granting women both the vote and "co-partnership" in marriage.[3]

In March, Rose gave two anti-slavery speeches in New York City, and in May she attended the American Anti-Slavery meeting there, where she asked questions but did not lecture. On May 30, she made a major address to the New England Anti-Slavery Convention in Boston and then held forth for two hours that evening on women's rights. In July, she sent the *Boston Investigator* a letter about a new, progressive college in Kirtland, Ohio, and early in August spoke at an "Anti-Slavery Excursion and Pic-Nic" on Long Island. Later that month, she attended a Woman's Rights Convention in Saratoga, New York, presenting one of the "longest and principal addresses." A few days later, she went to the Convention of the Friends of Progress in Waverly, New York, where she gave "some concluding remarks" and was asked to name a baby girl. She called her "Ernestine Frances."[4]

In September, Rose began a two-month lecture tour. She first went to Salem, Ohio, where she spoke at a second Convention of the Friends of Progress. She then gave speeches throughout Michigan on women's rights, anti-slavery, and "the fundamental evils of society." Without returning home, she proceeded on to the two-day Sixth National Woman's Rights Convention in Cincinnati, Ohio, where she spoke both about the progress of the movement and women's right to equal education. While in Cincinnati, she sat in on a series of classes in the new field of anthropology. "I was exceedingly interested, and most truly regretted that I would not remain and attend the whole course," she wrote the *Boston Investigator*. "The subject is of vast importance." She also visited Frances Wright's grave there with an English clergyman turned freethinker, Joseph Barker.

The Cleveland journalist Lemuel E. Barnard interviewed her at length that autumn, publishing his piece on her early in 1856. Rose went on to lecture numerous times in Indiana and Ohio, returning to New York City in early November. Next she published a lengthy letter to Barker praising Wright's novel, *A Few Days in Athens*, and attempted to organize a World's Bible Convention. Bible Conventions, held periodically in the United States, brought believers and freethinkers together to debate the validity of scripture. Rose then gave two anti-slavery talks in Bangor, Maine, in late December, followed by one in Portland.[5]

How was she able to accomplish all this? Her most important support, both emotional and financial, came from her husband, William, whom she "chose with her heart." They had identical values. Both revered Robert Owen and his principles, free thought and Thomas Paine, anti-slavery and women's rights. William helped organize the Paine banquets and often made toasts there, although he never gave speeches. In 1859, for the first and only time, he toasted his wife, "Ernestine L. Rose—The courageous opposer of a corrupt clergy and a corrupter religion, and the faithful and devoted advocate of universal mental freedom." He clipped and saved newspaper articles about her. His jewelry store carried Women's Rights Petitions and portraits of Frances Wright he had published, in addition to the "mounted canes" ornamented with gold and silver he manufactured. He also made "dressing cases, whips, smelling bottles, fancy ivory turning and metal gilding" to order, as well as repairing jewelry. "In this competitive State of ours, few have any money to throw away," Ernestine remarked at a convention. "My husband is a mechanic who works for all he gets"—a mechanic being someone who worked with his hands. An accomplished silversmith, William Rose was commissioned by a group of Indiana women to make a pitcher honoring Robert Owen's son, Robert Dale Owen, for his work to pass legislation giving married women property rights in their state. The 1851 presentation praised the pitcher as "the finest specimen of silver plate we have ever seen . . . chased in the richest and most beautiful manner" with vines, tendrils, and bunches of grapes, adding that "the workmanship reflects the highest credit on the artist." Susan B. Anthony, Ernestine Rose's closest friend in the women's movement, wrote that Ernestine "was idolized by her husband," who "gladly furnished her the means of making her extensive tours, so that through his sense of justice she was enabled to preach the Gospel of Woman's Rights, Anti-Slavery and Free Religion without money and without price."[6]

Rose confirmed Anthony's account in her 1856 interviews with the French feminist Jenny d'Héricourt. Although others in the women's movement were "paid and reimbursed for all the expenses of their lectures," Rose never wanted to support her beliefs "except with her health and out of her own purse." When she was not traveling for her causes, she did the housework, cleaning, and cooking so that she could forgo "the money she might pay a servant to finance her trips and rent the halls where she lectures." This constituted a major sacrifice. Most middle-class families had at least one servant to do the dirtiest chores, from emptying and washing chamber pots, to heating water, carrying in wood or coal and hauling out ashes, in addition to cleaning up the resulting smoke and soot. Even with running water and indoor toilets, doing heavy cleaning and laundry and preparing food from scratch remained arduous tasks. "Mrs. Rose, aside from the obligations imposed by her mission . . . sees few people, and does not make social calls," d'Héricourt wrote. "She doesn't just take care of her housework, she enjoys hearing her kettle sing . . . with the same ears which just a few hours earlier were deafened by the clapping of four thousand hands. Yes, Mrs. Rose does not look down on cleaning her home or cooking and finds time to help her excellent husband with his work." In turn, William almost certainly assisted with the housework, which he had to do by himself during Ernestine's numerous tours. The Roses moved their home and business almost yearly during the 1840s, usually living in an apartment over the jewelry store. In the 1850s, they only changed residences twice, but this did not mean they liked their homes. "We live (I speak from experience) in uncomfortable houses for years, rather than move, though we have the privilege to do so," Ernestine said in 1860.[7]

Overall, their egalitarian marriage provided the bedrock for Ernestine Rose's feminism. Following Owenite precepts, Rose consistently argued that "a true and natural marriage" consisted of "an exclusive conjugal love based on perfect equality between one man and one woman." Rephrasing Justice Blackstone's oft-cited legal formula that "husband and wife are one; and that one is the husband," she maintained that it should rather be interpreted to mean that the couple's "interest ought to be one." This "conveys to my mind the idea of perfect equality," she told a women's rights convention in 1853. "No jarring between them of mine and thine, all is ours, their interests, rights, privileges, enjoyment, happiness, are identical, the same, no more and no less but perfect equality." William's steadfast support enabled Ernestine to pursue her unconventional career, just as calling herself "Mrs. Rose" gave her respectability. Using both her married name and her title—unlike Elizabeth Cady Stanton or Lucretia Mott—also provided the women's movement with credibility. Its adherents were often ridiculed as "old maids," considered "entirely devoid of personal attractions" who sought "revenge upon the sex who have slighted them."[8]

Well aware of how others perceived her unorthodox religious beliefs, which she downplayed at women's rights events, and of her unique position as a foreigner among native-born Americans, Ernestine Rose always dressed conventionally. In an 1856 black-and-white lithograph of her by the well-known artist Leopold Grozelier, she wears a long skirt of moiré silk and a matching top banded with black velvet. This may be the "russet gown" mentioned in an article about the Worcester convention. In a photo from the same year, she wears a black satin dress with white lace at the bodice and sleeves. Unlike a number of her women's rights colleagues, Rose never adopted the "bloomer costume" some began wearing in 1851. Elizabeth Cady Stanton, Susan B. Anthony, Lucy Stone, the Grimké sisters, Amelia Bloomer herself, and others discarded the cumbersome tight-waisted, full-skirted fashions of the day in favor of a modest knee-length dress worn over straight ankle-length pants. Far more comfortable and less restrictive than the long, heavy skirts which swept up dirt and needed to be lifted to go up or down stairs, "bloomers" occasioned such severe public scrutiny and criticism that the women who wore them all stopped doing so after a few years. Although Rose defended those women who switched to the costume, she never put it on herself, nor did she cut her hair short as some did. Not wearing a bonnet had distinguished Rose in the 1830s, but customs changed. An 1869 portrait of seven "Champions of Woman's Suffrage" shows more than half—including Rose—drawn with bare heads. "Mrs. Rose appeared very much like other women," a Maine newspaper wrote approvingly in 1855. "She is of medium size, dresses 'neat but not gaudy,' not *en bloomer*."[9]

In this era, women wore dresses for many years and wardrobes remained small. Donning one of her outfits and perhaps carrying the other in a valise, Ernestine Rose set off on her numerous speaking tours. Travel arrangements took a great deal of effort. To set up a single lecture in Taunton, Massachusetts, in 1855, Rose wrote at least five letters to a Charles H. Plummer to fix the date and subject of her talk. She usually traveled on trains, which went about twenty miles an hour. Three railroad lines served New York City, connecting it to New England, the Midwest, and the Mid-Atlantic states. The system did not run on Sundays then, catering to Christians' belief in the sanctity of the sabbath. Rose consistently argued that such interference violated the consitutional separation of church and state. For shorter journeys, she took slower horse-drawn coaches or carriages.[10]

Once Rose arrived at her destination, she did not know how she would be housed. On her upstate trip in January 1855, she stayed first in a home with "everything in beautiful order." But the following evening, she and Anthony were given

> a little room not 11 feet square, containing bed, Cooking Stove, beauro, table & three or 4 chairs—on the stove was a pot boiling some kind of fresh meat—the floor was strewn with papers, chips & straws—gave evidence of not having felt the impress of a broom for weeks.

"After learning of the state of things I went out & hired a carriage to take us to the Canandaigua Hotel," Anthony wrote. But Ernestine Rose continued to tour. "She has travelled alone, for months together," Joseph Barker wrote,

> along rivers and lakes, through the towns and cities, the woods and swamps of that vast continent, under a burning sun, amid winter storms, exposed to the deadly vapours of unhealthy regions, lecturing

in Legislative halls and rude log huts, to the highest and the lowest, the richest and the poorest, to the most refined and learned, and to the rudest and most neglected of her species.[11]

During this time, Ernestine Rose established her reputation as an outstanding orator. An Ohio newspaper praised her 1852 Thomas Paine address as "an offhand, able, and spirited speech . . . the equal of which few men are competent to make." Listeners most frequently praised Rose's spontaneity as well as her "argumentative power" and called out for her when more tedious lecturers held forth. "I was infinitely relieved when Mrs. Ernestine L. Rose took the floor," a female reporter wrote about the 1860 National Woman's Rights Convention.

A good delivery, a forcible voice, the most uncommon good sense, a delightful terseness of style, and a rare talent for humor, are the qualifications which so well fit this lady for a public speaker. In about two minutes she managed to infect her two-thousand-fold audience with a spirit of interest—an audience which mere dry morals and reason had succeeded in reducing to a comatose state.[12]

Rose often began with the Owenite premise that women's rights were human rights and she usually cited the Declaration of Independence to prove her case. By doing so, she expressed the views of a large majority of her colleagues, many of whom still disavowed the US Constitution for countenancing slavery. We claim our rights "upon the ground" that "our rights have already been conceded by the Declaration of Independence," Rose argued repeatedly throughout the 1850s. "For is woman not included in that phrase, 'all men are created free and equal?'. . . And if she is, what right has man to deprive her of her natural and inalienable rights? . . . Upon that just and eternal basis do we found our claims for our rights; political, civil, legal, social, religious, and every other." Rose periodically challenged those who opposed women's rights by asking, "Is woman alike human with man, or is she not? I would say to our opponents, *choose your alternative*: say yes or no, and we are willing to abide the consequences," she argued at the Fourth National Convention at Cleveland in 1853. If woman is "equally a human being with man," then she deserves the rights he has. If she is "*not* the same," then how can man "rightfully legislate for a being entirely different from himself?"[13]

Of the many benefits of democracy, Rose valued suffrage the most. "The ballot is the focus of all other rights, it is the pivot upon which all others hang," she declared in 1856. "The legal rights are embraced in it, for if once possessed of the right to the ballot box, to self-representation, she [woman] will see to it that the laws shall be just and protect her person and her property, as well as that of man." Rose refused to predict how women would use their rights. The entire purpose of rights was the freedom to legally employ them—just as men did. She consistently maintained, as she stated at Worcester in 1851, that "humanity recognizes no sex," that women and men come "involuntarily into existence" and both experience "life and death, pleasure and pain, happiness and misery." Directly attacking the common argument that physical difference "in the organic structure of the sexes militates against the rights of woman," she reasoned that "human rights and justice do not depend on the size or structure of the limbs, but on the simple yet all-sufficient authority of a human being, male or female." Rose's arguments for female equality mirrored those she made for black equality. "Like or unlike, he ["the colored man"] is a human being, and I will use the same argument with regard to him that I use when pleading—no, not when pleading—when *claiming* the rights of woman," she declared in 1855.[14]

Ernestine Rose always rejected the argument that men were oppressors and women victims. As an Owenite, she held that social conditions determined human character. "I blame no one," she affirmed at Cleveland in 1853. "My creed is, that man is precisely as good as all the laws, institutions, and influences allow him to be." That is why current conditions must be changed, through education and agitation. When Susan B. Anthony declared at the Eighth National in 1858 that the meeting was "a woman's rights convention," "Mrs. Rose wanted to amend that suggestion, because this was a human rights convention too, and the men ought not be afraid to speak out also." Applause followed her comment. Rose and many others believed that "woman must go hand in hand with man in every great and noble cause, if success would be insured." It then followed that "the beneficial result" of giving women their rights "will not be for herself alone" but for men as well. Many abolitionists held that slavery harmed slave owners as well as slaves. Rose applied this argument to men and women. "Woman is a slave, from the cradle to the grave," she asserted at Syracuse in 1852. "In claiming her rights, we claim the rights of humanity; it is not for the interest of woman only, but for the interest of all. The interest of the sexes cannot be separated—together they must enjoy or suffer—both are one in the race."[15]

Ernestine Rose's sympathy for men and her camaraderie with male allies did not prevent her from mocking those who did not give women their due. Early in 1852, she took on the eminent reformer Horace Mann, who in his

"Hints to a Young Woman" maintained that since God created man and woman different in body, mind, and soul, woman "unsexes" herself by claiming equal rights. "He admits woman is oppressed and degraded by man, but to claim and vindicate her right to call conventions and appear on the forum where she would have a chance to be heard, then 'she unsexes herself,' etc." Rose rebutted, "But what does the Hon. Lawgiver really mean by that term? I fear we will have to send to Washington for Congressional deliberation." A few years later, she wrote Joseph Barker, who finally read the novel about ancient Athens by Frances Wright that Rose had recommended to him, but blamed his delay on Rose not telling him enough about it. She replied, "What a comfort it is, when we feel guilty, to lay the blame on someone else! . . . Was it the fact that the book was written by a woman, and recommended by a woman, that misled you so . . . ? (for how indeed could the mind of a WOMAN penetrate the mysteries of the Grecian schools and their philosophy?)."[16]

At the 1852 National Convention in Syracuse, Rose argued similarly against the Liberal British M.P., J. A. Roebuck. Asked if women should have the vote, Roebuck replied that although "there is no man who owes more than I do to woman," he could not support female suffrage, since after a hard day at the House of Commons, he needed to find "a nook and shelter of quiet comfort" at home.

> My head rests upon a bosom throbbing with emotion for me and our child; and I feel a more hearty man in the cause of my country, the next day, because of the perfect soothing, gentle peace which a mind sullied by politics cannot feel. Oh! I cannot rob myself of that inexpressible benefit, and therefore I say, NO.

"Well, this is certainly a nice, little, romantic bit of Parliamentary declamation," Rose scoffed. "What a pity that he should give up all these enjoyments, to give woman a vote. Poor man! his happiness must be balanced on the very verge of a precipice, when the simple act of depositing a vote by the hand of a woman, would overthrow and destroy it forever." Rose and her colleagues continually had to deal with this division into "separate spheres."[17]

Often voicing majority views within the women's rights movement, Rose joined with her colleagues in deciding not to form a permanent organization to promote their cause at the 1852 National Convention. "Organizations were like Chinese bandages [used to bind women's feet]," Rose argued; "in Political, Moral, and Religious bodies, they had hindered the growth of man." Recalling the bitter split in the anti-slavery movement that led to women being excluded as participants, others supported this position. "We are not the lifeless staves of a barrel, which can be held together only by the iron hoops of an Artificial Organization," the anti-slavery activist Angelina Grimké Weld wrote in a long letter. When another participant argued that "organization and order" were necessary and cited Lucretia Mott's presidency of the convention to prove her point, Rose replied, "We all acted freely and spontaneously in that matter, and, because she had our confidence, we elected her unanimously. We have been brought together by the magnetism of the cause. If you have a permanent organization, you cannot be free." The convention upheld her and decided to urge women to hold meetings in individual states and counties to claim their rights rather than creating a national organization.[18]

But within the women's movement, Rose remained both an outsider and an insider. After being introduced by Mott at the 1852 meeting as "a Polish Lady and educated in the Jewish faith," she maintained that her origins testified to "the universality of our claims" and "asked for some charity on account of speaking in a foreign language." A few sentences later, she mispronounced "hen-pecked" as "hen-picked," which occasioned "great laughter" at her expense. In addition to being singled out as the lone foreigner, Rose could not completely avoid the topic of religion at the convention, since her co-worker Antoinette Brown introduced a motion that the Bible, especially the New Testament, endorsed female equality. Educated in theology at Oberlin College, Brown had preached at various Congregational churches and would become the first ordained female minister in the United States. Despite their religious differences, she and Rose had a cordial friendship. Calling Brown an "able Theologian," Rose opposed her resolution on the grounds that the Bible "is so obscure and indefinite as to admit of different interpretations." She then turned to US history and argued that if the rebellious American colonists had consulted scripture, it would have "answered them, 'submit to the powers that be, for they are from God.'" "No!," she concluded, "on Human Rights and Freedom—on a subject that is as self-evident as that two and two make four, there is no need of any written authority." The convention supported her position.[19]

The topic of biblical authority for the women's movement persisted. As radical Christians, most proponents of rights for women repeatedly cited scripture to support their views. They argued that the first Bible verses about creation—"male and female created he them"—took precedence over the more familiar but later account of Adam and Eve. They reasoned that Eve's divinely sanctioned subordination to Adam—"thy desire shall be to thy husband and he shall rule over thee"—represented a fallen state rather than an ideal one. They repeatedly quoted the New Testament dictum that "there is neither Greek nor Jew, neither slave nor free, neither male nor female, but all are one in Christ Jesus." Most conventions opened with a prayer, and the Syracuse meeting ended with members singing the Christian hymn "Old Hundred":

> *Praise God, from whom all blessings flow;*
> *Praise him, all creatures here below;*
> *Praise him above, ye heavenly host;*
> *Praise Father, Son, and Holy Ghost. Amen.*

At the Fourth National in 1853, a great deal of time was spent arguing about biblical authority for women's rights. William Lloyd Garrison, Stephen Foster, and Joseph Barker debated so heatedly with the clergyman Dr. Nevin that immediately following the meeting, Nevin "seized" Garrison "by the nose and shook him vehemently." At the Fifth National in Philadelphia, where Ernestine Rose presided, Henry Grew, an abolitionist Baptist minister, cited Bible verses to support his view that women should not speak in public. After hours of debate, the convention passed resolutions declaring that "the most determined opposition" to our "sacred cause . . . is from the clergy" and that no matter "whatever any book may teach, the rights of no human being are dependent upon or edified thereby."[20]

Ernestine Rose herself easily cited scripture for her own purposes. She often referred to Solomon, saying "There is a time and a season for everything," usually to dismiss discussion of the Bible at women's rights meetings, and always adding "and it is a good saying, not because it comes from him, but because it is *true*." At Syracuse, she quoted Genesis to argue that "'tis not well for man to remain alone," going on to assert that woman must be with man "to keep him in his proper sphere"—a backhanded reference to the separate spheres ideology. "Do you doubt it?" Rose continued; "then look at exclusive assemblies of men, and even among the best you will perceive the rude, uncultivated nature of Adam, before mother Eve civilized him, by making him partake of the Tree of Knowledge." During Bible Conventions, she quoted from the Gospels as easily as from the Hebrew Bible to prove her points. When the lights briefly went out at the Hartford Bible Convention in June 1853, Rose won "laughter and applause" from her largely hostile audience by remarking that "it reminded me of one of the true things that we find in the Bible, that some there are 'who love darkness better than light,'" a phrase from the Book of John.[21]

Hartford was the first of two difficult conventions Ernestine Rose spoke at in 1853. "Bible Conventions" had been held in the United States since the 1820s and allowed freethinkers and believers to debate whether the Bible was true. At Hartford, a number of other women attended, but Rose was the only one who spoke. She of course defended free thought, which she called a movement "of the highest and greatest importance that has taken place in our age—of more importance even than . . . the rights of woman." She began by using arguments aimed at women that she had made for years: since they especially had been "enslaved" by the Bible and "churches have been built upon your subjugated necks," women "must trample the Bible, the church, and the priests under your feet." Arguing that the "Good Book" had been written by man and for man, who "had made God in his own image," Rose excoriated the figure of God portrayed in Genesis. Calling him a "bad father," she said that "any earthly parent" would have corrected Adam and Eve for their disobedience in eating the "forbidden fruit," rather than pronouncing "curses and heavy penalties . . . against them, and not only against them for life, but on the whole unborn race to come after them." "This is Bible justice and Bible mercy," she concluded.

Students from a nearby theological seminary disrupted the convention while Rose spoke, hissing, shouting, calling her "mother," "old gal," and telling her to "go home." They finally extinguished the gas lights, throwing the hall into darkness. "Strange to say," her fellow participant William Lloyd Garrison wrote later, "the worst and grossest of interruptions were directed against a woman, Mrs. Ernestine L. Rose." But attacks on women freethinkers often exceeded those made on men. "We know of no object more deserving of contempt, loathing, and abhorrence than a *female* Atheist," a Bangor clergyman wrote a local newspaper about Rose when she was scheduled to speak there in 1855. "We hold the vilest strumpet from the stews to be by comparison respectable." Rose drew a sympathetic audience and gave a successful lecture despite this defamation. At Hartford, she did not lose her sangfroid. "During this melée . . . I stood upon the platform with my arms around Mrs. Rose," another female participant remembered,

> she saying to me, "*This is nothing, I'm not frightened.*" As the gas was lighted, I stepped back, and there stood the heroine, all alone, Bible in hand, in her fearless majesty! I shall never forget her terrible invective, in these words, as she held it up before the gallery students, and shook it in their faces, exclaiming, "*Yes, you are fit representatives of your book,*

you illustrate your religion by your mobocracy!" She then proceeded with her discourse, which was a scathing one.

Susan B. Anthony later wrote on Rose's copy of her Hartford speech, "Bravest and fearless of all women—Mrs. Rose." Rose attempted to organize subsequent Bible Conventions, but none took place because believers refused to participate.[22]

Further disruptions occurred at a women's rights convention held three months later, in September 1853 in New York City. Timed to coincide with the first US World's Fair, an anti-slavery meeting, and a World Temperance Convention, the women's rights event took place in the large Broadway Tabernacle—the same venue where Rose had been shouted down in 1837. This time, a gang of male hooligans attended, making so much noise they eventually overwhelmed the convention's speakers, earning the meeting the nickname "Mob Convention." Faced with these rowdies as she gave her speech, Rose "preserved the utmost calmness during the uproar." As hisses drowned her out at the end of the first evening, she declared, "As for hissing, what are hisses? It tells us that woman must assert her rights, unflinchingly, fearlessly. . . . [T]he beneficial result will not be for herself alone, but for such men as these!" The following day, the tumult increased. Sojourner Truth, the formerly enslaved New Yorker turned abolitionist, rebuked the audience for "hissing like snakes and geese" during her speech, but the noise grew even louder when Rose came onto the platform accompanied by a fellow immigrant, the German feminist Mathilde Franziska Anneke. "Horrible noises; everybody on his or her feet. Rapping of canes, clapping of hands, shrieks, and groans, and sneezes," reported the hostile New York *Express*, "in the midst of which a very, very masculine and 'strong-minded' looking woman . . . went on to address the audience, *in German*!"[23]

Rose's attempt to translate Anneke's speech—which proclaimed that "the women of my country look to this country for encouragement and sympathy"—brought the meeting to a flash point. Anneke represented the tens of thousands of foreigners who had poured into New York since 1848, giving rise to massive anti-immigrant sentiment. As Rose rendered Anneke's words into English, the uproar became unmanageable and she called on the police to intervene. They did nothing. The Boston abolitionist Wendell Phillips then attempted to calm the commotion, to no avail. Jeers drowned out the rest of the speakers and Rose adjourned the convention. "I surrendered with the courageous band of my comrades-in-arms," Anneke remembered, and we "quickly left the tabernacle, still constantly in danger of being insulted by the threatening crowd on the streets." Three years later, Ernestine Rose asserted that "with my well-known heresies on religion and society, I have *never* been disturbed in *any* of my meetings, except at the Hartford Bible Convention by some young clerical rowdies; at an Anti-Slavery Convention in Boston [in 1855] . . . and by a few silly boys at a Women's Rights Convention in the city of New York. With these exceptions, I have always been treated by audiences with attention and respect."[24]

Anneke and Rose became close allies, united not only by feminism but also by free thought. In Germany, Anneke had written a treatise titled *Woman in Conflict with Society* in 1847 in which she proclaimed that "I believe neither in a personal God nor a universal spirit. . . . Why is such a confession from the mouth of a woman so strongly forbidden?" Anneke and her husband emigrated to the United States in 1849, following the defeat of the German revolution they had fought for. They initially settled in Milwaukee, where Anneke defied convention by giving a public lecture while pregnant. In 1852, she began publishing her monthly *Deutsche Frauen=Zeitung* [*German Women's Newspaper*], in which she first praised Ernestine Rose. Translating and reprinting Rose's 1851 Worcester speech in German, Anneke wrote that Rose was not only "one of the foremost battlers for women's rights," but also "one of the very few . . . to fight openly against . . . religious cant in this 'land of freedom.'" Like Rose, Anneke believed that women "maintain the delusion" that they can fight for their rights "without fighting the bitterest enemies of their cause, the bitterest enemies of all freedom and independence . . . *Religion, Priestcraft*, and *the Bible*." Anneke recalled that aside from herself, "only Ernestine Rose, who though Polish, but spoke here and there in German . . . agitated openly for our cause" among German-Americans. When the two re-met at a women's rights convention years later, Anneke wrote that "Ernestine Rose was very happy to hold me in her arms again. She is still the same old wise and witty campaigner."[25]

A month after the 1853 Mob Convention in New York, the Fourth National Woman's Rights Convention convened in Cleveland. Rose spoke frequently at this gathering, praising the Declaration of Independence and condemning the attempted use of the Bible. She commented on a remark Antoinette Brown had made about divorce—Brown advocated "legal separation," in which the parties would not be allowed to remarry, for cases of "habitual drunkenness." Rose deferred discussion of the issue, although "it is of vital importance," since "this subject will encounter more prejudice and in consequence more difficulties than any subject hitherto brought before the public." But she did raise the issue of "whether, what is wrong in one sex, can be right in the other?" Wording her statement very carefully, Rose asked if it were right that a woman who "is drawn down to sin . . . should be cast out of the pale of humanity—while he who led her into it . . . shall go free?" Never mentioning sex out of wedlock or prostitution, Rose argued that women's "ignorance and dependence" produced this double standard of sexual morality. Being more specific would have tainted the convention with accusations of supporting "free love," since, as Rose declared, "man, from the time of Adam to the present time, has had utmost license, while woman must not commit the slightest degree of 'impropriety,' as it is termed." But she continued to refrain from blaming either men or women for this situation.[26]

Through her work for women, Rose became accepted and liked by many. At a Women's Rights Convention in Rochester, New York, held a few weeks after the Cleveland meeting, Rose met Sallie Holley, an ardently Christian abolitionist. Holley wrote a friend that "Ernestine L. Rose is a charming woman and at times playful." Knowing that Rose did not believe in an afterlife, Holley said that she thought they would meet in heaven. "Then you will say to me, 'I told you so,' and I shall reply, 'How very stupid I was!'" Rose joked. Holley concluded, "She seems to me to be a candid, reverent, loving spirit."[27] During these years, Rose also became acquainted with the poet Walt Whitman, who listed her in his address book from 1855 on and called her "a first rate lady friend." At that time, Whitman associated with a number of female reformers who discussed women's rights with him. In 1857, Ernestine Rose filled the poet in about Frances Wright's later, unhappy years. Throughout his long life, Whitman repeatedly remembered Rose speaking about the French Revolution—"one of the very few things which ruffle[d] her beautiful placidity." Rose declared, "What!—to be trod down and not turn! Were the people mere playthings? blocks of wood or boulders of stone?" "I put" these words "in my notebook," Whitman stated in 1890 and "have kept them all these years. . . . And today it applies as then." "She was a splendid woman: big, richly gifted, brave, expansive," he continued, explaining that she was "in body a poor sickly thing, a strong breath would blow her away—but with a head full of brains—the amplitude of a [Daniel] Webster. . . . I can see the flash in her eye now—the noble, containing eye!"[28]

Although most of Ernestine and William Rose's close friends came from free thought rather than feminism, Ernestine Rose did develop a lasting friendship with Susan B. Anthony, whom she first toured with in the spring of 1854. They met at the 1852 Syracuse Convention, shortly after Anthony joined the women's rights movement. Ten years younger than Rose, raised in a liberal Quaker family, and never married, Anthony had been active in the

anti-alcohol temperance movement until she attempted to speak at the organization's meeting, only to be told that "the sisters were not invited there to
speak, but to listen and learn." Although Rose occasionally spoke in favor of
temperance and believed that "healthful amusements" should be substituted
for "alcoholic stimulus," she never embraced the issue as a number of her feminist allies did. Rather, like Anneke and most new immigrants, Rose thought
drunkenness an American problem, caused primarily by "puritanism." The
United States "prohibited enjoyments" while nations like France drank wine
sparingly with daily meals. Rose thought this resulted in European sobriety
and American inebriation.[29]

Despite their disagreements on issues like temperance and the bloomer
costume, the two feminists became staunch allies. Rose rarely toured with
others, but she and Anthony linked up early in 1854 to address the New York
State Legislature in Albany and then went on to the mid-South, with Rose
lecturing and Anthony making arrangements. Beginning in Washington,
DC, they had great difficulty finding a venue that would give Rose a platform. When Anthony asked the Speaker of the House to let Rose use the
Capitol building, he referred them to the chaplain, who said he could not
"allow her to speak there because she was not a member of some religious society." Although Anthony remonstrated with him about religious freedom, he
did not change his mind. Also denied access to the Smithsonian Hall, because
"they had to be very careful whom they permitted to speak there," Rose
instead lectured three times to small audiences at the cramped Washington
Theatre. Rose next spoke twice in Alexandria, Virginia. The two women then
traveled to Baltimore, where they stayed in a boarding house staffed by slaves,
whose lives they found "wretched."[30]

In Baltimore, Ernestine Rose and Susan B. Anthony had an intimate conversation, reported at length in Anthony's diary. On Sunday, April 9, they
attended a Universalist Church, hearing a sermon on "Woman's Sphere."
Afterward they had a discussion about the Know-Nothings—the new nativist political party that sought to exclude immigrants and keep them from voting or holding office. Rose criticized two women's rights stalwarts, the Boston
brahmin Wendell Phillips and the popular speaker Lucy Stone "with regard
to their feelings towards foreigners," Anthony wrote in her diary. "Said she
heard them both express themselves in terms of prejudice against granting
to foreigners the rights of Citizenship." Anthony remonstrated with Rose,
expressing "disbelief as to either of them having that narrow, mean prejudice
in their souls." But Rose was correct. While calming the mob in New York
the previous autumn, Phillips repeatedly contrasted "the illiterate Irishman"

and other male "foreigners from Europe," who could vote after five years in the United States, to "American women," who could not. He also frequently opposed "the Saxon race," which he argued "led the van" on women's rights to "the Jewish—yes, the Jewish—ridicule which laughs at such a Convention as this." Considering St. Paul "Jewish" despite his conversion to Christianity, Phillips concluded, "It is Paul versus the Saxon blood; it is a religious prejudice against the blood of the race."[31]

Lucy Stone, also native-born, had spoken similarly in Rose's presence, reviling "the foreigner, who can't speak his mother tongue correctly" but who could vote when native women could not. Stone graduated from Oberlin College—the first co-ed and interracial institute of higher learning in the United States—and in these years embodied radical feminism by bobbing her hair and wearing bloomers. Beginning as an anti-slavery lecturer, she soon joined the women's movement. By the early 1850s, she had become one of the most famous women in the nation.

Eight years younger than Rose, Stone was also a superb orator. Both women admired William Lloyd Garrison and adopted his position that the states should separate rather than remain in a union with slaveholders. But they differed deeply on religion, with Stone having a lifelong "deep and abiding faith in divine justice." This belief, coupled with her appearance and voice, drew audiences to her. Stone was "a tiny creature with the prettiest pink color," "the sweetest, modest manners," and a voice "like a silver bell." Invariably described as "sweet" and "little," Stone not only won over audiences but she also made a great deal of money from her speaking, first as a paid lecturer for anti-slavery and women's rights, then by charging for her lectures. Contemporaries invariably preferred her to the atheist and "exotic" Ernestine Rose. Thomas Wentworth Higginson, a friend of both women, reported that Stone convinced his sisters to support women's rights, because they found her "so lovely," with "her winning voice . . . whose very look suggests a home and a husband and a baby," even though Stone was single at that time. "The public mind instinctively fastens upon this little person . . . as being the heart and soul of this crusade," the *New York Tribune* concluded.[32]

In 1855, Lucy Stone sent Susan B. Anthony a long letter about the women's movement in which she severely criticized Ernestine Rose. Although Rose "spoke well" at the Sixth National in Cincinnati, Stone began, "there are so many mean Jews" there "and her *face* is so essentially Jewish, that the people remarked the likeness and feared her." Stone went on to paint a picture of Rose complaining about how much her travel, speaking, and clothing had cost her. She asserted that Rose gave "a tirade about the low fee, said it was

shameful" and insisted she would never take on the responsibility of organizing a convention as Stone had done.

These charges are the only ones of this nature ever made against Ernestine
Rose. Even in Stone's letter, she wrote that it was only Joseph Barker who
insisted that Rose be paid, while Rose herself consistently refused to take any
money. "My advice to you is not to let Mrs. Rose do anything," Stone concluded. A few years later, Stone again urged Anthony not to let Rose speak
at a convention since she is "*known*" and "about 30 people will stay away,
who see her name where 10 will be attracted by it." Stone's criticisms—that
Rose looks Jewish, that she is avaricious and only out for herself—constitute
antisemitism. Others consistently praised Rose's self-sacrifice. In 1886, sum-
ming up Rose's career, the *Boston Investigator* wrote that she was "one of the
most prominent and ablest female lecturers in this country, and probably the
most generous, for she lectured at her own expense."[33]

Most important, Susan B. Anthony paid no attention to these charges,
consistently scheduling Rose as a speaker, praising her, and remaining her lifelong friend. In their 1854 conversation about nativists in the women's movement, however, Anthony wrote about her disagreements with Rose:

> I said Mrs. Rose "there is not *one* in the Reform ranks, whom you think
> true, not one but whom panders to the popular feeling—She answered
> I can't help it, I take them by the words of their own mouths. I trust all
> until their words or acts declare them false to truth & right, & con-
> tinued she, no one can tell the hours of anguish I have suffered as one
> after another I have seen those whom I had trusted, betray falsity of
> motive, as I have been compelled to place one after another on the list
> of panderers to public favor. Said I, do you know Mrs. Rose, that I can
> but feel that you place *me too* on that list. Said she, I will tell you when
> I see you untrue—

A silence ensued. To Rose, any denigration of "foreigners" meant her—the
only foreigner within the movement. To Anthony, Rose was unduly suspi-
cious, unable to "ascribe *pure motives* to any of our Reformers." The women's
friendship survived and they toured amicably together again early the next
year. But despite her heartfelt sympathy, Anthony could not help offending
her freethinking companion. Hoping to make Rose feel better, Anthony copied out a verse from the liberal, not explicitly Christian hymn they heard earlier that morning, "All Equal before God," and inscribed it "for her dear friend,
Ernestine L. Rose." But however egalitarian its lyrics, the hymn glorified

God. Tears came to Rose's eyes as Anthony gave it to her. "Said I, Mrs. Rose, have I been wicked and hurt your feelings?" Anthony wrote. "She answered, no, but I never expect to be understood in this lifetime. Her anguish was extreme." The two women wept together. Anthony added, "Mrs. Rose is not appreciated nor cannot be by this age—She is too much in advance of the extreme ultraists even, to be understood by them."[34]

Ernestine Rose's chief defense against her ultraist, outsider status was an intense desire to be correct at all times. Such moralism could easily shade into self-righteousness. At Worcester in 1851, for instance, Abby Kelley had argued that women must first fulfill their duties before they deserved their rights. Rose challenged her, asserting that "this is an error, a very prevalent error, and therefore the more necessary to be corrected . . . as it is, while man enjoys all the rights, he preaches all the duties to woman." Give women our rights, and then we "will not fail in the performance of our duties." At the Mob Convention, Rose spoke about women's inability to write wills in New York. Lucy Stone intervened, stating that women could write wills in some other states. Rose replied, "I did not say this was the universal law; I said it was the law in the State of New York." Rose may have been harsher because the speaker was Stone, but she saw her desire to always be right as a virtue. "If, in expressing my opinions, I have been severe alike on friend and foe," she wrote in 1856, "it is because in principle I know no compromise."[35]

After Rose's springtime tour with Anthony, she developed an "inflammation of the lungs," which prevented her from participating in a women's rights convention at Saratoga Springs, New York, that summer. In early October, she wrote the *Boston Investigator* that she might be too ill to attend the Fifth National Woman's Rights Convention in Philadelphia. But she recovered, and with Anthony's support, became president of the meeting. Some objected to an atheist presiding over a women's rights event, but Anthony argued that "every religion—or none—should have an equal right on the platform." As president, Ernestine Rose spoke only briefly at the convention, but she was praised in a resolution thanking her "for the courtesy, impartiality and dignity with which she has presided over the proceedings."[36]

At Philadelphia, Rose made one of her many references to foreigners. She reviewed "the relative political position of women in this country and Europe, illustrating her remarks by a description of the horror of a Hungarian lady on discovering that, in this country, in the State of New York, she had no *legal* right to her children." As a "foreigner," Rose had many more contacts with Europeans and also a wider and more international perspective than her co-workers. For one example, the Englishmen Joseph Barker and

John Finch—an Owenite friend of hers from London—gave the freethink-ing German doctor Augustus Theodore Stamm letters of introduction to Rose. Stamm, Rose, and others then fruitlessly attempted to organize a "World's Bible Convention." Rose also came in contact with Ottilie Assing, a Berlin Jew who emigrated to the United States in 1852. Assing reported for a liberal German newspaper and, like Rose, believed in free thought, women's rights, and anti-slavery. She praised Rose as an "elegant German-Polish lady with long greying hair and traces of bygone beauty" who "takes an active role in the conventions," while "she tactfully avoids any appear-ance of eccentricity." Although the two women met a number of times, they never became friends. In her articles, Assing complimented Rose's "broadly educated, independent, and lucid mind," asserting that "her knowledge of two continents has broadened her horizon; experience and understanding have matured her opinions."[37]

Ernestine Rose's European background, her contacts, and her principles made her an internationalist. She believed that the causes she supported could only succeed if they crossed national boundaries and had universal appeal. She often quoted Thomas Paine's motto, "The world is my country and to do good my religion." Rose stressed internationalism at women's rights meet-ings, joining a committee in 1853 to address "the women of Great Britain and the continent of Europe," since "this great movement is intended to meet the wants, not of America only, but of the whole world."[38] Throughout the early 1850s, she strenuously urged the United States to support the revolutionary European republics, arguing that the War of Independence against Great Britain would not have succeeded without French aid. "Non-intervention!—There is no thing as non-intervention," she proclaimed at the 1852 Paine dinner. "What kind of aid does the Czar of Russia require to crush freedom in Europe? Precisely such as England and this country give him—a passive consent to his active intervention, in violation of the laws of nations as well as of humanity." She continued to denounce both European despotism and American Know-Nothingism during the Crimean War of 1853–56, when Britain, France, and the Ottoman Empire fought Russia. At the 1855 Paine dinner, she maintained that it would be easier for the allies to defeat the czar "than to conquer minds filled with Know-Nothingism. It requires far more true courage and persevering heroism to carry on a moral war than a physical one."[39]

After her hectic year of touring, Ernestine Rose's health deteriorated and she and William decided to visit Europe for six months to "renovate a once exceedingly strong and enduring constitution, so as to enable me to perform my part in the great drama of life a few years longer." The couple left New York for London in May 1856, almost twenty years to the day after they arrived in the United States. Using an uncharacteristic military metaphor, Ernestine Rose wrote the *Boston Investigator* that "as a volunteer soldier in the cause of Truth," she looked forward to a "furlough" so she could "gather fresh strength for the glorious battle of freedom."[40]

6

A Minority of One

ON A "SWELTERING" Friday morning in late June 1858, two years after she left to visit Europe, Ernestine Rose mounted the platform under a large tent at a new gathering—a "Free Convention" held in Rutland, Vermont. The invitation to this unique meeting asked "the Friends of Human Progress" to come together in "the unanimous movement of those who hail from every section of the great Army of Reform and who have no watchword save *Humanity*." Especially concerned about female participation, the organizers urged "woman" to "vindicate by her own eloquence and zeal, the social position she is so nobly and rapidly winning for herself." To further this end, they scheduled Rose to speak immediately after the reading of the convention's diverse resolutions. Rose merged free thought and feminism in her brief opening speech, as she often did in these years. "This being a *Free Convention*, and as we hope, composed of *Free Men and Women*, and as we have no Pope to govern us, it is hoped that every question presented will be taken into consideration by all persons present," she began. Then turning specifically to women, she encouraged them to speak out and vote on the issues they "have at heart." "It is high time the ladies learned to say No," she declared. "Therefore if you mean yes, say yes; and if you mean no, say no; though you find yourself in a minority of one."[1]

The only "Free Convention" ever held, this gathering brought together a wide variety of reformers: freethinkers and anti-slavery activists, women's rights workers and spiritualists, free love advocates and radical Christians. Yet even among this maverick group, Ernestine Rose herself constituted "a minority of one." The only female freethinker among both the feminists and the abolitionists, she remained the sole foreigner in this host of native-born Americans. She was also the only participant to openly denounce the popular new belief in spirit communications between the living and the dead that dominated much of the convention's proceedings. Yet even those participants who disagreed with her still respected her. "She [Rose] has spoken to this people the words of truth and freedom, and noble words of love of humanity," asserted Mary Davis, a lecturer and wife of a leading spiritualist, Andrew Jackson Davis.[2] This combination of esteem and isolation even within radical circles characterized Rose's life in the late 1850s.

Mainstream US society of course denounced all the participants at Rutland as "a convention of moral lunatics." "We do not remember to have read of a greater exhibition of mingled nonsense, indecency, insanity, and blasphemy," wrote the *Burlington Free Press*, while the *New York Times* declared that "it was to be expected that various funny people would come together. The expectation was not disappointed." Both the *Times* and other major newspapers specifically attacked the women present. The *New York Tribune* disparaged their looks: "If any one of them should ever be accused of being what people of carnal minds call 'good-looking,' not a jury in the land but would instantly acquit her of that unfounded charge." The *Times* devoted the entire front page of its June 29 edition to Rutland, headlining the second and third days' proceedings as "A Spicy Time on Free-Love" with the sub-head "A Small Bit of Abolitionism, Touches of Spiritualism, and a Great Deal of Woman's Rights." The article lambasted Rose as "a native of Poland. She speaks broken English, and labors under disadvantages as a public expounder of her speciality—Woman's Rights." After criticizing her as "very stout" and having short hair—descriptions that never appear in any other source—the paragraph concluded that "Mrs. Rose is a scoffing Infidel, is always a prominent actor at the anniversary of Tom Paine, and apparently delights in sarcasms upon the Bible and Christianity."[3]

Between 1855 and 1861, Ernestine Rose remained much the same. She knew she held a unique position as "a minority of one" and perhaps used this phrase to refer to Thoreau's dictum about abolitionists in *Civil Disobedience*: that "any man more right than his neighbors constitutes a majority of one already." But whatever Rose's confidence in the correctness of her beliefs, the nation changed around her. Both the women's movement and free thought began to falter in the face of the growing pressures that led to the Civil War. Her views about that impending struggle increased her isolation. Not only did she ardently oppose slavery, but she also believed in "Disunion," being willing to divide the nation if it meant liberating the free states from an immoral connection with the slave ones. This conviction separated her from most Americans and the majority of abolitionists. Mrs. Rose "said that there was no argument that could have a feather's weight in the balance against human freedom," Susan B. Anthony wrote William Lloyd Garrison—also a disunionist—in 1854, just after the two women had made a trip south. "If she were convinced that slavery could be abolished by a dissolution of the Union, she would rather see, not only the North separate from the South, but State from State, and city from city, than that the curse of slavery should longer continue."[4]

This isolation, which led to "severe reproach, slander, and persecution" for her beliefs, as Rose wrote in her "Farewell Letter" to the *Boston Investigator*, added to her decision to visit Europe at the height of her career in 1856. Complaining that her health had been "greatly impaired by too long continued exertions and exposure," Rose again adopted the male remedy of travel to cure illness. Journeying for one's health legitimized what may have been simply a wish to leave the fray for a while. In addition, the Roses could easily finance both their sea voyage and their numerous and lengthy journeys throughout Europe. During these years, Ernestine Rose "had a portrait of Thomas Paine painted for her by Jarvis." Buying, much less commissioning an oil painting, demonstrates that the couple had disposable income, perhaps from investments in real estate.[5]

Ernestine Rose had arranged to write public letters about her journey to the *Boston Investigator*. Before her first missive from Europe arrived— communications took about three weeks to cross the Atlantic—the *Investigator* reprinted a "Biographical Sketch of Mrs. Ernestine L. Rose," written by the liberal journalist Lemuel E. Barnard. Barnard, a Vermonter who settled in Cleveland, had interviewed Rose during her visit there in the fall of 1855. He detailed her life until she came to the United States in 1836 and then briefly summarized her next twenty years here. Extolling her "active part in the great progressive movement which marks the present as the most glorious of historical epochs," Barnard praised Rose's accomplishments "for the elevation of her sex and the amelioration of social conditions, a work which can be ascribed to few women of our time." He concluded by hoping she would share more of her biography with others. "The history of her life and experience, as disclosed to the limited circle of her friends, is said to be highly interesting and instructive; but hitherto she has uniformly resisted all their solicitations to give it to the world. They are not without hope, however, that she may, at some future day, consent to do so."[6]

Ernestine Rose's eleven letters from Europe, however, reveal little about her life. Most are travelogues, describing major sights for those who could not go abroad. Her first letter told of their month-long voyage across the Atlantic, but as Rose herself commented, she wrote "so much" while saying "so little."

She mused at length about the ocean, interpreting it politically. "The ocean in repose looks beautiful, but yet I like it not," she wrote; it "looks to me like a nation which by long and unsuccessful attempts to free itself from the iron yoke of despotism, has subsided into apathy and inaction," like her native Poland. Their freighter carried only four other passengers, "one nice bright young girl" and an English family of three, "as interesting as ignorance, bigotry, and intolerance could make them." Ernestine and William Rose could not resist goading their co-voyagers. After the family praised the royal heads of Britain, France, and Russia, the Roses "nearly got ourselves into trouble by gently suggesting that these monarchs with all their religion, are not quite so virtuous and good but they might be a little bit better, which produced such an outburst of loyal indignation, that nearly threatened us with the fate of Jonah."[7]

More sympathetic allies in England had been alerted to their arrival. The most important was George Jacob Holyoake, a fellow Owenite who had been convicted of blasphemy in 1842 for denying God's existence and had served six months in prison. By the time the Roses arrived, he directed *The Reasoner*, a successful radical weekly with a circulation of 5,000 that coined the term "secularism" and advocated women's rights. In early June, he announced Rose's imminent arrival, praising her as "a lady with whose name the friends of American progress have long been familiar" and "one of the most courageous, honest, intelligent, and womanly of the woman's-right agitators." A few weeks later, he reprinted Barnard's piece as well as her May Farewell Letter from the *Investigator*. One reader wanted a public meeting to welcome Ernestine Rose; Holyoake wrote it would happen only if she wanted it, which she did not.[8]

A few weeks after arriving, the Roses traveled to see the eighty-five-year-old Robert Owen, then living on an estate outside London. Owen "exclaimed with much energy, 'Since I saw you, nine years ago, I have not spent an hour without laboring for the cause of humanity,'" a goal Rose tried to emulate. Owen wanted Rose to believe in spiritualism; she tried "to convince him *out* of it"—they "met with equal success." Although Owen still rode, walked, and wrote, the Roses "could see quite a change in him." But he had improved by the end of October, when he came to London to see the couple the day before they sailed back to New York. "I am happy to say that he was in excellent health and spirits," Rose wrote the *Investigator*.

His hearing is much better than when we saw him in June; he looks well and is as active as ever; he has called another World's Convention for next May, and has laid out work for me to do, enough to last me a lifetime, provided I live to as good an old age as he has reached, and then I fear I will have hardly begun my task.[9]

Owen died two years later at eighty-seven; Rose herself made it to eighty-two.

For the rest of the Roses' five weeks in London, they combined sight-seeing with contacting women's rights allies. For her American readers, Rose described Mme. Tussaud's waxworks, the British Museum, the Houses of Parliament, Westminster Abbey, and other tourist attractions. She was especially impressed by the Crystal Palace, a modern iron-and-glass exhibition space, built in 1851. To Rose it represented "all that is grand and beautiful in nature and in art, of ancient and modern times, of rude barbarity and the most refined civilizations." She asserted herself during this sightseeing. She sat in Napoleon's carriage at Mme. Tussaud's, "but I could feel none of the glory!" and in the coronation chair at Westminster Abbey, which "is very much dilapidated and full of dust, but I was in duty bound to sit in it!" She went even further at the House of Commons. Discovering that men could be admitted to parliamentary debates relatively easily, while women had to apply in writing and then wait two weeks for permission to sit in the tiny grilled balcony enclosure allotted them, she acted successfully on her own. "As I had a desire to hear the debate . . . I went in, and that without any permit." "Of the whole English policy it seems to me the strangest why woman should so entirely be excluded from the House of Commons," she wrote, "but let silly men do all they can to keep woman out, she can always outwit them! If she only wished to enter into the Garden of Eden, not even the cherubims with fiery swords could keep her out." Rose continually critiqued British society. "In reality, there is no middle class," she wrote.

> There are many castes and grades; each grade looks down with contempt on all those beneath, and with slavish subserviency on those above it. There is no more sympathy between any two of these grades than between the highest and the lowest. The people have not much energy or spirit. . . . Everything here is slow and heavy; it requires time, long, long time to move or change anything (except the weather).

"Reform movements are sound asleep," she continued, adding that for any change to be successful, it had to be championed "by some one of the higher ranks." She then mentioned going to "a fashionable dinner party" where she met both a member of Parliament and the well-known author Mary Howitt.[10]

A prolific writer and translator, Howitt and her husband William were ardent reformers. In December 1855, she helped form a committee to work for married women's property rights. When Rose visited London, Howitt introduced her to at least three other committee members, the younger feminists Barbara Leigh Smith, Bessie Rayner Parkes, and Eliza Fox. Rose referred to them in her speech at the Seventh National Woman's Rights Convention, held in November 1856, shortly after her return from Europe. She announced that "English women . . . were very active in forwarding the Woman's Rights movement throughout Great Britain," even though they had to contend with the English class system and, unlike Americans, had "no Declaration of Independence" to refer to. She praised Smith, Parkes, and Fox, who were all in their twenties, as "young and noble English girls—girls, who were too timid to take part publicly in the movement, but who were untiring and indefatigable in making converts and enlisting aid."[11]

Rose downplayed the achievements of these English feminists, perhaps because they did not lecture publicly as she did—she never explained her reasons. All became leaders of the 1860s English women's rights movement. Barbara Leigh Smith had attended a co-ed Owenite school before studying art at the new, non-denominational Bedford College for Women. Receiving a 300£ per year endowment from her father, she founded her own progressive co-ed school in 1853. The next year, she published a pamphlet, *A Brief Summary in Plain Language of the Most Important Laws of England Concerning Women*. Costing only a few pence, this work sold widely and caused a sensation, since it argued that women, but not men, were handicapped by bad laws which should be abolished. Leigh Smith challenged British statutes that gave child custody to fathers, transferred wives' property to husbands, and made divorce almost impossible. Within a year, the committee for a Married Women's Property Act had gathered 3,000 female signatures, many from prominent authors. It also allied with the powerful Law Amendment Society and enlisted male supporters to present its petitions to Parliament. Bessie Parkes, Leigh Smith's close friend, published *Remarks on the Education of Girls, with Reference to the Social, Legal, and Industrial Position of Women in the Present Day* in 1854. Aimed at a middle-class audience, it held that "women should be able to study anything" so they could do any work "they deem themselves fitted for." Eliza Fox's father, praised by Rose as "the celebrated W. J. Fox, the eloquent lecturer and Member of Parliament," aided his daughter and other budding English female artists by allowing them to sketch male models in his library once a week. The Royal Academy prevented women from drawing "undraped" men until 1893 and did not admit women as full members until 1922.[12]

In London, Ernestine Rose also visited the exiled French feminist Jeanne Deroin. Deroin and her associate, Pauline Roland, had written a letter of solidarity to the 1851 Worcester women's rights convention that Rose responded to in her main speech there. Roland had died; Deroin "supports herself and her two daughters and son," Rose told the 1856 Seventh National Convention. "She was educating them herself because she had no means to pay for their education. She filled their minds with noble thoughts and feelings, even to the very sacrifice of themselves for the benefit of the race, and more especially for the elevation of woman, without which she feels convinced that the elevation of man can never be accomplished." After Rose spoke, the convention passed a resolution in favor of "the supporters of the cause of women in Paris, worthy successors of Pauline Roland and Jeanne Deroin, who, in the face of imperial despotism, dare to tell the truth."[13]

Ernestine Rose herself experienced the censorship and surveillance of Emperor Napoleon III's government permeating French life. Although she and William arrived in Paris in early July, she did not send anything to the *Investigator* again until late August, when they reached Berlin. "I was advised not to write any article from Paris, as such article not only would be destroyed, but it might be dangerous," she told her readers, adding that although Holyoake had sent them copies of the *Investigator* and his *Reasoner* to Paris, "we received none." "Paris, with all her beauties . . . is at present little less than one vast barrack," she lamented. "The city is full of soldiers. . . . Nor is this the worst; for at any rate you see them, you know who is near you. But there is a much more formidable army, an *espionage*, against which you cannot guard except by a dead silence on all subjects connected with freedom." However, while in Paris, the Roses also "had the pleure to be introduced into a literary and reformatory circle" where they "spent several evenings together." "The members are free from all the shackles that fetter humanity," she explained, "they are universal in their ideas of freedom and rights, and of course perfectly divested from all the superstitions called religion." In this group, the Roses met Charles Lemonnier, a socialist, freethinker, and feminist, as well as other congenial reformers. But the most important contact was with the Frenchwoman Jenny P. d'Héricourt, who shared Ernestine Rose's core values of free thought, feminism, anti-slavery, and human rights. D'Héricourt published frequently, opposing "the masters, the nobles, the whites, the men, who have denied, deny, or will deny in the future, that slaves, bourgeois, blacks, and women are born for liberty and equality."[14]

Rose described d'Héricourt as "a physician, a woman of noble character, great energy and talents; she is a thorough reformer, particularly for women's rights and against priests and churches." Having played an active part in the Revolution of 1848, she belonged to the Society for the Emancipation of Women until the government excluded all members of the female sex from voting, running for political office, and finally, from attending any meeting where politics was discussed. During the early 1850s, d'Héricourt became a certified midwife. By the time she and Rose met, d'Héricourt had become a well-known figure in the international radical community—the same year Rose visited her so did the Russian reformer M. L. Mikhailov. But d'Héricourt remained under government scrutiny: Rose wrote that although she "writes a great deal . . . no journal in Paris dare publish her articles, so she has them published . . . in an Italian monthly journal and brought to Paris."[15]

For her part, d'Héricourt praised "Mrs. Rose, so justly famous in the United States of America," as "this admirable woman, who, during her mission of more than twenty years, has braved incredible rigors and dangers of every kind to follow the dictates of her conscience illuminated by reason." The two women spent time together during Rose's three weeks in Paris. D'Héricourt then immediately produced her eleven-page "biography" of "Madame Rose," which appeared in the September 1856 issue of the radical Parisian *Revue Philosophique et Religieuse*. D'Héricourt could publish pieces in this journal Lemonnier co-edited as long as they did not directly discuss French politics. In addition to her article on Rose, she wrote about the Bible's discrimination against women.[16]

D'Héricourt's portrait is the fullest contemporary account of Rose's appearance, life, philosophy, and struggles. The piece begins with a detailed description of Rose that emphasizes her gentility and femininity, perhaps to counter the stereotype of the mannish, "strong-minded" feminist. "Mrs. Rose" has "eyes of an extraordinary sweetness," her voice "never sounds a false or shrill note which might offend a musical ear," her "small hands are gloved in kidskin and her long skirt barely permits a glimpse of delicate shoes encasing her dainty feet." D'Héricourt then gives an admiring account of Rose's beliefs, politics, and goals. "Mrs. Rose's God is the *Living Universe*," d'Héricourt explains, "She is convinced that the Bible, the Koran, the Vedas, and all other books reputed to be divinely inspired are a source of slavery, despotism, intolerance, injustice, and errors; that humanity will never truly advance on the path of the true and the good until it rids itself of this sacred baggage which the past places on its shoulders." Rose's politics are "radical"—she believes that "all members of the human race" should have "equal political and social rights." Although d'Héricourt mentions Rose's opposition to "black slavery," she describes her work for female equality in much greater detail.[17]

The bulk of the article recounts Rose's early years in Europe and only briefly mentions her time in the United States. D'Héricourt exaggerates the dangers Rose faced—from "the brutality of a people for whom an individual life is at the mercy of the first gun drawn," which includes "the ferocious instincts of slaveholders who believe they have the right to kill those who speak in favor of blacks" and "ministers of all denominations, and all the believers who do not fail to arm themselves against impiety." In concluding her article, d'Héricourt also overstates the success of the women's rights movement in America. She claims that "one hundred thousand women" and "a hundred and fifty thousand men" support "the banner raised by Mrs. Rose," among them "the intellectual, moral, and political leaders of the country." She also asserts that "women doctors are now accepted," that "soon there will be female lawyers," and that Rose lectured successfully to "seventy-six members of Congress." It is impossible to say what caused all these distortions. D'Héricourt may have wanted to herald US accomplishments to encourage her countrywomen; she and Rose may have misunderstood each other or had translation problems.[18]

After they left Paris, the Roses traveled extensively throughout Europe. They spent at least four weeks in Berlin, but Ernestine Rose wrote nothing about Germany. Although she initially hoped to visit Poland, she wrote that it could not "be much gratification to me, except I could find it in a happier condition, or could be instrumental in placing it in one." There is no evidence that she traveled there, although at some point she did re-establish contact with her father's family, since she left her estate to his descendants. Her final letter described Italy's "miserable aspect of idleness, beggary, cruelty, and priests." After a brief return to Paris, the Roses traveled back to New York from England. This voyage took only twelve days and when the passengers entertained each other on the final evening aboard, Ernestine "spoke on the rights of man as the basis of the rights of woman."[19]

Less than two weeks after they returned, she played her usual active role at the Seventh National Woman's Rights Convention in New York City. Held at the end of November, the meeting might have been delayed to allow Rose to participate. She spoke frequently and eloquently, sounding familiar themes and displaying no fatigue from her travels. After praising the progress made since 1850—"no other reform ever agitated had gained so much ground in so short a time"—she informed her co-workers about the state of women's rights in Europe. She then dealt with a seeming contradiction within feminism. A male supporter asserted that men backed women's rights far more than women themselves did. Rose agreed, first remarking that men were more accustomed to thinking about rights than women. She then argued that "the subject, whenever presented to the mind of woman in its proper light, would not fail to find an echo in her heart." Although a woman might initially "smile" or "sneer" when asked if she needed rights, if you "put to her a few common-sense questions" about property, child custody, self-government, and voting, "the smile disappeared" and most women would give "an immediate, hearty, and warm assent" to the movement's demands.[20]

In her chief address, delivered on the convention's final evening, Ernestine Rose argued strenuously for US women's claims to better education, decent jobs, the vote, and legal equality. Comparing male and female development, she sketched how a boy went to college, which prepared him for many fields, "and if he finds one does not answer his purpose, he can change it for another." In contrast, "the girl, even in the most favorable position," whose education is finished at sixteen "with her mind undeveloped, her powers uncultivated, without a knowledge of herself or society, imbued with the erroneous idea that her whole and only aim and end in life is to please man" was limited to "the kitchen, the needle, and the school-room." And "even here on this narrow and constricted platform," men earned far more than women for the same work.

Urging her audience to give money to support female education rather than male missionary activity, Rose went on to champion women's suffrage. "I know there is great prejudice against our claim to political rights," she declared. "It requires a great moral courage . . . to say to those who believed themselves the only lords of creation, 'Stand aside; give us space to grow.'" She then contrasted the relatively easy "heroism of the battlefield," which was encouraged and rewarded, to "the amount of moral courage and true heroism" it took "to face the fire of an unjust and prejudiced public opinion, to attack the adamantine walls of long-usurped power, to brave not only the enemy abroad, but often that severest of all enemies, your own friends at home." That effort demanded "a heroism that the world has never yet recognized, that the battle-field cannot supply, but which woman possesses." Rose ended on an optimistic note, referring obliquely and modestly to both Frances Wright's and her own efforts on behalf of women in the 1830s:

> To see such an audience before us, listening with evident interest to what we have to say in support of our claims, you cannot realize what it was twenty-five and twenty years ago to call public attention to these wrongs, and prepare the way for such conventions, and such audiences; and yet woman had the moral courage to do it, and do it as fearlessly as now; for though she had nothing else to support her, she had the consciousness of possessing the might of right to sustain her.[21]

In the course of this speech, Rose felt compelled to raise the issue of prostitution. By the middle of the nineteenth century, respectable women were not supposed to even refer to any aspect of sexuality. But it proved impossible to discuss women's rights adequately while avoiding all mentions of sexual behavior. Rose had raised the issue of the double standard of sexual morality at the 1853 National in Cleveland; now she argued that the limited number of poorly paid jobs available to women often produced "the last, sad alternative: to sell herself in marriage, or out of it." Referring sarcastically to men's supposed "protection" of women, Rose openly discussed prostitution. "Go into your streets at night—look at the wretched beings who wander them, in many cases the only home they possess—and you will have the practical evidence of this protection," she declared before going on to denounce society's hypocrisy. "What a bitter mockery it is, to make a being helpless—to tie hand, heart, and head, and tell him that it is from pure affection, so as to have the pleasure of protecting him! [Like most of her contemporaries, Rose used the masculine pronoun to refer to all.] When our opponents ridicule the Woman's Rights movement—or even with their best feelings, tell us that if woman gets all her rights equal with man, particularly if she should come in contact with him in the forum, at the ballot-box, or in the legislative halls, that she might lose her modesty, innocence, and virtue; do they ever remember that these wretched victims of wrong are women too?"[22]

Such remarks instantly made the women's movement notorious. Even though Ernestine Rose and the women's movement attempted to avoid sexual topics, they were repeatedly charged with endorsing "free love" anyway. In its lead article on this convention, the *New York Herald* ran the sub-head "Speeches, Rich, Rare and Racy—Free Love Advocated and Endorsed." Much public opinion conflated women's rights with "free love" and the article itself stated, "We beg respectfully to inquire the precise difference between Woman's Rights and Free Love, or where one commences and the other ends?" The charge of "free love"—that is, heedless, animalistic fornication— had been hurled at reformers since the 1820s and was used to discredit any sexual behavior outside of marriage or any mention of such behavior—premarital sex, cohabitation, adultery, prostitution, or divorce—as well as any reference to contraception or abortion. In the late 1850s, a number of women's rights advocates and their allies felt it essential to raise these issues. This tainted the entire women's movement to many and was a reason it failed to enlist new members and grow during these years.

Ernestine Rose's views on sexuality and marriage came from Owenism. Like Owen, she believed that marriage should be a civil rather than a religious ceremony and that divorce should be allowed as long as the desire for it was mutual and any children were provided for. But she knew the "prejudice" and "difficulties" that any mention of divorce would provoke and so avoided the topic until others raised it. The same was true of birth control. Male freethinkers in both Britain and the United States had pioneered publishing contraceptive manuals, believing that it liberated women especially from unwanted pregnancies and from the Christian doctrine that sex within marriage should only be for procreation. Both Rose's English acquaintance, Richard Carlile, and Owen's son, Robert Dale Owen, published birth control guides, the first in 1826, the second in 1831. Gilbert Vale, Rose's chief supporter when she first came to New York and editor of the free-thought *Beacon* newspaper, updated Dale Owen's book in 1858. The *Boston Investigator* continually advertised these books and sold them very cheaply. By the late 1850s, many other treatises on contraception had been published, chiefly for "the preservation of the wife's health."[23]

It seems likely that Ernestine and William Rose used some form of birth control. They presumably continued to have sexual relations after the early deaths of their two children, but no other pregnancy is known to have resulted. The methods recommended in contemporary manuals—douching, sponges, partial or complete withdrawal, and expensive condoms made from animal intestines—although not completely reliable were better than nothing. But whether she used birth control or not, Rose avoided any public mention of this significant topic because of the avalanche of disapproval she knew would follow. After Robert Dale Owen published his contraceptive manual, the *New York Times* excoriated him as "A man who . . . would disgrace the gallows. It is the sentiments and precepts of Carlile . . . calculated to effect the same fiendish purpose, the destruction of the social compact, and the substitution of promiscuous concubinage." Dale Owen probably wrote his book in response to his associate Frances Wright's unwanted pregnancy in the spring of 1830. But Wright herself never spoke publicly about contraception—it was too controversial a subject even for her. When she criticized "ignorant codes of morals" that "condemn one portion of the female sex to vicious excess, and another to a vicious restraint," she was denounced as "a voluptuous preacher of licentiousness," a "harlot," and a "procuress."[24]

At the 1858 Free Convention in Rutland, Vermont, the medium Julia Branch made an impassioned speech declaring, "It is the binding marriage ceremony that keeps woman degraded in mental and moral slavery. She must demand her freedom; her right to receive the equal wages of man for her labor; *her right to bear children when she will, and by whom she will.*" In the ensuing debate, Rose took a strait-laced position, declaring that if Branch "meant to let loose the untamed passions either of men or women; if she meant that, I totally and utterly disagree." Branch replied that "I did not mean it in that light" and Rose went on to argue that "I for one, have never introduced the question of marriage into our Conventions, because I want to combat in them the injustice of the laws." Dealing with specific laws, like married women's property rights, exposed women to far less criticism than any reference, no matter how guarded, to sexual behavior. Instead, Rose proposed adding the words "based on perfect equality" to the convention's resolution on marriage so that it read "*Resolved,* That the only true and natural marriage is an exclusive conjugal love based on perfect equality between one man and one woman; the only true home is the isolated home based on this exclusive love." This resolution passed and Rose asserted that if the laws applied equally to women and men, all inequities "would be righted."[25]

Despite Ernestine Rose's clear support of conventional marriage, the *New York Times* reported that both she and Branch "go for free love on principle." Rose immediately wrote the newspaper that "I have never advocated these sentiments, from the simple reason that I do not believe in them." But this libel persisted. In 1869, the clergyman L. P. Brockett published a book on women in which he wrote: "Mrs. Rose scoffs at marriage, though she herself has been married for thirty years, and declares that each woman is free to choose the father of her children." The *Boston Investigator* instantly repudiated these charges on Rose's behalf. Rose herself wrote from Europe accusing Brockett of "slander," maintaining that she "never advocated any principles I need be ashamed of," and asking the *Investigator* to reprint her 1858 letter to the *Times*. Brockett agreed to remove her name from his paragraph, but added that he had included her because Rose "had been repeatedly charged with advocacy of these views."[26]

In the course of this skirmish, a longtime correspondent to the *Investigator* defended Rose by reminiscing about a visit they had paid to the Long Island community of Modern Times in the mid-1850s, "when Modern Times was supposed to represent the extreme point of *practical Free Love.*" At the community, in existence from 1851 to 1857, "the arrangements of marriage were left entirely to the individual men and women," allowing couples to join up or separate at will. After their trip, her companion asked Ernestine Rose, " 'What are now your ideas of Free Love?' 'Free Love!' she replied with ineffable scorn, 'I see nothing here but animalism! It is quite near to blasphemy to call these disgusting exhibitions of lust by the sacred name of *love!* '" Mrs. Rose "left Modern Times with as deep disgust for that new conservator of Woman's

Rights, Free Love, as she ever manifested for chattel slavery or ecclesiastical despotism," he reported.[27]

The commune of Modern Times had been founded by Stephen Pearl Andrews, an eccentric reformer. Before creating this model village, Andrews attempted to turn Texas into an abolitionist territory and then tried to promulgate "phonology," a shorthand system he hoped might lead to a universal language. He instituted a non-profit, "cost the basis of price" economy at Modern Times and considered the free love principles enacted there to be "the antithesis of enslaved love." In 1858, the year after the community closed, Andrews raised an equally taboo subject—contraception—at the Eighth National Women's Rights Convention. He spoke during the opening session to urge that "the vital question of marriage be considered." After apologizing for having "opinions more radical than those held by this convention," using terms vague today but clear to his audience, he declared:

> One of the dearest rights of woman was that of the maternity of the coming generation, and to change the conditions of that maternity, to experiment, as he would say, and to decide as to the best method of siring and generating the forthcoming population. (Sensation.) Until this radical question was touched the vital point of woman's rights was not reached.[28]

That discussion never happened. Martha Wright, Lucretia Mott's sister, wrote Susan B. Anthony, who had presided, that she was "sorry for all that had been said" because "it is a subject that no Conventional or Legislative action can reach." Corresponding with a friend who was "full of wrath over Pearl Andrews, and our free platform," Lucretia Mott asserted, "Never fear for our cause. We can 'live down' all the harm that 'free-love' or the 'Maternity-question' can do us, only let not our faith fail us." When Ernestine Rose spoke shortly after Andrews at the convention, she made no reference to his remarks. But the issue of "free love" did not go away. In 1869, Rose unsuccessfully opposed a resolution at a women's rights meeting that asserted that feminists did not support free love—which they had been accused of—on the grounds that it was "in effect a plea of guilty." "If a man says to me he is not a thief, I would immediately look out for my pocket-book," she argued. "The prominent workers in this movement have been before the nation a long time, and none dare assert that their moral characters are stained. It was not the thing now . . . for the women who desired simply equal political rights for their sex to come out and voluntarily declare that they were not prostitutes."[29]

Just as any reference to preventing pregnancy provoked the charge of "free love," so too did the subject of divorce, which is why Ernestine Rose and other US feminists avoided the topic throughout the 1850s. But in Great Britain, the issues of married women's property rights and divorce became intertwined. When Parliament received the petitions for property rights amassed by the feminists Rose met in London, its members refused to act on them. Instead they amended Britain's stringent divorce law in 1857. It had mandated that each divorce required a separate act of Parliament, restricting divorce to a few wealthy men. The new law allowed men to divorce their wives for adultery; women who wanted a divorce had to prove adultery plus another crime, like incest, bigamy, or bestiality. The all-male legislature reasoned that since wives could now extricate themselves from the worst situations, they no longer needed property rights within marriage. Rose responded furiously to this maneuver. "The vitiated taste, the unblushing shamelessness exhibited by these civil and ecclesiastical law-givers in thus shielding and fencing around the depravity and corruption of their own sex, to the detriment of ours," she wrote the *Boston Investigator*, "far outdoes in impudence the Mormons themselves, and is a disgrace alike to the age, the country, and the sex."[30]

In the United States, individual states determined divorce laws, which varied widely. Indiana had very liberal statutes; New England allowed divorce on many grounds; New Yorkers could divorce only for adultery. After passing a strengthened Married Women's Property Act in the spring of 1860, the Albany legislature considered adding desertion and cruelty as justifications for ending a marriage. Horace Greeley, editor of the *New York Tribune*, vehemently opposed this measure, arguing that "my one ground of Divorce [adultery] is that expressly affirmed to be such by Jesus Christ, to the exclusion and negation of all others." He then denounced Indiana as "the Paradise of free-lovers, where the lax principles of Robert Dale Owen" prevailed. A few months later, at the Tenth National Woman's Rights Convention in May 1860—the first national woman's rights meeting she attended—Elizabeth Cady Stanton decided to throw "a bombshell into the center of woman's degradation" by presenting a series of resolutions advocating divorce. Using terms similar to Greeley's, but championing the other side, Stanton invoked both gender stereotypes and Christian imagery to support her case. "If in marriage, either party claims the right to stand supreme," she argued, "to woman, the mother of the race, belongs the sceptre and the crown. . . . Willingly do we drink the cup in the holy sacrament of marriage in the same faith that the Son of Mary died on Calvary, knowing that from our suffering comes forth a new and more glorious resurrection of thought and life." The minister Antoinette

Brown Blackwell followed Stanton and opposed her, maintaining that since marriage law came from God, it was "sacred and inviolable." She concluded that couples might separate, but had to live chastely, since anything else would weaken "the true ideal of marriage."[31]

Ernestine Rose spoke after Blackwell and finally gave voice to the principles of Robert Owen she had adopted thirty years earlier. Calling Blackwell's speech "a sermon," she asserted that marriage is "a human institution, called out by the needs of social, affectional human nature, for human purposes, its objects are, first the happiness of the parties immediately concerned, and secondly, the welfare of society." This secular, utilitarian approach demanded divorce if a marriage failed to meet these goals. Rose argued that cruelty, desertion, drunkenness, "or any other vice which makes the husband or wife intolerable and abhorrent to the other, ought to be sufficient cause for divorce. I ask for a law of Divorce," she continued,

> so as to secure the real objects and blessings of married life, to prevent the crimes and immoralities now practiced, to prevent "Free Love," in its most hideous form, such is now carried on but too often under the very name of marriage, where hypocrisy is added to the crime of legalized prostitution. "Free Love," in its degraded sense, asks for no Divorce law. . . . I believe in true marriages, and therefore I ask for a law to free men and women from false ones.

Rose concluded by urging society to "educate woman, to enable her to promote her independence, and she will not be obliged to marry for a home and a subsistence." "Loud applause" greeted her speech.[32]

But by 1860, the women's movement itself had begun to subside. In part, charges of "free love" weakened women's rights. Its advocates also divided over the new spiritualist movement, which grew explosively in these years. Spiritualism provided a powerful feminist alternative to male-dominated churches, giving women an important new role as mediums who could contact dead loved ones. It appealed especially to progressives, since it both rejected traditional religions and supported women's rights. After Rose and Anthony's speaking tour south in 1854, they went on to Philadelphia, where they attended a dinner party at Lucretia and James Mott's house. We had a discussion, "spiritualism as usual being the principal topic," Anthony wrote in her diary. She and Sarah Grimké had "an intuitive feeling that we were not to cease when the body dies." Ernestine Rose, "believing the spirit inseparable from the body, of course, was on the unbelieving side," she wrote. At the 1858

Rutland Free Convention, spiritualism dominated. Its adherents could lecture as long as they wanted, while non-spiritualists were limited to ten minutes each. Two female "trance speakers" closed the first evening session with lengthy talks presumably dictated to them by "the spirit world." Later that summer, Rose furiously denounced spiritualism in print for being "as foolish in sentiment as it is false in principle and pernicious in practice." "I dislike to have to do with ghosts," she wrote a few months later, since "there is not substance enough in them to form an idea from, or to base an opinion on. The subject is too slippery; it is like a live eel."[33]

By the late 1850s, the growing pressures over issues leading to the Civil War—from the Dred Scott decision reinforcing slavery to struggles over Kansas being a free or slave state—helped weaken the women's rights movement. Conventions became increasingly tedious and repetitive. "At this stage of the proceedings, whatever branch of the subject connected with Woman's Rights I speak upon, I necessarily repeat some of the ideas that already have been advanced," Rose stated at the 1856 National, "yet it is necessary to do so, as I doubt not that there are some here . . . who have not been at previous meetings." The organizers decided to forgo gathering in 1857. "We should let Conventions 'slide' this year," Lucretia Mott wrote Lucy Stone. "We have had so many, & such a repetition of the same speakers, that I fear they are costing more than they come to—." They scheduled the next meeting for May 1858, during the "Anniversary Week" celebrating abolitionism, in the hopes of attracting a larger audience. But nothing worked. Attendance declined; participants were either true believers or opponents who came to heckle. Stalwart activists often droned on too long. Sarah Grimké lost the audience at the Eighth National in 1858. "Why it was dreadful," Martha Wright wrote Lucretia Mott, "sheet after sheet closely written and monotonously read till all who were awake were out of all patience. Such helpless looks as passed around the platform." Organizers decided not to publish these proceedings, instead printing *The Woman's Rights Almanac of 1858. Containing Facts, Statistics, Arguments, Records of Progress, and Proofs of the Need of It.* The most impressive part of this thirty-five-page pamphlet was its title: it consisted of a jumble of ill-assorted paragraphs, with little on women's rights. Half its pages reproduced charts giving the phases of the moon.[34]

The Ninth National in 1859 met for only a single day. Audiences called out for different speakers, including Ernestine Rose, but also disrupted Rose's lecture, where she repeated points from 1856. Attending the 1860 Tenth National, a sympathetic female reporter wrote that "I felt much dashed in spirits. The speaker was declaiming in a monotonous voice, a most logical but dreary speech . . . which consisted in enumerating . . . why woman is entitled to the same natural rights as man . . . the same things in substance, that have been said, and resaid, and said again, year after year, in these conventions." An Eleventh National one-day convention was supposed to meet on May 9, 1861, and was advertised as late as May 1, even though civil war had been declared on April 12. The organizers canceled the convention at the last minute and did not schedule another until the war ended.[35]

Ernestine Rose consistently argued that women's rights and free thought constituted a single cause, although this made her "a minority of one" in both arenas. Freethinkers attempted to revive their stalled movement in the late 1850s, with little success. In 1857, ten years after their last national meeting, "the friends of Mental Liberty" convened in Philadelphia. Too ill to attend, Rose was occasionally cited during the proceedings, chiefly for wanting the group to meet in New York. Only forty-nine people signed on as members and arranged to meet again in Philadelphia, which had replaced New York as the center of organized free thought in the United States. Ernestine Rose attended in 1858 and 1860 and remained the only woman who spoke, although she did so infrequently. These conventions followed familiar patterns, as freethinkers lamented religious faith, debated a constitution, and passed numerous resolutions impossible to fulfill. From their 1857 revival on, these Infidel Conventions proved to be as numbingly formulaic as previous ones.[36]

Ernestine Rose, however, continued her individual battles against religion. In November 1857, she published a furious letter denouncing a New York minister who had blamed those who lost money in the recent financial panic for not having enough "faith in God" and "breaking 'God's Sabbath.'" "From this same reasoning," Rose sneered, "every one who goes in a mail steamer and breaks 'God's Sabbath' on the ocean, must be a criminal too, then it is quite right they should all get drowned." "Enough of this pious trash," she concluded. But Rose had difficulty attracting an audience. Her "Sunday lectures" on the merits of religious belief and disbelief, biblical heroes, and the moral life were "concluded for the present" in 1858, since "they did not receive the attention expected, or that might have been given." The Thomas Paine celebrations also declined. When she first attended in 1840, more than 800 freethinkers participated; by the years before the Civil War that number had dwindled to just under 200. Ernestine Rose continued to be the event's chief speaker until its final New York meeting in 1861. Her lectures followed her usual trajectory of extolling Paine and denouncing his critics, but in 1859 she raised a new international cause célèbre, the Mortara Case. A six-year-old Italian Jewish boy had been taken from his family by the pope's police because a servant had given him an "emergency baptism" when he was sick. The pope, who still governed parts of Italy as well as the church, ruled that the boy need not be returned to his Jewish family since the baptism made him a Catholic. Mortara provided Rose with fresh ammunition against religion. Criticizing the "despotic government" of Rome, she quickly segued to religious interference in American life. "The Constitution has divorced that unnatural marriage—the union of Church and State—but by government it is reunited," she declared. "In Washington chaplains' pray[ers] open Congress, while the members prey upon the people; our State governors issue out annual mandates for fasts, feasts, and thanksgiving over roast turkeys, which is quite an improvement on the 'Pope's bulls,' for it is certainly pleasanter to roast a turkey than to be roasted."[37]

Ernestine Rose never divided free thought, women's rights, and anti-slavery into separate causes, seeing them all as part of one great struggle for human rights and freedom. In her 1858 Paine speech, she made this unity clear. After praising the Declaration of Independence, she stated that "as long as woman was forced to pay taxes without the right to representation—as long as the colored man is transformed into a piece of chattel because his face is darker than his owner—as long as an honest, conscientious avowal of a disbelief in the fashionable superstition called religion is a crime," the Declaration remained "a dead letter." During these years, Rose spoke only infrequently on the struggles leading to the Civil War. At the 1857 Paine dinner, she denounced "the cowardly, dastardly" beating "in our own Senate" of "the heroic Charles Sumner" by a southerner outraged by his criticism of the attempts to make Kansas a slave state. Late in 1859, she mentioned John Brown's recent execution for trying to foment a slave uprising in Virginia. "I said that if the Harper's Ferry insurrection was to be regretted," she wrote the *Investigator*, "the cause that produced it was infinitely more so, and I greatly feared we would have to regret many more unhappy results springing from the same miserable cause" of slavery. She consistently supported "Disunion," maintaining that slavery contaminated not only slaveholders but also the "falsely so-called free states" of the North. "I say *falsely so-called*," she declared to an Antislavery Convention in 1855,

> for if they were truly free, there would be no slavery in this country. . . . [F]reedom and slavery can no more exist together than truth and falsehood. It is all true or all false; all free or all slave, and as we are not all free, we are all slaves and we are all slaveholders to some extent; at any rate in aiding and abetting, unless we raise our voice against it and

use the utmost efforts in our power to disunite, to break that unholy Union—of wickedness, of crime, of sin, and of shame. A Union of freedom and slavery cannot exist any more than fire and water.[38]

By endorsing this uncompromising position, Rose allied herself with the most extreme wing of the abolitionist movement. As war drew closer, she became even more militant, appearing at anti-slavery rallies, including one at Boston in October 1860, where she was placed on the Executive Committee, and another at Albany in February 1861. In her final Paine address, given in late January 1861, after Lincoln's election and South Carolina's push for seces-sion, Ernestine Rose condemned any union of the free North and the slave South as "a Union with a vengeance; like that of husband and wife; with all the rights on one side and all the penalties on the other." On the eve of the war, she embraced the struggle to come—in part because the rebellion had been led by South Carolina, which she had despised since her 1847 visit there. "South Carolina set up an independent empire!" she exclaimed to the 1861 Paine audience. "For my part, I would give her a passport to Heaven to keep her away from us. But whether the South is allowed to drift to her downward destiny, or forced into submission, let the watchword be 'No more compro-mise!'"[39] Embracing the coming Civil War, she did not realize how much it would harm the causes she held dear.

7

Dissention, Division, Departure

ERNESTINE ROSE FOUND the 1860s a difficult decade. From 1861 to 1865 the Civil War upended her life, even though she remained in the North and had no male relative or friend engaged in the fighting. The women's movement voluntarily suspended its meetings for the war's duration, instead organizing a "Loyal League" to support the Union. Once the war ended, feminists split irrevocably over whether black men should get the vote before them. The free-thought movement continued to decline as the war revived religious devotion. Antisemitism also increased and Horace Seaver, head of the *Boston Investigator*, published editorials denouncing Jews, which Rose rebutted. Throughout the decade, she became increasingly ill, but periodically recovered. In 1869, the Roses left for Europe to try to restore her health.

Throughout this period, Ernestine Rose continued to work for her principles, ardently supporting women's rights, anti-slavery, and free thought even under adverse conditions. She actively participated in conventions, wrote numerous letters, and gave many speeches, even though she could no longer manage the extensive tours she had previously undertaken. In 1860, for instance, she triumphed over a hostile Long Island minister who urged the women of his congregation not to attend a lecture of hers. Instead, "the disobedient daughters of Eve" thronged to her talk and refused to leave when she spoke about religion. "Had the minister simply refused to read the notice, and only left me . . . alone, I don't think I would have had any audience at all," Rose wrote in a public letter she titled "The World Moves!" "I would have confined myself to the subject of education, without touching religion . . . while as it was, I thought as he opened the ball, I would let him dance to his own tune," she jested. "I have been requested to speak again as soon as they can make arrangements.... They had never heard a woman nor an Infidel speaker before."[1]

Such triumphs encouraged Rose to complete *A Defence of Atheism*, her short but powerful free-thought credo. First delivered in Boston on April 10, 1861, two days before the declaration of Civil War, this speech was reprinted three times as a twenty-four-page pamphlet by Rose's friend, Josiah Paine Mendum, publisher of the *Investigator*. In it, Rose marshaled arguments from science, everyday life, and biblical criticism to prove her case that God does not exist. Rational and logical, but laced through with her trademark sarcasm and humor, *A Defence of Atheism* intermingled the latest scientific theories with older arguments against religion she had made in earlier years. It is written in the formal masculine voice, using "he" to stand for everyone, and capitalizes both "God" and "Atheism."[2]

Rose begins by surveying the sciences. She rapidly concludes that none provides any evidence for the existence of a deity and that all disprove biblical accounts of creation. Geology refutes the possibility that the world was made in six days, since "it requires thousands of ages to form the various strata of the earth." Chemistry "says that Nothing has no existence, and therefore out of Nothing, Nothing could be made." Anthropology, illustrated by the missionary/explorer David Livingstone's recent journeys in Africa, found "civilized, moral, and virtuous" tribes who "have not the remotest idea of a God," proving that religious belief is not universal. Asking why "man thought or wrote about God at all," she answers her own question by declaring that people worship because "Ignorance is the mother of superstition.... Before electricity was discovered, a thunder-storm was said to come from the wrath of an offended Deity."[3]

Rose then turns to the story of Adam and Eve, using it to show that the God presented in the Bible was not all-knowing, all-powerful, or all-good:

Did God know when he created the serpent that it would tempt the woman, and that *she* was made out of such frail materials (the rib of Adam), as not to be able to resist the temptation? If he did not know, then his knowledge was at fault; if he did, but could not prevent that calamity, then his power was at fault; if he knew and could, but would not, then his goodness was at fault. Choose which you please, and it remains alike fatal to the rest.

As she continues through the Hebrew Bible, sarcastically deconstructing the story of Noah—"so he [God] destroyed everything, except Noah with his family, and a few household pets. Why he saved them is hard to say"—one hears echoes of the young Jewish daughter arguing with her rabbi father. As a mature atheist, however, Rose had mastered an equally thorough knowledge of the Gospels, which she used to indict Christianity. God "was forced to resort to the last sad alternative of sending 'his only begotten son,' his second self, to save" the world. "Did he succeed even then?" she asks rhetorically. "Is the world saved? *Saved*! From what? From ignorance? It is all around us. From poverty, vice, crime, sin, misery, and shame? It abounds everywhere. Look into your poor-houses, your prisons, your lunatic asylums; contemplate the whip, the instruments of torture, and of death . . . and tell me from what the world was *saved*!" Rose concludes this section by arguing that the promise of justice in an afterlife is at best a sham. "If a rich parent were to let his children live in ignorance, poverty, and wretchedness, all their lives, and hold out to them the promise of a fortune at some time hereafter, he would justly be considered a criminal or a madman."[4]

In the second half of her *Defence*, Rose justifies Atheism, concluding that atheists are more moral than believers. Countering the standard religious argument that God cannot be understood, she asserts that it is unreasonable "to expect me to believe—blame, persecute, and punish me for not believing—in what you have to acknowledge you cannot understand." She then argues that the fact that the world exists "does not prove a Creator"; it only shows that contemporary knowledge is deficient. Next, Rose asserts that religion is not "natural." If "the belief in a God were natural," she reasons, "there would be no need to teach it. We don't have to teach the general elements of human nature,—the five senses. . . . They are universal; so would religion be were *it* natural, but it is not. On the contrary, it is an interesting and demonstrable fact that all children are Atheists, and were religion not inculcated into their minds, they would remain so."[5]

Rose then questions the supposed link between religion and morality, which contemporaries took for granted—even the Italian revolutionary Guiseppe Mazzini, for example, who had radical social ideals, declared, "An atheist can have no sense of duty." Instead, Rose maintains, "Morality does not depend on the belief in any religion. History gives ample evidence that the more belief the less virtue and goodness." To prove her case, she cites the biblical justifications of slavery used by southern apologists. "Look at the present crisis—at the South with 4,000,000 beings in slavery, bought and sold like brute chattels under the sanction of religion and of God . . . and the South complains that reforms in the North are owing to Infidelity." In her conclusion, Rose reverses the religious view of atheists as immoral to argue that religion has made people worse, not better:

Teach man to do right, to love justice, to revere truth, to be virtuous, not because a God would reward or punish him hereafter, but because it is right. . . . Let him feel the great truth that our highest happiness consists in making all around us happy; and it would be an infinitely truer and safer guide for man to a life of usefulness, virtue, and morality, than all the beliefs in all the Gods ever imagined.

Rose remained satisfied with this essay. Over thirty years later, when she was eighty-two, a friend wrote, "She gave me a copy of her 'Defence of Atheism,' and said she had nothing to alter."[6]

In *A Defence of Atheism*, Ernestine Rose limited herself to her topic, but in real life she attempted to unite her three causes of free thought, feminism, and anti-slavery. None of these efforts succeeded. Despite Rose's muting of free thought at feminist meetings, many women's rights activists continued to shun her because of her lack of religious belief. "There are so few who dare to be friendly to her," feminist Martha Wright wrote her sister Lucretia Mott in 1858. "I should feel better satisfied, if I had taken more pains to see Mrs. Rose," Mott replied. "There is too much truth in thy remarks. It *is* too bad for such a *woman*, to have to feel neglected." Five years later, little had changed. "My frd. Erneste. L. Rose has suffered, from the bigotry of very frds," Mott wrote her cousin in 1863. "As to Mrs. Rose's . . . atheism—people will cry 'Mad dog' when doctrines or sentiments conflict with their cherished ideas." Mott repeatedly hoped that the time would come when Rose, Owen, and other freethinkers would be appreciated and "the denunciations of bigoted Sectarianism fall into merited contempt."[7]

During these same years, freethinkers resisted supporting anti-slavery, which Rose passionately championed. In January 1862, she sent a toast to the Thomas Paine celebration in Boston calling for President Lincoln to "awaken from the lethargy in which the opiate of slavery has so long kept him" and to remove the "cancer" of slave ownership from the nation. A regular correspondent wrote the *Investigator* objecting to "E. L. Rose and others" prodding the newspaper "to do service for abolitionism." He did not want Infidels to be "drawn into the Christian error of attributing the war to slavery" and thought that "long will be the fight if abolitionism is the Northern object." Anti-slavery was an overwhelmingly Christian movement. Its religiosity inspired the most popular war song in the North, Julia Ward Howe's "Battle Hymn of the Republic." Written in 1861 to the tune of "John Brown's Body," the anthem merged anti-slavery with Christianity in both its chorus of "Glory, glory, hallelujah" and many of its verses:

Mine eyes have seen the glory of the coming of the Lord,
He is trampling out the vintage where the grapes of wrath are stored,
He hath loosed the fateful lightning of His terrible swift sword:
His truth is marching on.
. . . .
In the beauty of the lilies Christ was born across the sea,
With a glory in his bosom that transfigures you and me:
As he died to make men holy, let us die to make men free,
While God is marching on.[8]

At the Infidel Convention in 1862, however, Ernestine Rose tried to sever that connection by presenting an anti-slavery resolution: "Whereas, Religion is the primary cause of all slavery . . . it is the bounden duty of every lover of freedom and justice . . . to aid in emancipating the slaves wherever found, and of whatever color." Despite Rose's prestige—the *Investigator* wrote that "her attendance at the Convention will greatly contribute to its interest"—a heated debate ensued, although the resolution eventually passed. Some objected to "Infidels meddling with the slavery question"; others "regarded the discussion of slavery as irrelevant"; still others opposed "running the country into a prolonged civil war, where twenty-six millions of people are undergoing all the miseries and horrors of war, for the freedom of three and a half millions of aliens, and foreigners by nature, and who too are undoubtedly of an inferior quality." Rose herself knew she was correct and "defended her resolution as being the legitimate result of Infidelity. What is her infidelity? UNIVERSAL MENTAL FREEDOM! How can slavery exist with universal mental freedom which wages unceasing war upon *all* oppression?" Her heightened tone came from both her sense of righteousness and her unwillingness to compromise on such an important issue.

Free thought continued to decline. "The war has nearly broken up our organization, or rendered it inoperative," the group's president Horace Seaver lamented in 1863. The movement lost a prominent adherent when Joseph Barker abandoned free thought to return to religion. Barker had first come to the United States in 1851, where he actively supported both anti-slavery and free thought, and Rose had once praised him as "*the* man for us." But the two had no further contact after Barker returned to both Christianity and England.[9]

Just before the war and during its early years, Ernestine Rose fought especially hard for the controversial topic of abolition and the even more unpopular cause of integration. "Mrs. Rose will come" to a series of meetings in upstate New York in 1861, Susan B. Anthony wrote Elizabeth Cady Stanton, "she never felt so strong—to speak on Anti-Slavery." Riots erupted when those meetings convened. Even in the North, most white Americans considered blacks inferior and opposed freeing the slaves. In Albany, when Rose objected to "the [segregation] laws that regulate steamboats, hotels, and public meetings . . . clamor and confusion rung in the hall, and for a time interrupted the proceedings of the Convention." Although the mayor called on the police to keep order, hisses, groans, and stamping drowned out the speakers. Abolitionists canceled their anniversary meetings in the spring of 1861 because of the war, but when they convened again in 1862, Rose played an active part. At the American Anti-Slavery Society meeting early that May in New York City, she not only "urged the duty of the Abolitionists to stand firm to their principles and methods of action" but also spoke for "the publication in pamphlet form" of the African American abolitionist William Wells Brown's address. Rose "considered it the most important speech of the day— excellent as were the others—and she wished it published and laid upon the desks of the Members of Congress, and others, who may still be troubled with the absurd idea that the slaves, if set free, cannot take care of themselves." She closed by offering to donate money to publish his speech.[10]

A few weeks later, Ernestine Rose traveled to Boston to present her abolitionist resolution to the Infidel Convention. She also made a forceful speech at the New England Anti-Slavery Convention, harshly denouncing Lincoln for not having already freed all the slaves. Rose underestimated Lincoln's political and logistical difficulties: he had won only a scant majority of northern votes in the 1860 election, the North did badly in the first year of the war, and he wanted to prevent the slave-owning border states from joining the Confederacy. As a disunionist, Rose condemned Lincoln's and Congress's insistence that the war was only being fought to preserve the Union, not to free the slaves. "Lincoln must answer to the ages for the use of the power he has taken and will not wield aright," she charged. "If the President cannot move without pushing, push him on. I stand here to push you on." When Rose questioned the president's honesty, she was hissed by her fellow abolitionists. By this stage in her career, Ernestine Rose was so accustomed to thinking herself as right and "a minority of one" that she took opposition as a sign of her correctness: "I am proud to think I have said the best thing in the Convention—*ecce signum*! [behold the proof]," she declared after being hissed. She concluded by re-stating her disunionist principles, maintaining that a real "Union" did not exist, since the North had acquiesced to southern slavery rather than creating "a union based on reciprocity. Union can only be formed, not restored among us." After this convention, Rose made at least one more anti-slavery speech, in Ellenville, New York, at the end of August.[11]

Much changed between then and Rose's next public appearance almost a year later in May 1863. The Confederate army advanced to within twenty miles of Washington, DC. The Union's victory at Antietam that autumn convinced Lincoln to issue an Emancipation Proclamation, nominally freeing the slaves in the states still in rebellion on January 1, 1863, and allowing the enlistment of blacks into the previously all-white Union forces. The proclamation disappointed Rose and some others for leaving slavery intact in the border states, but both Frederick Douglass and William Lloyd Garrison praised the measure for heading in the right direction.

Rose and a number of other feminist abolitionists felt excluded from the war effort. Believing that northern women should pressure the government for immediate emancipation of all slaves and inspired by the male Loyal and Union Leagues that coalesced during these years, Stanton and Anthony created the Woman's National Loyal League in the spring of 1863. They convened a meeting of over a thousand women on May 14 in New York City. Their goal was to bring women into the public sphere by organizing them to submit mammoth petitions to Congress from every state in the Union to support complete freedom for all slaves. Rose played a major role at this convention, where she spoke frequently and was on its influential Business Committee, which produced the League's resolutions.[12]

All seven resolutions presented proposed full emancipation for blacks and called on northern women to support the war—except the fifth resolution. It held, "There can never be a true peace in this Republic until the civil and political equality of every subject of the Government shall be practically established," which implied that women, both black and white, and black men, as citizens, should be allowed to vote. This issue occasioned considerable debate, while all the other resolutions passed unanimously. The delegate from Wisconsin stated that although she herself agreed with the resolution, "We all know that Woman's Rights as an *ism* has not been received with entire favor by the women of the country, and I know that there are thousands of earnest, loyal, and able women who will not go into any movement of this kind, if this idea is made prominent." Rose replied, "I, for one, object to throwing women out of the race for freedom. And do you know why? Because she needs freedom for the freedom of man. . . . Woman, as well as the negro, should be recognized as an equal with the whole human race." As debate continued, Rose spoke again. Convinced she was correct, she became condescending. "It is exceedingly amusing to hear persons talk about throwing out Woman's

Rights, when, if it had not been for Woman's Rights, that lady would not have had the courage to stand here and say what she did," she began. "I think it will be exceedingly inconsistent if, because some women out in the West are opposed to the Woman's Rights movement—though at the same time they take advantage of it—that therefore we shall throw it out of this resolution." The measure eventually passed, but not unanimously.[13]

Rose devoted her set speech that evening to a harsh and detailed critique of Lincoln's conduct of the war, similar to the one she gave a year earlier. Provocatively declaring that she was "not unconditionally loyal to the Administration" since "we women need not be, for the law has never yet recognized us," she attacked most of the president's previous policies, from his choice of generals, to not freeing slaves in the border states, to the composition of his cabinet. Showing a detailed knowledge of the government's military tactics, personalities, and policies, she closed with her unpopular position that emancipation took precedence over union: "Why this hue-and-cry for Union, *Union*, UNION, which is like a bait held out to the mass of the people to lure them on. . . . I would rather have a small republic without the taint . . . of slavery in it. . . . Our work must be mainly to watch, and criticize, and urge the Administration to do its whole duty to freedom and humanity." Rose's views were so extreme and her denunciation of Lincoln so unsparing that Lucy Stone, the convention's president, rebuked her, declaring that "all the loyal women will agree with me that we owe to the President and the Government . . . words of cheer and encouragement; and as events occur one after another, our criticisms should not be harshly made." The Convention then adjourned.[14]

The next day, the Business Committee met to create a platform for the League. They resolved to back conscription, to advocate black men's participation in the fighting, and to organize Women's Loyal Leagues throughout the nation to support 'OUR COUNTRY RIGHT, not wrong.'" Stanton then proposed a declaration that "our work as a National League is to educate the nation into the true idea of a Republic." "Considerable preliminary debate, in which many ladies joined, took place on details of form and phraseology," Anthony reported, and the group finally added the word "Christian" before "Republic." Ernestine Rose almost certainly took part in this discussion and of course would have opposed the addition, but she remained isolated in her beliefs. Throughout the Convention, Christian doctrine and language predominated. Stanton's lengthy Opening Address equated civilization with Christianity. All the letters sent to the Convention and almost all the speeches invoked religion. "Our Declaration of Independence was the very first national evidence of the great doctrine of brotherhood and equality which Jesus Christ had taught the world," Angelina Grimké Weld stated in a typical intertwining of American values with Christendom. The organizers concluded that "A deep religious tone of loyalty to God and Freedom pervaded the entire meeting." This spirit was in tune with the times. Church membership rose dramatically during the war, as did efforts to christianize the nation. In 1863, the National Association to Secure the Religious Amendment of the Constitution organized, with its goal of rewriting the Preamble so that it read

> We, the people of the United States, recognizing the being and attributes of Almighty God, the Divine authority of the Holy Scriptures, the law of God as the paramount rule, and Jesus the Messiah, the Savior, and the Lord of all, in order to form a more perfect union . . .

The Loyal League's final goal of endorsing a "Christian Republic" both reflected that religious outlook and ignored women's rights. None of this spared the League from criticism. "The whole affair brought up vividly before the mind the funny women's rights conventions of former days," jeered the *New York Herald*, adding that the event "has been distorted into an atheistical revolutionary woman's rights movement under the leadership of Lucy Stone, Susan B. Anthony, and Ernestine L. Rose."[15]

Two months after this Convention, violence connected to the Civil War erupted in New York City. Prompted by the institution of a draft in mid-July that allowed wealthy men chosen by lottery to either hire a substitute or pay $300 to exempt themselves while poor men had to serve, riots broke out in Manhattan. Mobs of white workers, many of them Irish immigrants, stormed federal buildings, pro-war newspaper offices, and police stations, setting fires and erecting barricades. They especially attacked black New Yorkers, lynching at least ten of them, burning down the Colored Orphan Asylum, and completely overwhelming the city's police. In these Draft Riots, 120 New Yorkers died. Living at 95 Prince Street, just a few blocks from police headquarters, the Roses would have been near this mayhem. Union army troops, fresh from the Battle of Gettysburg, finally restored order.[16]

Simultaneously, Ernestine Rose encountered antisemitism from an unexpected source: the pages of her beloved newspaper, the atheistic *Boston Investigator*. Antisemitism directed at the ancient Hebrews and their Bible had a long tradition within free thought. Many men of the Enlightenment, including Thomas Paine, reviled the Jews of the Bible and their religion as the chief source of Christian "superstition." They reserved special scorn for Moses, whose character Paine declared was "the most horrid that can be imagined" since he "committed the most unexampled atrocities that are to be found in the history of any nation." Rose shared Paine's opinion of religions as pernicious superstition and she had severely criticized both the God of the Bible and biblical figures in her *Defence of Atheism.* But she distinguished between the ancient Hebrews who created religion and contemporary Jews, whom she did not write about.[17]

Ernestine Rose and the *Investigator's* editor, Horace Seaver, had a lengthy and warm relationship. She began reading the weekly *Boston Investigator* in 1837, the year he started working for the paper. He published Rose's speeches at the Paine dinners and Infidel Conventions regularly from the 1840s on and printed her letters, usually with her name in the headline. In 1856, he reproduced a unique acrostic poem from a correspondent to "our mutual and noble friend," Ernestine L. Rose, which despite its heartfelt admiration characterized her as both "God-inspired" and having a " 'Jewish' face."

> *Earnestest, bravest, best in speech of womankind,*
> *Right in the face of error—champion of mind*
> *Never faltering—God-inspired, so bold and true,*
> *Excellence, sure, is but a synonym for you!*
> *Significant, and most promising for the race,*
> *To me, is the sight of thy soul-lit "Jewish" face!*
> *I hail thy coming as pledge of the "better day"*
> *Now so much talked about, for which we all do pray,*
> *Erst dreamed of and oft sung by the prophets of old ...*
> *Lo! in thee its hopeful dawn we may behold!*
> *Ring out the old, and ring in the better new,*
> *Oh! burst in glory upon our enraptured view,*
> *Selectest of day! Of all that have gone before,*
> *Earnest of blessings, innumerable in store!*

In turn, Rose helped raise money for a benefit to aid Seaver in 1858. In her solicitations, she praised his "talents, sound principles, good judgment, refined taste, and gentle spirit" as well as "his disinterested and unremitting labors for over twenty years in *our* cause." Seaver warmly thanked "the estimable lady ... who manifests in this case what is usual with her, a disposition that delights in contributing to the welfare of others." Throughout the decades, the newspaper treated its Jewish Infidel correspondents, both Ernestine Rose and the Baltimore man who published as "Philo-Spinoza," with admiration and respect.[18]

But the *Investigator* combined this regard for individuals with a routine antisemitism that permeated segments of US culture. In 1860, most Americans would never have met any Jews, who numbered only about 150,000 persons in a population of 31.5 million. Jews, however, were generally viewed both as "Christ-killers" and through the lens of Shakespeare's character Shylock, known for his love of money and hatred of Christians. The *Investigator* regularly printed crude antisemitic (and anti–Irish Catholic) jokes. A typical one featured Christians pushing a Jew under water. The third time, he says he will convert, so he is then "drowned as a Christian." The *Investigator* also published harsh denunciations of the ancient Hebrews, for their "ridiculous customs, murderous propensities, disgusting ceremonies, and determined scoundrelism."[19]

In addition to strengthening Christianity, the Civil War heightened antisemitism. A number of northern newspapers alleged that the "descendants of Shylock" sold goods to the enemy, speculated in gold, and opposed the end of slavery. The most notorious result of these charges was Ulysses Grant's General Order #11, issued in December 1862, which commanded that "the Jews, as a class" be "expelled" from Kentucky, Tennessee, and the Union-occupied sections of Mississippi "within twenty-four hours" for trading with the Confederacy. Although President Lincoln rescinded this widely criticized order within a few weeks, it signaled an intensification of anti-Jewish sentiments under the pressure of war. Horace Seaver shared these feelings and in 1863 began publishing lead editorials that expanded attacks on the ancient Hebrews to include modern Jews. Rose was roused to reply to one that appeared on October 28, 1863.[20]

First denouncing the ancient Jews as "about the worst people of whom we have any account, and the poorest guides to follow," Seaver then turned to "the modern Jews," expressing relief because they had lost power and were "scattered among other nations, which rendered them comparatively harmless." He condemned them for "clinging with wonderful tenacity" to their religion with "all its absurd rites and ceremonies," while maintaining that "neither the Protestants nor Catholics can vie with them in this regard." Next, Seaver deplored the replacement of a Universalist church in Boston by "a large synagogue," since Universalism, a Christian denomination that held that all would go to heaven, was "liberal, democratic, equal, and saves the entire race," while Judaism was "bigoted, narrow, exclusive, and totally unfit for a progressive people like the Americans, among whom we hope it may not spread."

Ernestine Rose brooded over this editorial for a number of months. She gave her first critical letter the most significant date in the free-thought pantheon: Thomas Paine's birthday, January 29. Challenging Seaver's remarks about modern Jews, she teased him by writing, "Mr. Editor, I almost smelt brimstone, genuine Christian brimstone, when I read" your statement that they are unfit for this country. How "would you prevent their spreading? Would you drive them out of Boston, out of 'progressive America,' as they were driven out of Spain?" Rose then used her considerable knowledge of contemporary Jewish life in both the United States and Europe to rebut Seaver. She argued that in American cities Jews "have synagogues, and have no doubt spread as much as they could, and no calamity has yet befallen any place in consequence of that fact." She maintained that Jews assimilated to the culture they lived in, that wherever they are "they act just about the same as other people. The nature of a Jew is governed by the same laws as human nature in general." Where they "are still under the Christian lash . . . self-preservation forces them to be narrow and exclusive," but

> in other countries more civilized and just, they are so too; they progress just as fast as the world will permit them. In France, there is hardly any difference between Jew and Christian. The Jews occupy some of the highest positions in the Army, the State, in literature, the arts, and sciences; the same is the case more or less in Germany and other enlightened countries. Are then the Jews in Boston so much worse, that their spread is dreaded even by Infidels?

After mocking an antisemitic letter in the *Investigator* which maintained that the author knew what Jews were like since he lived "in a street where there are" several Jewish families and "they carry out the old Levitical law . . . not omitting circumcision and other barbarities," Rose reasserted that the Jews are "as intelligent, social, and friendly" as other Americans. The weakest parts of her rebuttal were her attempts to defend Judaism, which she no longer believed in. She argued, unconvincingly, that circumcision hurts less than having one's ears pierced. She insisted that Judaism was morally superior to Universalism because it worshipped only one deity rather than "three Gods" and did not believe in either a savior or an afterlife. She undermined the standard antisemitic charge that Jews were "cunning sharp traders" by pointing "to the renowned 'Yankee,' who, it is admitted by all, excels the Jew in that art," a common observation. The English traveler Frances Trollope had written thirty years earlier that "I never met an individual in any part of the Union who did not paint these New Englanders as sly, grinding, selfish, and tricky. The Yankees . . . will avow these qualities themselves with a complacent smile, and boast that no people on earth can match them at over-reaching in a bargain." Rose then ended on a conciliatory note. "I know there are honest, honorable Yankees as well as Jews: the Editor of the *Investigator* is one of the very best," she concluded. "Then let us, as Infidels . . . not add to the prejudice already existing towards the Jews, or any other sect." She signed her letter "Yours for Justice" and then sent another letter a few days later with $5 to support the *Investigator*, twice the amount of a yearly subscription.[21]

Ernestine Rose assumed she had convinced Seaver that he had been "too hasty" in making his "sweeping denunciation against the modern Jews." Instead, Seaver repeated his original argument that Universalism was superior to Judaism, insisted that he had "nothing against a Jew personally," and wrote that he never "intimated" anything about driving "the Jews out of Boston"— "what could have put such an idea into her head?" He called Rose "his too sensitive sister" and declared that if she wanted to see Judaism spread "she is more friendly to superstition than we supposed her to be." Referring to Rose's presumed relations with her own family, he added, "We have heard it said that if a Jew or Jewess forsake their religion, they are disinherited by the family and regarded as dead forever afterwards. If this be true," Jews "are not equal . . . to the Universalists, for they are more forgiving than to act in this manner." His ugly final riposte showed he had been stung by Rose's charges against the Yankees. "If the Yankees, as a class, like money as well as the Jews we question whether so many of the former would be found in the ranks of the Union Army," Seaver concluded. "They would be more likely to stay at home to deal in 'old clothes,' at a profit of 'fifteen per shent.'" Adding injury to insult, he engineered the format unfairly, dividing Rose's not very long letters into two parts so he could rebut each half separately and at length. "Our friend Mrs. Rose did not have the benefit . . . which she would have had if her matter had been published in a more connected manner," one of the few correspondents supporting Rose wrote. "You had a decided advantage of the arrangements . . . enabling you to make your responses more effective." This tactic not only weakened Rose's arguments but also put her in the difficult position of responding late to many of Seaver's criticisms.[22]

This debate by correspondence continued for eight weeks, with Rose sending four letters in all. She became furious when Seaver wrote that because of her defense of Judaism, he had thought that "Sister Rose" might "leave us and go to Rome or Judea." "No! 'she is not yet disposed to give up the ship,'" Rose replied. "'She' has held fast to it long before she knew you, and as you did not at all help her to get on board of it, nor depend upon your piloting, she is not likely to slip off, however unsteady you may navigate the 'ship.' " This led Seaver to accuse Rose of demonstrating that "she can scold bravely, if she cannot use convincing arguments." He wrote that their discussion had become repetitive and then proceeded to repeat all his previous points at great length. In her final letter, Rose defended her "scolding"—"perhaps if you had received a little more scolding from women, the right kind I mean, you might deserve it less now." She ended by writing that she was "quite willing to leave it to the readers of the *Investigator* to judge who used the most 'invectives,' who possessed the most 'equanimity,' and whether you fairly answered my questions." Seaver claimed the last words, again accusing Rose of delivering "a scolding tirade," and also left it "to our readers to decide which of the twain has preserved the better temper."[23]

If Rose's letters had been written by a man, he might have been accused of arguing or disputing, but not of scolding. Most of the *Investigator*'s correspondents, all of them male, sided with Seaver, accusing Rose of not only "scolding like a termagant" but of writing "spleeny inanities" and being "personal, abusive, and ill-natured." Rose did have a few defenders, however. Philo-Spinoza charged Seaver with "slandering a whole race of people," and William Wood, who had criticized Seaver's format, wrote that the editor "was not entirely rid of the old Puritanic notion that the whole of their race is only capable of Christ-killing." He went on to say that he admired Rose's "progressive liberality of sentiment, and her independence in its expression" so much "that some years since I named my only daughter ERNESTINE ROSE WOOD." The *Jewish Record*, a religious newspaper, also praised Rose, who even if she no longer believed in Judaism, still possessed "some of the leaven of the Jewish spirit."[24]

This passionate and lengthy interchange of letters with Seaver remained the only time Ernestine Rose ever wrote about contemporary Jews and modern Judaism. Horace Seaver did not change his views at all, continuing to publish antisemitic diatribes against Moses. Early in 1867, he visited the synagogue whose replacement of a Universalist church had prompted the editorial Rose first responded to. Ignorant that Jewish men's heads must remain covered, he "acted as a gentleman should" by removing his hat upon entering and then took great offense at being told, as he put it, "I vant you to put on yourn hat!" He continued to deny that he treated "*modern* Jews unfairly, though such a charge has before been preferred against us."[25] For her part, Ernestine Rose never mentioned this matter again, and in later life, she wrote warmly to and about Seaver. It seems not to have affected her close friendship with J. P. Mendum, publisher of the newspaper, and Seaver's good friend. Rose continued to subscribe but ceased her frequent writing to the *Boston Investigator*. For almost five years, from April 1864 until February 1869, she did not send a single item to the newspaper.

Without Rose's letters to the *Investigator*, few sources exist for her life during the tumultuous final years of the Civil War. The couple moved uptown in 1864, from Prince Street in Soho to Broadway north of Washington Square. Ernestine Rose made "a soul-stirring speech" at the large first Anniversary Meeting of the Woman's National Loyal League on May 12, 1864, in New York City. The group "nearly filled" the liberal Church of the Puritans close to her home, but the proceedings were not published and her speech has not survived. Large parades took place in lower Manhattan before the presidential election in November 1864, but it is not known whether Rose backed Lincoln. Early in March 1865, a "National Jubilee" parade celebrating Lincoln's second term stretched for seven miles through lower Manhattan. The Civil War ended on April 9, 1865, and New York City "exploded" with spontaneous victory celebrations. Less than a week later, Lincoln was assassinated. Crepe "completely darkened" the city, the daily *New York World* wrote. "There was not a store on Broadway that was not draped in deep black, mingled with pure white." William Rose's jewelry store, underneath the couple's apartment, probably joined in this public mourning. On April 24, Lincoln's body arrived in New York to lie in state at City Hall. The following day his funeral procession wended uptown, watched by close to a million people. Whether the Roses were among them remains unknown.[26]

A letter Ernestine Rose wrote declining an invitation to the Boston Paine celebration and Infidel Convention in January 1865 does survive. In it she joked that since Paine "*chose* to make his first appearance in the middle of winter," he must "dispense" with her presence, since she could not face "the still harsher climate of Boston, when even" in New York "the weather is too severe for me to battle with." Writing on her fifty-fifth birthday, she added, "I get every year a year older, (though ladies never get old) and what is worse, my strength does not increase with my years, though my love of liberty and hatred to superstition and tyranny does." She closed by urging infidels to oppose the proposed amendment to include God and Jesus in the US Constitution's preamble.[27]

From the late 1850s, friends commented on Ernestine Rose's ailments. "Mrs. Rose very poorly we hear (as usual), inflam[mator]y rheumm. &c. [*sic.*]," Lucretia Mott wrote her sister. "Who is there to take the lead?" "She has for some time been failing in health," the *Boston Investigator* reported in

1859. Ten years later, Stanton and Anthony declared that she "has long been an invalid." Sara Underwood, a journalist who interviewed Rose in 1868, wrote that "her health was so poor and uncertain that she was obliged to forbear taking much active part in the reforms so dear to her," but added that Rose "was not forced into quietude until the shackles had fallen from the black race forever"—presumably after the passage of the Thirteenth Amendment abolishing slavery in December 1865.[28]

As Rose's health deteriorated, others began to supplant her. Underwood started writing monthly articles for the *Boston Investigator*. Previously, Rose had been the newspaper's only regular female correspondent, but by the late 1860s, both the freethinkers Elmina D. Slenker and a woman who wrote as "Old Mother" also began publishing in the newspaper. During the Civil War, Anna Dickinson, a new young female orator, quickly captivated the public. Often called "America's Joan of Arc," Dickinson spoke in favor of the war, campaigned successfully for Lincoln and the Republican Party, and in 1864 became the first woman to address Congress. She had three chief advantages over Ernestine Rose in appealing to audiences: she was native-born, youthful, and not an atheist. But unlike Rose, Dickinson operated on her own and rarely joined forces with other women.[29]

Within the women's movement itself, Elizabeth Cady Stanton came to the fore during the 1860s. She and Ernestine Rose had many traits in common. Both lectured exceptionally well, their dramatic eloquence enabling them to hold audiences rapt for hours. Both had a keen sense of humor and a talent for sarcastic wit. Both swam against the mainstream, boldly defying contemporary beliefs. Both ardently opposed slavery and developed coherent philosophies of human rights and female equality. Both were seen as exceptional. Reporting on an 1868 convention, Underwood wrote that Rose and Stanton were the only women there who "would be singled out from a miscellaneous crowd as persons of mark," adding that "no young girl" was "ever more lovely, in my eyes, than are Mrs. Rose and Mrs. Stanton in the beautiful ripeness of life's autumn."[30]

But the two women also differed greatly, especially in social background. Stanton's father was a wealthy judge in upstate New York where her family owned slaves. Stanton possessed both her caste's prestige and some of its biases against foreigners, blacks, and the uneducated. Rose did not share Stanton's prejudices, wealth, or social status. She sought to win people over through reasoned arguments, but her militant atheism repelled many, no matter how much she downplayed it at women's rights conventions. Underwood wrote that if only Rose "had been less honest and conscientious" about her lack of religious belief, "she would today occupy a far higher position in public favor than she does." In contrast, Stanton always identified as a Christian, even as she moved away from orthodoxy. During the 1860s, she routinely wore a large cross around her neck and frequently invoked Jesus's authority to support her demands. She also had personal relationships with members of Congress and abolitionist leaders, made through her birth family and her husband, the anti-slavery politician Henry B. Stanton. As Rose's energy waned, Stanton rapidly became a movement leader. By the second half of the 1860s, Rose tended to follow Stanton rather than creating her own path.[31]

The end of the Civil War ushered in a critical and difficult time for women's rights. During the war, the movement had focused on freeing the slaves, but the end of slavery inevitably raised the issue of suffrage. Would every adult receive the vote, or only black men? Throughout her career, Ernestine Rose consistently argued, as she did in 1867, that all human beings deserved equal rights, which "do not depend on the shade of color, . . . on a somewhat different construction, or somewhat different shape of body, or somewhat different shape of mind." For a short time after the war, it seemed possible to gain the vote for all. Early in 1866, Congress received its first women's suffrage petition (earlier ones had gone to state legislatures) with Ernestine Rose's signature written on it in large letters using very black ink. The petition, signed by more than 10,000 women, received little support from the government. Stanton and Anthony then organized the Eleventh National Woman's Rights Convention—the first since 1860—to meet for one day in May in New York City. Rose's name led the announcement that advertised the featured speakers.[32]

But for the first and only time in her life, Ernestine Rose chose not to deliver her speech. She sat on the stage, listening initially to Stanton and then to three men: Theodore Tilton, editor of a popular newspaper; Henry Ward Beecher, a celebrated Brooklyn minister; and Wendell Phillips, the abolitionist whose anti-foreigner bias she had criticized in the 1850s. Stanton and Tilton championed women's suffrage. Beecher regaled the appreciative group for over an hour, sprinkling his lecture with anti-Irish remarks before concluding, "It is more important that woman shall vote than that the black man shall vote." In sharp contrast, Phillips harshly critiqued his audience, telling them how to act, which included "trampl[ing] mistaken Judaism under one foot." He then excoriated the entire female sex, saying, "Let woman know that nobody stops her but herself. She ties her own limbs. She corrupts her own sisters." By the time he finished, Ernestine Rose had "left the platform, because she said the subject was exhausted," the next speaker announced. She herself may have been exhausted. Or, she might have been fed up with listening to long-winded male authorities who preached Christian doctrine and felt free to tell women what to do. Rose never explained why she did not give her speech. At the end of the session, with Rose still absent, the group changed its name from the Woman's Rights Organization to the American Equal Rights Association, transforming itself from a feminist convention to one focusing on the vote for all. Rose agreed with its goals but did not make a financial contribution to the new entity, nor did she become one of its officers.[33]

She did not give another lecture nor attend another public meeting for a year, until May 1867. In the interim, two factions emerged from the old abolitionist-feminist coalition, one prioritizing black male suffrage, the other votes for women. The first, led by Phillips, who called 1865 "the [male] Negro's hour," included William Lloyd Garrison, Stephen and Abby Kelley Foster, and Frederick Douglass. Douglass, who still wanted the ballot for all, argued that the vote was "a question of life and death" for black men, while for women it was at most "a desirable matter." Leading the feminist faction, Stanton injected racism and elitism into her demands. "So long as he [the black man] was lowest in the scale of being we [white women] were willing to press his claims," she wrote in a public letter, "but now, as the celestial gate to civil rights is slowly moving on its hinges, it becomes a serious question whether we had better stand aside and see 'Sambo' walk into the kingdom first." Rose never shared this racism, but she allied herself with Stanton when Congress passed the controversial Fourteenth Amendment in 1866. That measure seemed to acknowledge that women were citizens, and as such, guaranteed "equal protection of the laws." But it also limited voting rights by adding the word "male" to the Constitution for the first time. Many abolitionist-feminists supported this amendment, but Stanton and Anthony praised Rose as being among the "few" women's rights advocates who opposed it, along with Lucretia Mott and Paulina Wright Davis.[34]

Conflicts between abolitionists and feminists worsened in 1867. At the May Equal Rights Association meeting in New York, Anthony announced that the organization badly needed money to campaign for women's rights. Able to lecture once again with her customary eloquence and energy, Ernestine Rose began her speech to the Convention with this issue. "If we only had sufficient of that root of all evil in our hands, there would be no need of holding these meetings," she declared. "Give us one million of dollars, and we will have the elective franchise at the very next session of our Legislature." After joking that if women had the ballot, "our Senators and our members of the House" would court us as they are now courting freedmen, Rose made

her familiar argument that all Americans deserved to vote. "We have proclaimed to the world universal suffrage; but it is universal suffrage with a vengeance attached to it—universal suffrage excluding the negro and the woman,
who are by far the largest majority in this country," she asserted. "White
men are the minority in this nation. White women, black men, and black
women compose the large majority of this nation." Sojourner Truth, formerly
enslaved in New York, followed up on the plight of black women: "If colored men get their rights, and not colored women theirs, they will be masters
over the women, and it will be just as bad as it was before." Although present,
Rose did not speak again at this meeting, but most of the participants ignored
Truth and other black women by advocating suffrage either for black men or
for white women.[35]

Desperate for money, Stanton and Anthony then allied themselves
with a wealthy, eccentric racist who funded their new feminist journal, *The
Revolution*. Beginning its weekly publication in January 1868, *The Revolution*
championed women's rights but also supported "educated suffrage," which
further alienated the abolitionists who wanted the vote for all black men,
regardless of how much education they had. Rose almost certainly read *The
Revolution*. She must have been pleased by the paper's announcement that
"elegant and attractive engravings" of herself and Frances Wright "now dec-
orate the walls of 'The Revolution' office." But she would also have been dis-
mayed by an 1869 article which argued that "the Jews and the Chinese" should
not be allowed into the United States, since "great harm accrues to us from
the vast accession of voracious, knavish, cunning traders, especially Jews,"
whom it characterized as "a race of mere bloodsuckers, especially gifted . . . in
grinding the faces of the poor American sewing women."[36]

In addition, Stanton continued to use racist language in these years, often
telling her audiences to "think of Patrick and Sambo and Hans and Yung
Tung, who do not know the difference between a monarchy and a republic,
who cannot read the Declaration of Independence or Webster's spelling book,
making laws for Lucretia Mott, Ernestine L. Rose, and Anna E. Dickinson."
Rose echoed her in an 1869 speech when she denounced Congress for ignor-
ing women's suffrage. "We might commence by calling the Chinaman a man
and a brother, or the Hottentot, or the Calmuck [Mongol], or the Indian,
the idiot or the criminal, but where shall we stop? They will bring all these in
before us, and then they will bring in the babies—the male babies." This is the
only racist remark of hers ever recorded. It may reflect her anger at Congress
or her increasing fatigue—caused by illness and age—which led her to copy
Stanton.[37]

Ernestine Rose's health continued to fluctuate in the late 1860s, but she felt strong enough to speak at two New York City conventions in May 1868: the Equal Rights Association and the Universal Peace Union the next day. Neither group published its proceedings, but Sara Underwood attended both meetings and found Rose "the best speaker among the ladies." She described her as "a woman of fifty [Rose was actually fifty-eight], with a slight lisp, and foreign accent, yet possessing all the fire and eloquence of youth. She was radical, sensible, forceful, and earnest." Underwood added that "all the force and fire of her enthusiastic nature seemed to flash up" when Rose spoke, making her listeners forget her lisp and accent, "or to remember them only as additional charms." Underwood described Rose's Polish patriotism:

> I remember well how she startled and electrified the members of the Universal Peace Society, in the midst of their mild platitudes and millenial dreams, by her description of the sort of peace *she* advocated—a peace brought with the sword! And with eyes flashing, her pale cheeks flushing, and her voice thrilling, she declared how she longed to plunge with her own hand, if need be, the dagger to the hearts of the enemies of her country's liberty and rights.[38]

Ernestine Rose's next burst of public activity came between January and June of 1869, when she published three public letters and made a number of speeches. The first letter justified her life as a champion of reform who "had educated society up towards justice" and suffered "misrepresentation, slander, and persecution" as a result. She sent this piece to the *Boston Investigator*, ending her five-year boycott of its pages. Her next letter unleashed her sarcastic invective on a New Jersey clergyman who held that women should remain in the domestic sphere, providing "ornamentation," while men alone went out to labor. "New Jersey is said to be out of the world; but where, Oh! where has Dr. J. T. resided? For if he had ever lived within sound, sight, or smell of a human habitation, he would have found out before 1869 that . . . poor woman like poor man has always been 'doomed to labor'; only she has not yet been doomed to be paid for it as well as he." Countering his assertion that women would lose their "delicacy" if they worked outside the home, Rose detailed the grosser side of housework, from "standing over kitchen fires," with their "fumes and odors of grease" to "washing, ironing, and scrubbing" while inhaling "the agreeable healthful odors of soiled linen." Instead, women would be far better off "in the mechanic's shop, the artist's studio, the chemist's laboratory, the merchant's emporium, the brokers' and bankers' offices, the jury boxes, the judge's chair, the legislative halls, and the pulpit."[39]

Her third letter went to the January 1869 National Woman Suffrage Convention in Washington, DC, convened by Stanton and Anthony. This new group's existence displayed the deepening division within the women's rights movement over the issue of the proposed fifteenth amendment, which gave the vote just to black men, leaving out all women. In November, New England abolitionist-feminists formed a separate organization to support this amendment. In retaliation, Stanton and Anthony convened their meeting, hoping against all political reality to gain the vote for women as well. Rose firmly aligned with them, regretting that "indisposition" prevented her from attending "perhaps the most important" convention "that was ever held." After repeating her standard arguments for women's suffrage, she turned to the Fourteenth Amendment's use of the word "male," which she thought "ought to be expunged from the constitution and the laws as a last reminiscence of barbarism—when the animal, not mind, when might, not right, governed the world."[40]

Although she did not feel well enough to travel to Washington, Rose addressed Stanton and Anthony's new, short-lived Working Women's Association in New York City in early January. She began by recalling her Owenite work with cooperative organizations in England but stated that this was the first time she ever spoke to a female labor organization. She advised the women to raise money by asking prominent male speakers to donate their time, "for money was power, and union was strength." She then recommended expanding jobs for women by forming both a female savings bank and an insurance company. She also advised women to train as watchmakers, jewelers, and in other "suitable industries."[41] Four months later, in May 1869, Ernestine Rose played an active role at the Second Anniversary Convention of the American Equal Rights Association. Clashes between the abolitionist and feminist factions over the Fifteenth Amendment dominated this tumultuous meeting. Stanton and Anthony were attacked for not supporting the vote for black men, which Rose never specifically opposed. These feminists insisted that if women did not get the vote then, they would remain disenfranchised for decades, which turned out to be the case. Ernestine Rose remained silent for the first day, although she sat on the stage, was placed on the Executive Committee, and was appointed both chair of the Committee on Resolutions and a "Vice-President at large."

The next day, however, Rose spoke a great deal: recommending that members not respond to the charge that they were "free lovers," urging that cooperative societies be formed to raise women's pay, insisting that the movement began not in Massachusetts but in New York when she circulated her petition for married women's property rights in 1837. She also corrected a minister who asserted that "woman's rights were founded on the New Testament" by declaring "that Testament was only 1,400 years old, but woman's rights were as old as woman herself." In the evening, perhaps to calm the meeting, Anthony scheduled two old acquaintances of Ernestine Rose who lectured in their native languages. Mathilde Franziska Anneke, now living in Milwaukee, addressed the group in German and praised Rose for helping her at the 1853 Mob Convention. Jenny d'Héricourt, residing in Chicago, did not mention Rose in her French lecture, but a few weeks later published a shortened English version of her 1856 biography of "Madame Rose." Rose spoke next. She began by enthusiastically claiming that "the world moves," since "their cause had been greeted by thrilling words, both spoken and written, from England, France, Germany, and Switzerland," as well as all sections of the United States. She then turned on Congress: "Why is it, my friends, that Congress has enacted laws to give the negro of the South the right to vote? Why do they not at the same time protect the negro woman?" Extolling the power of the ballot, that "great talisman" that "can unlock all doors" for women, Rose mocked the legislators for enacting "laws for the man and the brother," while they "had not yet found out there was a woman and a sister." She concluded by objecting "to the name of the Association, 'Equal Rights.' Congress evidently did not know what the word 'equal' meant. She proposed to change the name to the 'Woman's Franchise Association.'" This caught others by surprise. Lucy Stone opposed any such move "till the colored man gained the right to vote," while Stanton ruled that there had to be a month's notice before such an action. Rose then "explained that she by no means meant to throw the black man overboard. She merely wanted the Association to have a name that could not be misunderstood."[42]

The US women's rights movement split irredeemably after this stormy meeting, dividing into rival suffrage organizations. The two groups feuded for twenty-one years, until 1890 when they finally reunited. These conflicts would certainly have troubled Ernestine Rose, but she never commented on them. She also never explained the decision she and William made to leave the United States to travel in Europe a few weeks after this convention. She intimated that she left "in hopes that a voyage across the Atlantic and residence abroad a few months" would cure her ailments. "May her health be restored by again breathing her native air!" Lucretia Mott wished in a farewell note. Paradoxically, Ernestine Rose took out US citizenship in her own name only seventeen days before the couple left the country. William Rose had become an American citizen in 1845 and by law then a wife automatically assumed her husband's nationality. She never wrote about this decision either.[43]

Both Rose and her co-workers in the US women's movement assumed she would return when her health improved. Just a few days before she left, Stanton and Anthony's National Woman Suffrage Association made her a member of their Executive Committee. They also appointed her as a delegate to the Women's Industrial Congress meeting in Berlin that autumn. Rose delayed telling her friends and associates that she was departing but again never explained why. On May 17, she addressed the Sorosis Society, a professional women's organization founded in 1868, on the proposed creation of a foundling hospital for unwanted infants. "Mrs. Rose said she would advocate the Foundling Hospital with all her heart and soul, but she thought prevention better than cure. The evil would never be remedied until men were punished as well as women" for prostitution. A few weeks later, just before Rose's actual departure, Sorosis met again at Delmonico's Restaurant to honor her. Abby Hutchinson Patton, a former member of the Hutchinson Singers who had performed at many reform events, "was deputed by that body to present Mrs. Rose . . . with a testimonial of their regard enclosed in a beautiful basket of flowers. A card accompanied it bearing an appropriate inscription:— 'A basket of June roses to Mrs. Rose from Sorosis.' "[44]

Susan B. Anthony in New York and J. P. Mendum in Boston raised "handsome testimonial[s] in money, much to her surprise, for she was not aware that any movement of the kind was being made." Anthony "spent three very agreeable hours" with Ernestine Rose the evening before her departure. "Probably our last separation in this world and she thinks that there isn't another," Anthony remembered, "but I hope that she will discover that there is a life after death." On Monday, June 8, "Mrs. Rose went on board ship laden with flowers and very happy and grateful."[45] This departure began a new, transatlantic phase in Ernestine Rose's life.

8

The Heroine of a Hundred Battles

ERNESTINE ROSE'S TRAVELS to restore her health succeeded. After eighteen months of recuperation, during which she continued to write public letters, she remained surprisingly active throughout most of her sixties. For most of the 1870s, she effectively supported both free thought and feminism by participating in numerous meetings where she often made speeches. She also dedicated herself to the cause of peace, attending three European conferences. In addition, she made a host of new friends in England. And she continued to send many letters across the Atlantic, most to the *Boston Investigator*, but also to the National Woman Suffrage Association and especially to Susan B. Anthony. She remained a public personage both in the United States and Western Europe.

Initially, "Mrs. Rose was forced to try a complete change of air, by advice of her physicians," wrote *The Revolution*. "She came abroad, therefore, both for change and rest." A week after the couple's ship docked in France, they went to Luxeuil-les-Bains, a spa first developed by the Romans. Rose found it "the most curious and interesting town I have ever seen" and her health improved from "its various springs of hot and cold waters." Luxeuil had a reputation for aiding women with gynecological problems, but Ernestine Rose only referred to its "benefit" for "poor, miserable dyspeptics, and Americans in particular." Her own few stomach problems stemmed from seasickness, but the hot springs almost certainly helped her rheumatism. Even in Luxeuil, Rose encountered Europeans who "knew my name and heretical proclivities, which gave rise to very interesting conversations and discussions on religion and Women's Rights," she wrote the *Investigator*.[1]

After Luxeuil, the Roses traveled to Lake Lucerne in the Swiss Alps before wintering at Nice in the south of France. Kate N. Doggett, a feminist Chicago friend of Ernestine's, visited there in February 1870. Both Doggett and Rose had been selected by the National Woman Suffrage Association to be delegates to the Women's Industrial Conference in Berlin in the fall of 1869, but only Doggett had attended. From Nice, Doggett reported to *The Revolution* that Ernestine Rose's "friends will be glad to know that she is much better than when she left America last spring," adding that Rose planned to return the following year. "As I looked into her bright eyes and saw the color deepen in her cheeks as she talked in her animated way of the good cause she has by no means relinquished on this side of the Atlantic," Doggett wrote, "I could hardly persuade myself she was an invalid. She has nerve power now to supply a dozen average women, or men either, for that matter." The Roses and Doggett attempted to cross the Alps to visit Turin in northern Italy, but freezing winds forced them to return. "I wish to record the fact, for I think the mistral is the only obstacle by which Ernestine L. Rose was ever vanquished," Doggett concluded.[2]

That spring, the Roses visited Paris for seven weeks, "seeing some of the foremost men and women in the reformatory movements." They renewed their acquaintance with Charles Lemonnier and Charles Fauvety, radical editors whom they had met in 1856, as well as being introduced to the new women's rights activists Léon Richer and André Leo (Léodile Champseix). Then, since Ernestine had "not been very well since we left Nice," the couple visited Bad Homburg in Germany "to try what its famous waters will do for me."[3] The Roses continued their travel to spas by spending the winter of 1870–71 in Bath, England, famous for its hot springs and mineral waters. They despised it. "Every denomination can be found in Bath, but I greatly fear *not one* freethinker," Ernestine wrote the *Investigator*. "Is it not sad to see human beings so stupefied?"

Rose also disliked Bath because "we have no company, no friends, no acquaintances, and are not likely to have," adding that "in London we have quite a number of friends, but here we are entire strangers." The Roses were a gregarious couple, easily connecting with fellow reformers and liberals. Ernestine Rose maintained a number of friendships with US feminists, among them Anthony, Stanton, and Pauline Wright Davis, who visited her twice in London in the early 1870s.[4] But a number of close American friends began to die during these years. Rose lamented the "sad news that James Thompson was no more," explaining that "he was our oldest and most intimate friend in New York . . . and now we would be almost strangers in the city we have spent the best part of our lives—nearly 35 years." An English immigrant like the Roses, Thompson had often helped William Rose organize the Thomas

Paine dinners and was a noted chess master.[5] In the 1870s, however, these losses were balanced by their new transatlantic friends.

In London, the Roses already knew the free-thought Owenite editor, George Jacob Holyoake, from their 1856 visit. They soon became fond of his brother Austin, who shared their values. Austin Holyoake, a printer and author, warmly remembered how the Roses had "kindly made daily calls upon me" during his illness in the summer of 1872. He had also taught the English feminist Emily Faithfull how to set type, which allowed her to found the all-female Victoria Press. She became a correspondent to *The Revolution* and in 1871 she reported on Ernestine Rose's first "very telling" public speech in Bath on the issue of women voting for and serving on local boards of education.[6]

Parliament had recently passed a law allowing women who owned or rented property and had paid taxes for a year to vote and stand for office in many local elections. While the United States then restricted the suffrage by gender and age, Great Britain added home ownership or rental and tax payments to those requirements. Under them only about one-third of adult men qualified to vote in national elections. The Roses went to the first meeting in Bath to nominate female candidates for the School Board. Although many women attended, none spoke to the audience. "A lady" asked the chairman to read a widely publicized letter by Angela Burdett-Coutts, the wealthiest woman in England and a major philanthropist. Burdett-Coutts argued forcefully that although women could serve on subcommittees, they should neither hold public office nor participate in politics. This roused Ernestine Rose to address the gathering.

In 1870, women spoke publicly far less often in Great Britain than in the United States. "It required considerable courage then for a woman to sit on a public platform and actually to speak from one was considered almost indecent," writes an English historian. Rose began by explaining that "I have for all my life-time been interested in the education of all parties, particularly in the education of my own sex." She then asserted, "Yes, the world moves. Woman is actually beginning to be considered as a human being . . . who has influences beyond the boudoir, the ball-room, and the theatre, for those, until very recently, have been the only places assigned to her except the kitchen and the cradle." Supported by cheers, applause, and approving laughter from the audience, Rose argued that the United States could educate Britain on this subject:

> There it is almost a settled fact that woman is a human being; that she has a mind, and that that mind requires cultivation; that she has

wants and needs, which wants and needs require assistance. Hence, we are over there—don't be frightened at the name—a "woman's rights" people . . . and remember that "woman's rights" simply means "human rights."

Rose swayed the meeting, which then nominated two women to run for positions on the board. Finding them "quite unprepared with any plan for future action," Rose encouraged these candidates to hold another meeting where they would state their views. Overcoming their dislike of "the publicity of such a course," Rose gave another "one of her stirring and eloquent addresses, which roused the meeting to a pitch of enthusiasm quite unusual for a decorous English audience." The two women were then elected.[7] A few weeks later, Rose spoke at a Conference of the Women's Suffrage Movement in London, receiving praise from the atheist *National Reformer*: "The speech of the meeting was made by . . . Mrs. Ernestine L. Rose of New York. The good old lady, with her white curls, her erect, healthy looking body, her clear, distinct voice, her occasional quaint phrases, her stern determination, and her real genius as a speaker, won from those present a far more hearty and lengthy tribute of applause than was accorded to any one else."[8]

These speeches launched Ernestine Rose as a lecturer in Great Britain, as well as introducing her to numerous new reformist friends. One of the female nominees in Bath was Ann Ashworth, a member of a large radical family. Her uncle, the Liberal M.P. Jacob Bright, succeeded in getting the bill for women's local suffrage passed, in addition to supporting married women's property rights and women's national suffrage. Her aunt was Priscilla Bright McLaren, head of the Edinburgh Women's Suffrage Society.[9] In the spring of 1871, Rose spoke in Bristol as well as again in Bath before she and William moved to London in April. The editor of the *National Reformer*, who covered Rose's women's rights speech there so positively, was Charles Bradlaugh. He, and later his two daughters, became close friends and supporters of Ernestine Rose.

Bradlaugh and Rose knew about each other before they met, through the pages of the *Boston Investigator*, which covered both their careers in detail. A generation younger than Rose, Bradlaugh became an atheist as a teenager and by the mid-1850s had achieved prominence among English radicals. He spoke and wrote widely, often under the pseudonym "Iconoclast." Like Rose, Bradlaugh was a superb public speaker. "He was the most magnetic person I have ever known, and the greatest orator," playwright George Bernard Shaw later wrote; "Bradlaugh was the heavy-weight champion of the platform."[10]

He became editor of the weekly *National Reformer* in 1860 and helped found Britain's National Secular Society in 1866. The government prosecuted him for blasphemy and sedition in 1868. Although he was acquitted, his reputation as an atheist, a republican, and an agitator placed him outside traditional Victorian values. "As a mere speculative freethinker, Mr. Bradlaugh might possibly have passed muster," *The Times* of London wrote when he had been elected to the House of Commons in 1880, "but as a social reformer, with republican opinions and a very aggressive mode of displaying them he is thought to be deserving of Parliamentary ostracism." These beliefs, which made him unacceptable to *The Times*, endeared him to Ernestine Rose. "She was greatly attached to Mr. Bradlaugh, who in turn felt a thorough admiration and reverence for her," his daughter wrote.[11]

When the Roses moved to London in 1871, they also were befriended by Moncure D. Conway and his wife, Ellen. Conway was a radical minister who invited Ernestine Rose to speak a number of times at his extremely liberal South Place Chapel. Raised in a slaveholding Virginia family, he rejected his heritage early on, converting to both anti-slavery and Unitarianism in his twenties. In 1864 he and his wife, who shared his views, moved to London and in 1868 he was one of four speakers at the first British public meeting for female suffrage. In addition to women's rights, Conway shared Rose's devotion to Robert Owen and Thomas Paine. He moved his chapel away from Unitarianism to "the uttermost ends of Agnosticism," dropping formal prayer and reading from a variety of works, including Hindu scriptures and the poems of William Blake. Conway invited Rose to speak to his congregation about Robert Owen on Sunday, May 14, 1871, and wrote the *Investigator* that she was "something of a lioness in London." For her talk, the chapel "was crowded with a thousand people . . . and so completely did she charm the audience that three times applause began, and had to be checked."[12]

Rose's lecture took place on the actual centenary of Owen's birth; two days later a large "Festival" assembled to celebrate his life. Although many women attended, sang, and read poetry there, Ernestine Rose was the only female speaker. Owen was a "man of one idea, and that idea the happiness of the human race," she declared. "The time will come when that one idea will be understood," she continued, adding that "I have no doubt that he would have advocated the Woman's Rights Bill had he lived." After reminiscing about her years with Owen and praising his character and beliefs, she concluded by asserting that when the world followed Owen's principles, "we shall have a race of really superior, rational, healthy, and happy human beings." London liberal newspapers reported that "Mrs. Rose made *the* speech of the evening—the most appropriate one and the best delivered," while Moncure Conway wrote that "the enthusiasm at her burning words, her fine sarcasm, her clear statement was *so* great that the people pressed nearer and nearer, and fairly stood up. . . . In voice and manner she is one of the very few real orators I have ever heard." The following summer, Conway wrote that "some recent speeches of hers on the woman question have drawn about her such troops of admiring friends, that it is to be feared that she and her excellent husband will find it difficult to go home again."[13]

In fact, the Roses did remain in England, returning to the United States only for a visit in 1873–74. They never provided a complete explanation, and in her first years abroad, Ernestine made a number of contradictory statements on the subject. At the Owen centenary, she declared, "I am not an American, although I have my residence in the United States"—despite the fact that she had become a US citizen just before leaving for Europe. A few months later, *The Revolution* reported that Mrs. Rose "intends to remain abroad a year longer, when she will return to her American home." In 1876, Rose wrote Susan B. Anthony to "keep a warm place for me with the American people. I hope some day to be there yet." Her most complete rationale for living in England came at the end of 1870, in a letter to the *Boston Investigator*. "When you hire an apartment, (large or small), the people of the house engage to keep house for you without any extra charges," she wrote, adding that the couple lived in two large, well-furnished rooms, with "fire and gas, and all kinds of services." These included having the rooms cleaned, cooking food the Roses had purchased, and serving meals when and how they wished. "Thus we have all the real comfort of housekeeping without the trouble of it, or servants, and our expenses for living" were far less than in New York—$11 a week instead of $35. Never having employed a servant in the United States, the Roses were understandably reluctant to hire one in England. Yet they were getting on in years, and housework demanded a great deal of time and energy. US boarding houses required communal eating at set times and usually provided only a single room to live in. The "mode of living" she described "is peculiar to England only," Rose explained. "You cannot live the same way on the Continent, though you can live reasonable [*sic*] in many places."[14]

The Roses had a fair amount of money during their first two years in Europe, when they visited expensive spas and lived in tourist destinations such as Nice and Bath. This lifestyle continued through the summer of 1871, when they traveled to the mountain resorts of Petersthal in Germany and Lausanne in Switzerland. But the Great Chicago Fire of October 1871, and the equally great but less well-known Boston Fire of November 1872 hurt the

Roses' finances. The couple had invested heavily in real estate lost in these conflagrations. In 1873, Charles Bradlaugh wrote that he regretted "to hear that the bulk of the property belonging to Mr. and Mrs. Rose had been swept away in the late disastrous fires in Boston and Chicago," while in 1876, Ernestine Rose told the *Boston Investigator* that "as you know, the Chicago and Boston fires have crippled our means."[15] These losses made the relatively lower costs of living in London all the more important. The missing factor in these explanations for their life in England remains William Rose. William had been born in London and lived there until he was twenty-three, when he and his new wife emigrated to New York. Did he want to return to his native land? It is impossible to say, as no letter or remark by him remains from these years. Ernestine's mentions of him in her letters only deal with his health or send his "kind regards" to their friends.

Ernestine Rose occasionally commented on the differences between the two nations, although she consistently maintained that "neither in America nor England are the obstacles to free thought and free speech removed, and Liberalism triumphant." But in terms of government, Great Britain could not match the United States. Although royal power had diminished, a conservative monarch still reigned. The House of Lords held equal power with the House of Commons and British class divisions carried far more weight than those in the United States. Rose consistently championed American democracy, writing this on the centennial of the US Declaration of Independence in 1876: "The glorious day upon which human equality was first proclaimed ought to be commemorated . . . until its grand principles are carried into practice." Compared to the promise of the United States, England remained retrograde. "I see not much to admire in the English Government, though there are some very good people here," she wrote later. "But, you know, I am a republican or a democrat all through, and so as I 'put no faith in princes' nor priests either, I am deeply interested in all the affairs of America. . . . [M]ay kings and tyrants soon learn from its grand example that the only true or legitimate power to rule is in the PEOPLE and not in any pretended 'right Divine.'"[16] Both nations continued to be extremely religious, but only Great Britain maintained a state church. "The Church of England would, if she could, stamp out every vestige of Free Thought rather than give up her strong hold on the State," Rose wrote in 1877. The British government prosecuted both Holyoake and Bradlaugh for blasphemy and convicted the editor of *The Freethinker* for that crime in 1883. He served a year in prison.[17]

Still, British free thought grew dramatically under Bradlaugh's leadership in the 1860s and 1870s. His National Secular Society came to have thousands of members meeting weekly in numerous Halls of Science. In 1872, the American reformer Thomas Wentworth Higginson, a friend of Ernestine Rose, attended a London meeting of the Society where Bradlaugh spoke, followed briefly by Rose. He described a group of about 1,500 people "in the grasp of a born orator. . . . Nine-tenths were men; almost all were well-dressed. They looked as if all classes might be represented there, and while the majority were plainly artisans, I was afterward told that a peer of the realm stood just behind me." In addition, Bradlaugh's *National Reformer*, established in 1860, became Britain's premier and longest-running free-thought journal, achieving a position similar to that of the *Boston Investigator* in the United States. By the time Rose joined the British free-thought movement, biblical criticism and debates about Darwinism, churchly intransigence, and the growth of skepticism had created a congenial community of non-believers in England.[18]

In addition to championing free thought, Rose supported the related cause of opening secular institutions on Sundays. Early-nineteenth-century British sabbath societies had succeeded in forcing museums, galleries, and post offices to close on that day, as well as banning public music, dancing, theater, horse-racing, sailing, and rowing. This produced the notoriously tedious English Sunday—"this lugubrious holiday" as the *Boston Investigator* termed it.[19] In 1873, both Ernestine Rose and Moncure Conway contributed "some able words toward the laudable object of opening a large Museum on Sundays"—the Bethnal Green Museum, located in a working-class area of London. The next year, Rose sent the *Investigator* remarks that P. A. Taylor made on this subject in the House of Commons. "It is an excellent and unanswerable speech, which was listened to with great attention and warmly applauded, and yet lost by a great majority" she wrote, because "the power of the Church is very great here, and the members have not the moral courage to go against the theological Mr. Grundies." Rose went on to praise Taylor as "an independent member of the most radical type," and both he and his wife, the feminist Mentia Taylor, became her friends.[20]

The Taylors had long been active in the same radical causes as the Roses. In his parliamentary campaign, P. A. Taylor advocated the separation of church and state and the abolition of mandatory taxes to support the Church of England. Both the Taylors actively opposed US slavery. Wealthy and childless, the couple ran a school for working-class adults on the grounds of their home, Aubrey House, where they also hosted salons "open to all, friend and stranger, black and white, rich and poor," as Louisa May Alcott wrote after she visited in 1873. George Jacob Holyoake attended their "open evenings" from 1861 on.[21] Ernestine Rose met Mentia Taylor either through one of these mutual friends or in the English women's suffrage movement, which Taylor had helped to found. Mentia Taylor organized the petition for the women's vote, which John Stuart Mill, the writer and philosopher, presented repeatedly and unsuccessfully to Parliament during his 1866–68 term as a member. Mill's feminist prestige increased with the publication of his *Subjection of Women* in 1869; Ernestine Rose referred positively to him and P. A. Taylor in her 1871 Owen centenary speech. But Mill also caused problems within the early women's movement by insisting that it proceed slowly and focus only on the single issue of suffrage.[22]

This stricture arose because of a British feminist campaign that had no American equivalent. In the 1860s, Parliament passed the Contagious Diseases Acts to protect the military from venereal disease. These acts gave police the power to subject any woman in towns near military bases whom they suspected of being a prostitute to a pelvic exam in the station. If they found evidence of disease, the woman could be sent to a locked hospital; men were never inspected. Numerous English feminists, including Mentia Taylor, joined the Ladies' National Campaign for the repeal of these acts, which did not happen until 1886. Even though Mill himself testified against these acts in Parliament, he and others insisted that this campaign, which necessarily raised sexual issues, would contaminate women's bid for the vote. They succeeded in having Contagious Diseases activists removed as officers of the suffrage movement.[23]

Ernestine Rose never became involved in the Contagious Diseases campaign. Throughout her life, she avoided most public references to sexuality, correctly believing it would lead to the charge of supporting "free love." She also did not support this campaign because it invoked Christian beliefs and prayer even more than the US anti-slavery movement had done. Neither did she participate in the simultaneous push for married women's property rights in Britain. Instead, Rose focused on the ballot, as she had during her last years in the United States. American opposition to the woman's vote came naturally from conservative opponents, but also from feminists' allies—those abolitionists who put "the black man's vote" first. A similar situation prevailed in Britain, where many liberals working to extend the franchise to male citizens refused to include women. William Gladstone, the longtime Liberal Party prime minister, consistently opposed woman's suffrage on the grounds that it would "trespass upon the delicacy, the purity, the refinement, the elevation of her own nature, which are the present sources of its power." US feminists sometimes assumed that as a powerful female monarch, Queen Victoria would support their cause. The experience of Kate, Lady Amberley, among many others, proved this false. Amberley, who had visited the United States and remained in contact with women's rights leaders there, argued for the vote on the same grounds as Ernestine Rose, asserting that the ballot would "make the life of a woman of the higher and lower classes more complete, less dependent . . . and give her the chance of leading an honest and happy life." In a furious response, Victoria wrote, "The Queen is most anxious to enlist everyone who can speak or write or join in checking this mad, wicked folly of 'Women's Rights' with all its attendant horrors, on which her poor feeble sex is bent, forgetting every sense of womanly feeling and propriety. Lady Amberley ought to get a good *whipping.*" Many Britons shared these feelings, especially members of Parliament. In 1871, the M.P. Alexander Beresford Hope argued at length against enfranchising women, concluding that if it were done, "Our legislation would develop hysterical and spasmodic features, partaking more of the French and American system than reproducing the tradition of the English Parliament."[24]

Ernestine Rose repeatedly challenged Beresford Hope, first at a large London women's suffrage meeting in May 1872 where she pursued "the subject in a vein of pleasant irony which would not have caused that Hon. Gentleman quite so much amusement as it did the audience," the London *Telegraph* reported. She continued her attack during her time lecturing in Edinburgh in January of 1873 where she had been invited by Priscilla Bright McLaren, aunt of the candidate Rose had aided in Bath.[25] Rose mentioned that Beresford Hope opposed women's suffrage in part because it would "bring sympathy and consolation into parliament." "Mr. Beresford Hope; alas! What was in a name! he was exceedingly hopeless," Rose joked, before asserting that fearing sympathy in Parliament was "exceedingly illogical." This comment was a reference to parliamentary arguments that women should not be allowed to vote because they were "not logical." "I am not going to stand here and prove that I am logical," Rose declared. "The franchise was never given for logic. Had it been based upon logic, I doubt whether that member of Parliament would ever have been in his place." Her remarks occasioned "great laughter and applause." Rose went on to make points she had frequently used in her American speeches, maintaining that men and women should have equal human rights. She concluded by tackling the widely accepted view that "woman, if she got the franchise, would cease to be womanly":

She might become stronger in mind, more faithful in convictions; she might become more intellectual; she might take a greater and wider view of the duties and responsibilities of life; but would that unsex her? Would that change her nature? Would she be less a mother, less a sister, less a woman? No! Believe, trust in the right, do rightly, do justly, and leave all the consequences to themselves. (Loud applause.)

Rose repeated these points more briefly in speeches made over the next two days, asserting that she demanded justice for women "simply because she asked for it for men" and urging "those present to do all they could to elevate not women merely, but humanity at large."[26]

The US women's suffrage movement mentioned Ernestine Rose frequently, and American feminists kept appointing her to offices, hoping she might soon return. She remained on the National Woman Suffrage Association's (NWSA) Executive Committee and was designated its chairwoman in 1870 as well as being listed as a vice president of the New York State Suffrage Association. They placed her on the Committee of Arrangements for the 1870 "Decade Meeting" celebrating the "twentieth anniversary of a great national movement for freedom." She signed the Declaration of Rights of the Women of the United States, issued by the NWSA on the centennial of the Declaration of Independence and was listed as a vice president in the 1876 Constitution of the National Woman Suffrage Association. Rose appreciated these accolades. "I am glad to see my name among the vice-presidents of the National Association," she wrote Susan B. Anthony.[27]

The editors of the *Boston Investigator* often mentioned Rose as well. Rose and Horace Seaver had put their 1864 battle over antisemitism completely behind them. In 1873, Austin Holyoake wrote that the Roses spoke to him "of the devotedness, the self-sacrifice, and the untiring energy of both Mr. Mendum and Mr. Seaver. Mr. and Mrs. Rose have been intimate friends of both gentlemen for years, and they say that more worthy members of society do not exist in the States." As well as publishing all of Ernestine Rose's letters, the *Investigator*'s editors periodically praised her contributions to the US women's movement and deplored her exclusion from its tributes. "Certain it is that when the Woman's Rights Party, of which she was almost or quite the originator, count up their jewels, she seldom if ever shines among them in their papers," they wrote in 1870, criticizing *The Revolution*; "but to omit *her* name from the catalogue, is like playing Hamlet with the character of Hamlet left out." The *Investigator* repeatedly argued that Rose was ignored because she "is not a Christian, and for this reason is not appreciated by her sex as her merits deserve. . . . At present, all bigotry is not confined to the masculine gender."[28]

The *Investigator* also reported frequently on Rose's health, hoping that "it may soon be fully restored, so that when she returns home she may be able to pursue the useful mission of social and religious reform to which her life has been constantly and successfully devoted." From her departure in June 1869 through the summer of 1871, Rose wrote about her ailments, particularly her rheumatism. But from then on, she mentioned no health problems and spoke more frequently in Britain. In July 1873, the *Investigator* announced that the Roses had bought steamship tickets to return to the states, adding, "They were in tolerably good health, and had found many friends in England where they had enjoyed a very agreeable city and country residence. Our readers will join with us in wishing them a pleasant and a safe passage home."[29] When the couple arrived in September, the editors expressed their pleasure at the return "of these well-known and much esteemed Liberal friends, after their long absence in Europe. 'Welcome home.'" The Roses seem to have intended to live in the United States, but their situation changed dramatically in November when Ernestine fell "seriously ill" with an unnamed malady. "She has not been able to leave her room for some weeks, or even to sit up long at a time," the *Investigator* wrote. "We sincerely hope that her sickness may not prove fatal."[30]

Ernestine Rose slowly recovered, but her illness contributed to the Roses' decision to return to England for good. By January 1874 she became able to write letters again from New York City, sending greetings to the NWSA Convention in Washington, DC, as well as articles and letters to the *Boston Investigator*. She detailed the views of Sir James Stansfeld, a radical M.P. friend, who supported votes for women as well as non-religious schools, rare then in Britain. "I am very much interested, as you well know," Rose wrote, "in secular education and woman's suffrage, and perhaps some of your readers might be interested in seeing that these two great Reforms are gaining ground in England." (Neither would be achieved until the twentieth century.) A week later, Charles Bradlaugh, then on a speaking tour of the United States, wrote the *National Reformer* that the Roses met him when he arrived in New York City. Remarking that the sixty-four-year-old Ernestine's "page of life was nearly filled," he added that "Mr. and Mrs. Rose intend to make England their permanent abode, and I trust that returning health may enable the heroine of a hundred battles to sometimes gratify us with her presence at the New Hall of Science" in London.[31]

The Roses spent the spring of 1874 winding up their affairs in the United States. In May, Ernestine Rose spoke at her last American convention, the Sixth Annual meeting of the National Woman Suffrage Association in

New York City. On the first day, Rose declared that "suffrage was the true right of woman, and to refuse it to her was an injustice which men were not able to defend." She then told the group that "ill-health would prevent her from ever again appearing in public, and on retiring she was roundly applauded." On the convention's second day, she gave "a short but impressive address." The male speaker who preceded her declared that women were essentially different from men. Rose vehemently disagreed, asserting that just as it "was very difficult to make European monarchs recognize the fact that they were not better than the people for whose purpose they were instituted," so it was "equally difficult to inspire into men's minds the idea that women were other than their help-mates, and were not created for the same glorious destiny." Let men make "whatever laws they pleased, but let them make them alike for men and women. What right had men to make laws" for women anyway, she then asked rhetorically. "The laws were as binding on her as on man, and all she asked was participation in their formation." Assessing the overall impact of the US women's movement, Ernestine Rose declared, "The wonder was not that they had not accomplished more, but that they had accomplished so much."[32]

Before the Roses left for England in June, they donated four oil paintings depicting Thomas Paine, Robert Owen, Willam Rose, and Ernestine Rose to hang in Paine Hall, a major new edifice built as the *Investigator*'s headquarters in Boston. The Roses, "always ready to lend a helping hand in every good work, and who, though in another part of the world, are interested in all Liberal measures going on at home," contributed to this project, which was completed when a wealthy California investor gave Mendum and Seaver land to fund it. The building's cornerstone was laid on July 4, 1874, over a box containing photographs, including one of Ernestine Rose, to "inform the Liberals of 1974 or 2000" that "we met ... to honor Thomas Paine." Rose immediately wrote back from London, congratulating the editors "and through you, all friends of progress" and hoping that they might "live to see many more temples dedicated to freedom and humanity." Paine Hall was inaugurated on January 29, 1875, the anniversary of Thomas Paine's birthday, and Ernestine Rose wrote regretting that she and William could not attend the ceremony. "But that cannot be, though perhaps if the Atlantic were as accommodating to us as the Red Sea is said to have been to 'the children of Israel,' we might cross over and arrive just in time to take you all by surprise. But as we do not belong to 'the household of faith,' we cannot expect such a watery miracle on our behalf." However, their portraits—described as those of "Mr. and Mrs. Ernestine L. Rose"—graced the scene and the editors used an engraving of Paine Hall as part of the *Investigator*'s masthead from April on. Mendum and Seaver hired Paine Hall out to numerous groups and speakers, including Susan B. Anthony, who began her 1876 lecture there by referring to Rose's portrait "opposite her on the wall, saying that she was always glad to be in the same vicinity with a picture of that noble worker for the cause of woman's freedom." Ernestine Rose donated money to fund the building for many years and urged other subscribers to do the same.[33]

From the Roses' return to England in 1874, Ernestine alternated complaints about her health with accounts of speeches she made, which implies that she periodically recovered. The couple spent the winter of 1874–75 in Brighton, "a very healthy place," but one they found "very dull, very religious, and very anti-progressive." In November, they attended an "*anti*-Woman's Rights lecture," given by a minister. "The whole thing was made up of Biblical quotations, misrepresentations, downright falsehoods, insults, and flattery," Rose wrote the *Investigator*. After the minister cited John Ruskin's pronouncement that "woman is Queen in *her husband's house*—Queen over the crockery, jewelry, china, etc.," Rose added, she "spoke about fifteen minutes, and told him he made a mistake to think that not a Women's Rights woman was present." Two months later, in January 1875, she wrote that she was "too ill to ... even" write a speech for the Paine Hall dedication. She was still sick at the end of March 1875, describing herself as "a prisoner" of the London weather, "not yet well enough to go out in this wretched north east wind which has now lasted over six weeks, with hardly a gleam of sunshine, and the Lord only knows (if he knows anything) how much longer it will last—What an awful climate!" In October, her ill health was confirmed by the London *National Reformer*: "Unfortunately, the party lost the services of one of its bravest and most eloquent platform advocates, the Mrs. Ernestine L. Rose, who worked with so much intrepidity and power. Now and then we notice an article from her pen in the *Investigator*, but ill health prevents her from using her tongue in the cause."[34]

But Rose continued to rebound. She wrote that 1876 was "a very sick year throughout," but also mentioned that she had given two speeches in Yorkshire, "notwithstanding all the scolding about my heresies, for the people there are very religious." The Roses had gone north to recover in Ilkley and Harrogate, where William "was taken very sick from drinking a little of what was called sulphur water, but which was more like poison, for it nearly killed him. . . . The anxiety and exertion of taking care of him pulled me very much down again." Rose added that when they returned to Brighton that fall, they both felt better. George Jacob Holyoake, writing about the same period, said,

"Mention is made of her delicate health, which 'prevented her from speaking with her wonted effect.' It is pleasant to report that . . . she is still a speaker of remarkable power."[35]

Given the vague language Ernestine Rose used to describe her symptoms, it is impossible to diagnose her ailments. The cause of her nearly fatal illness in 1873 remains unknown. She certainly suffered from rheumatism, which caused her "my full share of aches," but at the same time she asserted that "my general health is pretty good." In a letter to Susan B. Anthony, dated July 4, 1876, she wrote, "I suffer from great debility and dizziness in my head, which prevents me from much mental labor." Her dizziness came and went. A year later, in July 1877, she wrote the *Investigator* that "I can think, and think all the more because I cannot work," but then in 1879, she complained to the Conways that "my Head *swims* badly today, but I hope it will get steady again." She called her most constant symptom "neuralgia," which might be what is today known as fibromyalgia, but it too was not constant. "I have suffered so much all the winter, and do now from neuralgia in my head, chest, and the whole upper part of my body," she wrote in the summer of 1877, "and am so weak, that I can hardly write. . . . I keep up, but suffer constant pain."[36]

Her last major recovery came in 1878, when she spoke at length over two days at the London Conference of Liberal Thinkers in June. Moncure D. Conway had organized this meeting "for the discussion of matters pertaining to the religious needs of our time, and the method of meeting them." He cast his net widely, inviting liberal clergymen and rabbis, Britons and foreigners, as well as freethinkers like Holyoake and Rose, resulting in "the most inclusive group of its kind ever assembled." Speaking forcefully on the afternoon of the first day, Ernestine Rose began by declaring her militant atheism: "I belong to no religious sect; I profess no religion; and I have long ago discarded even the name. It is too indefinite and misleading, and is only calculated to divide the human family instead of uniting it. Well may we exclaim, 'Oh! religion what crimes have been perpetrated in thy name.'" Rose then criticized the US Free Religious Association (FRA), touted by the previous speaker. Founded by liberal Unitarians, the FRA included Lucretia Mott, Rabbi Isaac Meyer Wise, and Ralph Waldo Emerson, among others. "Free is all right. But what is Religion?" Rose asked rhetorically, before proposing a name for the group, a gambit she had used many times before, from naming the Infidel Society in 1845 to suggesting that US women change their "Equal Rights Association" to the "Woman's Franchise Association" in 1869. Suggesting that this group "unite in a Society of Friends of Progress," she maintained that then "the Christian, the Mahometan, the Jew, the Deist, and the Atheist" could "reform the laws so as to have perfect freedom of conscience, the right to think and to express our thoughts on all subjects. Progress opens as wide a field as the human race—it endeavors to remove the obstacles that prevent our growth." Rose, however, had trouble being open-minded about clergymen and she then turned on two ministers who had spoken before her, saying that if they were "not too fixed in their bigotry" they could "all unite with us to form a union which should give us strength, strength not to injure anyone, not even to prevent the irrational views that some of the religionists have of their god, but a strength to take care that as long as they have them they should have a perfect right to express them." One of the clergy she mentioned was the Reverend Charles Voysey, who had been expelled from the Church of England for his radical views. He did not return on the Conference's second day.[37] Rose steamed on, declaring that the strength provided by such a union

> shall enable us to assist each other to improve the world, to obtain rational and consistent laws, laws that will not deprive a mother of her child—(loud and continued applause)—as has been done to Mrs. Besant, simply because she thinks differently from the judge; laws that will not incarcerate an innocent, respectable man, simply because he sold something he conscientiously thought would benefit society.

Here, Ernestine Rose alluded to a cause célèbre of the previous year—the trial and conviction of Annie Besant and Charles Bradlaugh for publishing a book on birth control. Annie Besant had become a prominent lecturer and journalist in British free thought—she had written the 1875 *National Reformer* article saying that Rose was now too ill to continue speaking in public. Almost forty years younger than Rose, she was married at twenty to an Anglican clergyman. Besant (who always used her married name) left her husband and son five years later, taking her daughter Mabel with her. She and Bradlaugh decided to bring a test case on contraception by reprinting the American Charles Knowlton's 1832 book as a cheap pamphlet in 1876. Anglo-American freethinkers had often published birth control manuals, but they were in book form, which made them unaffordable to many. Hundreds of thousands of copies of Bradlaugh and Besant's low-priced work sold and the two were then tried and convicted of obscenity. The verdict was overturned on a technicality. Frank Besant sued for custody of his daughter Mabel and won. Rose's American friend Thomas Wentworth Higginson, who attended this trial as well as the Conference of Liberal Thinkers, said the judge "damned" Besant "for her infidel opinions," ruling that the girl could "not be brought up in opposition to the view of mankind generally as to what is moral, what is decent, what is womanly, or proper merely because her mother differs from these views. . . . [T]he child might even grow up to write such things herself!" Mabel was taken away just a few weeks before Rose referred to the case.[38]

At the Conference, Rose used Besant's ordeal to show why women needed equality. "I want that woman should have the same rights as a human being," she declared. "Now when a judge says that if this woman had been the father instead of the mother, the child might have been left with her, I think that is one of the laws that should be altered." Higginson, a longtime activist reformer in the United States, had helped write the Call to the 1850 Worcester National Woman's Rights Convention where Rose spoke; he had also led a black Union regiment during the Civil War. Following Rose as speaker, he first praised "my dear old friend Mrs. Rose, whom we used to be proud for so many years to claim as an American, while her sonorous eloquence filled our halls, and whom you, I suppose, now try to claim as an English woman, though she is not"; he then criticized her proposal for a Society of Friends of Progress. Having been active in the US Free Religious Association, he argued that "if our experience has proved anything, it has been this: [L]imit your aims a little and not . . . expect to do everything at once, and with one organization." Asserting that this was almost the only point "on which I should dissent from the position taken by my old friend Mrs. Rose," he added that if they followed her strategy, in five years they would regret creating so broad a group. He closed by using the image of "Esquimaux" sled dogs pulling together. "I am not a Radical dog in the least," Rose responded, "but it is just as well to know, in the cause of freedom and expression of opinion, that 'we may aim at the sun, and at least hit the moon.'" "That was quite what I was afraid of," Higginson replied.[39]

On the Conference's second day, Rose again spoke at length. Conway and others attempted to organize the group as the Association of Liberal Thinkers with its goals as both the "collection and diffusion of information concerning world-wide religious developments" and "the emancipation of mankind from superstition." One speaker asserted that "what Mrs. Rose calls the service of humanity, and what others call the service of God are identical. The names are different, but the goodness is the same." Rose disagreed. Declaring that she was "glad to see so good a meeting come together" and that she supported "all parts that . . . benefit the human family," she invoked her familiar stance of preferring to be right than to unite with those whose views she could not support: "I am placed in a peculiar position, for there are some parts that I entirely differ from, and I fear that when it comes to a vote on such parts that I shall be a minority of one, and if it should be so, it would not be the first time, and I would much rather be in a minority even of one, for the right, than in a large majority for wrong and oppression." Rose insisted that she could not support any mention of religion, because "in my convictions, in my conscience, I call all religions superstitions, and consider them merely as superstitions. I cannot vote for what appears to me the great curse of the human mind, the great standing block in the way of human progress."

Yet Rose was torn, as so many good friends—from Higginson to Conway, both extremely liberal Unitarians—supported the inclusion of religion. "If you will allow me with all my heart to aid and assist you, I can say,—I wanted to say, 'God speed,'" she blurted. At this, "the audience burst into roars of laughter," the male reporter for the English *Unitarian Herald* wrote, adding, "It was the most extraordinary speech I ever heard from a woman; and coming as it did from a lady of advanced years, and spoken as it was with a really deep earnestness, it could not but touch all who listened sympathetically." The remainder of the Conference politely and lengthily debated the wording of its proposals. Ultimately, "religion" was completely removed. Moncure Conway suggested that Ernestine Rose be nominated to a committee to implement the group's aims, but Rose replied that she could not serve. However, she seconded the motion thanking Conway for the meeting "with a great deal of pleasure" and "the resolution was carried by loud acclamation."[40]

The good feelings aroused by this Conference in June 1878 did not last and the group disbanded the following year, unable to agree on a program. Ernestine Rose's health continued to fluctuate. On July 4, she wrote Susan B. Anthony that "I should like to write to you of the future, as well as of the present and the past. But I am too feeble, having hardly recovered from a severe illness, to even do that." She and William then "left London for the sea shore ... which made us feel a little stronger." In August they traveled to Paris, for the Exposition Universelle—the third Paris World's Fair. "The whole ensemble was grand and magnificent beyond description," Rose wrote the *Investigator*. "The whole world seemed to be represented in it." The couple remained in Paris five weeks, attending a peace conference there at the end of September.

This International Congress of the Friends of Peace was Ernestine Rose's fifth peace conference. In the United States, she and William had been among "the first members of the Universal Peace Union [UPU]," going to meetings in both New York and Philadelphia. The UPU affiliated with various French peace groups in the late 1860s, among them the one directed by the Roses' friend Charles Lemonnier. He published a pamphlet advocating a *United States of Europe*, believing that a single, republican, federal nation would do away with war. The Roses went to a Congress he helped organize at Lausanne in the summer of 1871 where Victor Hugo presided. The next summer, Ernestine attended a Woman's Peace Congress in London, organized by Julia Ward Howe, who also spoke at Conway's South Place Chapel. Howe remained traditionally religious and Conway criticized her for it. The *Boston Investigator* wrote that he "throws cold water" on Howe's proposal to organize a "great prayer for peace" in London, adding, "He says that praying people generally believe the Lord is a man of war, a God of battles and all that sort of thing. Only Quakers and Infidels are in favor of peace."[41]

In Paris, both Howe and Rose represented the United States at the International Congress of the Friends of Peace. Thanking the group for "allowing her the honor of saying a few words on this subject of peace, which is very dear to my heart," Rose apologized both for her poor French and for not being "strong enough to speak for long." She then expressed feminist concerns. "I just want to say that women should be represented in these universal peace societies," she stated, to shouts of "Very good, very good!" War is worse on women, she continued, "because if it is unfortunate to lose one's life, it is even more unfortunate to lose one's dear ones." After expounding on war as "the crime of crimes," Rose maintained that peace could not exist without justice, since "one cannot remain quiet when one is under the yoke of oppression. Let us then do everything that we can for freedom and against war, and everywhere men and women will unite for this goal! (Lively applause.)" Other women supported her position, which resulted in a proposal that every peace society must include a "Women's Committee." After reassuring the women present that they had the right to vote, the group passed this resolution unanimously. These brief remarks were Rose's last public speech.[42]

Forced to retire from the platform because of her illnesses, Rose began to be commemorated by the free-thought and feminist communities. Sara Underwood's glowing twenty-six-page tribute, which praised Rose as "an earnest and indefatigable worker in behalf of all reforms for the greater part of her lifetime," appeared in her 1876 *Heroines of Freethought*. The freethinking author D. M. Bennett used Underwood's chapter for Rose's entry in his encyclopedia, *The World's Sages, Infidels and Thinkers*, and Elmina D. Slenker praised her book in the *Boston Investigator*. "Among them all none stands more conspicuous than your old and beloved correspondent, Mrs. ERNESTINE L. ROSE—she whom every reader of the *Investigator* has learned to love as a real human goddess of Freethought, and whose old-time enthusiasm has not waxed old, nor waned in brightness even to this day." Elizabeth Cady Stanton and Susan B. Anthony began trying to gather information on Rose for their *History of Woman Suffrage*, writing to Robert Dale Owen and Ernestine Rose herself. Dale Owen knew little and Rose could not provide much help since, as she wrote Anthony in 1877,

> I have nothing to refer to. I have never spoken from notes; and as I did not intend to publish anything about myself, for I had no other ambition except to work for the cause of humanity, irrespective of sex, sect, country, or color, and did not expect that a Susan B. Anthony would wish to do it for me, I made no memorandum of places, dates, or names; and thirty or forty years ago, the press was not sufficiently educated in the rights of women, even to notice, much less to report speeches as it does now; and therefore I have not anything to assist me or you.

Anthony ended up reprinting Lemuel E. Barnard's 1856 essay on Rose in volume 1 of the 1881 *History of Woman Suffrage*, supplementing it with Rose's letter and some brief reminiscences of her own. In addition, she contributed a short and extremely inaccurate paragraph on Rose to *Johnson's Universal Encyclopedia*, first published in 1876. The *Boston Investigator* also reprinted Barnard's piece the week after it published a toast sent by Rose for Thomas Paine's birthday in January 1877. "The Paine Memorial Building," she wrote, "May it be instrumental in promoting *Common Sense*, which is very uncommon,—*The Rights of Man*, women included, and *The Age of Reason*, in place of superstition."[43]

Ernestine Rose continued to write letters to both the *Investigator* and the US and British women's movements. At the end of 1878 she began a long missive to the *Investigator* by congratulating them for working "for the repeal of bad laws," referring to the Comstock Act. Passed to suppress "Trade in, and Circulation of, Obscene Literature and Articles of Immoral Use," the law was widely used to prevent any distribution of contraceptive information as well as pornography. She then discussed her visit to Paris and the peace conference before adding that although "I am against war . . . I am not a 'non-resistant,' for self-defence is the first law of nature and when Russia, or any other highway robber attacks us we must defend ourselves." Rose remained focused on Russia because it still ruled Poland. She then praised the German scientist Carl Vogt's *Man, His Place in Creation and in the History of Earth* and quoted at length from its free-thought conclusion which excoriated the religious for attacking "Materialism and Darwinism." She gave a brief anecdote from a German satirical journal and concluded with a short reminiscence of the English free-thought publisher Richard Carlile. Rose's letters to women's groups focused on the suffrage. Writing in 1880 to decline the invitation of the Manchester Women's Suffrage Association to attend their demonstration, she hoped that it would be "grand." "But our cause does not depend upon numbers, but on justice," she commented. "That all women do not ask for the suffrage doesn't make the demand of it less just. *All* the slaves did not ask for their freedom." A few months later, she wrote Elizabeth Cady Stanton, saying that although it was impossible for her to travel abroad, she sent her "voice across the Atlantic to plead for Human rights without distinction of sex and to swell the grand chorus in the demand of Justice to Woman by declaring her right to the suffrage and proclaim her a citizen."[44]

Most of Ernestine Rose's energy when she felt well went into her English friendships. "We enjoyed ourselves very much at your house yesterday," she wrote the Conways in 1879, enclosing two of her speeches on divorce and slavery with the letter. She became especially close to Charles Bradlaugh, who supported the same causes she did: republicanism, free thought, and universal suffrage. In the United States in 1875, Bradlaugh declared to a feminist goup that "the Woman question is no American question, no national question; it is a question for the whole world. . . . [W]henever woman suffrage is debated, my voice is at their service." Bradlaugh ran unsuccessfully three times for Parliament from Northampton, a manufacturing center northwest of London, before being elected in 1880. Conservative members of the House of Commons, as well as Queen Victoria, who wrote almost daily to the Liberal Prime Minister Gladstone, held Bradlaugh's republicanism and support of birth control against him almost as much as his atheism. By then, affirmation rather than swearing a religious oath was allowed by many British institutions, but not Parliament. In an unprecedented move, the House of Commons refused to let Bradlaugh either affirm or take its oath, which he offered to do. Nonetheless, he still gave his maiden speech in June of 1880, standing behind the bar that blocked his way into the chamber.[45]

A few weeks later, the American reporter Kate Field, "curious to know what Mr. Bradlaugh's sensations were on this historic occasion," interviewed him. "Why should I have been agitated? I was not in the wrong," he answered. "Remember my life and remember I have gone through far worse ordeals. I confess, however, that I was touched when, in going out of the House, Mr. [P. A.] Taylor and several others shook hands with me. Kindness moves me far more than anything else, and I very nearly broke down completely when, in the lobby, Mrs. Ernestine L. Rose kissed me." Vehement opposition to his taking his seat prevailed, even though he was repeatedly re-elected. Bradlaugh's case lasted six years, until the House of Commons finally seated him in 1886. "Suppose Northampton had selected a woman as its representative," one parliamentary enemy declaimed. "Are we to be told that female suffrage is to be immediately established because a constituency has thought it proper to act in violation of the law?"[46]

Rose also became close to Bradlaugh's two daughters, Alice and Hypatia, named after a female Greek philosopher stoned to death by Christians. Both young women began studying political economy at the City of London College with Joseph Hiam Levy, a Jewish free-thought lecturer. Both also were musical: Alice played the piano, and in 1878 she founded the London Secular Choral Union, while Hypatia sang.[47]

These friends and others sustained Ernestine Rose through the great tragedy of her life: William's unexpected death from a heart attack in London on January 25, 1882. "He had gone into the city on some little business when he fell in the street," the couple's attorney wrote, "and although carried immediately to St. Bartholomew's Hospital, he died ere he reached it." "As soon as the sad news reached me, I hurried to the residence of Mrs. Rose," Charles Bradlaugh wrote, "and found the good old lady very brave but very heartbroken at the loss of her faithful partner." Moncure Conway "spoke a few words" at William's funeral in Highgate Cemetery, which was "attended by Mrs. Besant, Mr. Bradlaugh, Miss Bradlaugh, and a large number of members of the London Branches of the National Secular Society, as a mark of respect to the deceased and of sympathy with Mrs. Rose," the *National Reformer* reported. "Mr. Rose was a very worthy man in all the relations of life," Josiah Mendum wrote in the *Boston Investigator*:

> Pleasant in his manners, prompt in all his duties, and remarkably kind and benevolent in his disposition, he was greatly esteemed by all who enjoyed the pleasure of his acquaintance. He was a genuine and intelligent Liberal, made so by reading and reflection, and although quiet and unassuming, yet his upright example and kind deeds spoke louder than words of the purity and goodness of his mind and heart.... Mr. Rose was greatly respected by all who knew him.[48]

William died at sixty-nine; he was three years younger than Ernestine. "She depended so much upon him," an Englishwoman wrote to Mathilde Franziska Anneke a few weeks later, urging her to send Rose a letter of consolation. "He was the younger and has always been the stronger. As her long avowed unbelief in a future state forbids her the prospect of meeting him in the future, they say she is very wretched." This correspondent added that Rose "will not consent to anything that will help her in any way, that she will not ride or walk—or anything her friends wish, and they say she has many friends and very good ones." There is no doubt that William's death transformed Ernestine's life. Hypatia Bradlaugh later wrote that since he died "—a shock for which she was totally unprepared—Mrs. Rose has never been the same. She has been slowly and lingeringly dying, and always wishing for death." However, with support from friends both in England and the United States, she never lost her spirit completely and maintained her values of idealism and activism.[49]

Epilogue

"I HAVE LIVED"

WILLIAM'S DEATH INITIALLY devastated Ernestine Rose and it took her quite a while to resume even some everyday activities. When Susan B. Anthony visited her in March 1883, she wrote in her diary that Rose "threw her arms around my neck and her first words were: 'O, that my heart would break now and you might close my eyes, dear Susan!'" When Anthony saw her again that summer, she wrote, "It is very sad to see so great and grand an intellect . . . so incapable of making the *best* of the *inevitable*—accepting it cheerfully"; two days later she added, "Nothing I could propose seemed possible or attractive to her—She mourns her loss of her adoring husband—he was never exhaust[ed] in doing for her." Anthony also hoped that she herself would "not live to feel that no one cares for me or can help me to conditions of enjoyment," a sentiment Elizabeth Cady Stanton expressed in slightly different terms when she visited Rose in December 1882. Although she found Rose "as bright, witty, and sarcastic as ever," she added, "It is sad to be as alone in the world as she is, with not one soul with a drop of her blood in their veins living, no one life-long friend at hand on whom she can call."[1]

Seeing Rose relatively soon after her husband's death, both Stanton and Anthony overestimated her isolation in England. Unlike Stanton, with her six children, Rose had not had anyone in her close circle "with a drop of her blood in their veins" since she was seventeen. On her first visit to Rose, Anthony surmised that "she is vastly more isolated in England because of her non-Christian views than she ever was in America. Sectarianism sways everything here more now than fifty years ago with us." But Ernestine Rose retained a circle of extremely close friends in London. On a visit in October 1883, Anthony wrote, "Last evening at Mrs. Rose's I met the daughter of Charles Bradlaugh, a talented young woman, whom the college refused to admit to botany lectures because of her father's atheism." This was Alice Bradlaugh, who often called on Rose. Ernestine Rose was "very fond of my sister, who visited her frequently," Hypatia Bradlaugh later wrote. "On one occasion while my sister was with her, a lady—an old and valued friend—called. Mrs. Rose introduced my sister, who went almost immediately. When she was gone the lady said: 'Did you say that was Miss Bradlaugh—you don't mean any relation to *the* Bradlaugh?' Mrs. Rose answered: 'Yes, his daughter.' 'Then . . . you cannot expect me to come and see you Mrs. Rose, if you have such people as that here.' 'Then, my dear,' replied the old lady with spirit, 'you must stay away!' " This unnamed friend did stay away for a while because of the Bradlaughs' atheism. Alice Bradlaugh offered not to visit, "but Mrs. Rose would not hear of that." Finally the friend returned, allowing "the remembrance of a long-standing friendship to fortify her against the possible risks of contamination."[2]

Both Stanton and Anthony urged Rose to return to the United States, but she chose to stay in London, both because she wanted to lie in the same grave as William and because she "feared she had not strength for the voyage." At least she had "money enough to carry her along comfortably," Anthony wrote after she visited Rose's executor. Stanton remembered that when the pair made their final visit to Rose "a few days before sailing," we "found our noble coadjutor . . . though in delicate health, pleasantly situated in the heart of London, as deeply interested as ever in the struggles of the hour."[3] These interests, as well as emotional support from friends both in England and America, kept Ernestine Rose going. Major confirmation came from Charles Bradlaugh at the *National Reformer* and from Josiah P. Mendum and Horace Seaver at the *Boston Investigator*. Both free-thought journals printed some of her speeches as well as numerous tributes to her. In 1883, the *Investigator* published a letter from a Virginia man, saying he had named his daughter "Ernestine Rose Nock." "I think it will please Mrs. Rose to know she is remembered by her admirers in America," a Brooklyn woman then wrote. In addition, the *Investigator* printed almost every letter Ernestine Rose sent them. As she aged, the *Investigator* became increasingly important to her. "For many years, I have been a feeble invalid, almost helpless," she wrote Mendum in 1886, "yet in all that time I have managed to read, and with a great deal of pleasure, the good old *Investigator*, which I think grows better and better with its advanced age." On Rose's seventy-ninth birthday, in 1889, the *Reformer* wrote, "The brave old lady is sorely tried by the fogs of our London winter—the cold, damp air which chains her indoors despite her will. The *Boston Investigator* is each week greedily read by her as bringing news of her

Transatlantic Liberal friends, and thus lessening the loneliness of her indoor life."[4]

Despite her infirmities and sorrows, Ernestine Rose stayed engaged and kept up with new developments. From the late 1870s through the 1890s, Colonel Robert Ingersoll led the free-thought movement in the United States, championing women's rights and anti-racism as well. In 1885, Rose hoped Ingersoll would "visit her, should he ever go to England," but he never did. She then contributed $10 to the Ingersoll Secular Society and in appreciation that group proposed a toast to "Mrs. Ernestine L. Rose, dear to all American Liberals" at their annual meeting.[5] In 1887, Edward F. Strickland, a progressive clergyman, asked Rose for her photograph and autograph for his collection on women's rights leaders. "I am very glad that you and your dear wife take an interest in reform movements. For over fifty years I have endeavored to promote the rights of humanity without distinction of sex, sect, party, country or color," Rose wrote back. Two years later, in 1889, an English atheist, Joseph Mazzini Wheeler, included Rose, whom he knew personally, in his monumental *Biographical Dictionary of Freethinkers of All Ages and Nations*. He concluded his entry by writing, "Mrs. Rose has a fine face and head, and though aged and suffering, retains the utmost interest in the Freethought cause." That same year, Elmina D. Slenker, a US atheist, wrote a long article about Rose for her series on "Eminent Women," published in the American free-thought newspaper *The Truth Seeker*. Rose had visited her childhood home, Slenker remembered; "I had heard her lecture, and knew her for a really loving and lovely, womanly woman, and I felt indignant and hurt that anyone should so unkindly malign her, simply because she was a Radical reformer, and belonged to the sex which had no rights men were bound to respect." Slenker apologized for calling her "Mrs. Rose," as "we should insist on women keeping their own individual names, and being known by them whenever it is feasible" before explaining that Rose became famous under that name and made it "distinctively her own." Slenker concluded, "This good, brave worker for human happiness is still living in England, enjoying the supreme satisfaction of knowing she has lived down all the scorn and contumely of an ignorant past, and is now reverenced as one of the world's beloved and blessed saviors."[6]

Slenker was unduly optimistic. Freethinkers, no matter how aged, still remained vulnerable to attacks from believers. In 1887, Rose received a fifteen-page letter from a medical student, urging her to convert to Christianity. In reply, she sent him her *Defence of Atheism* and her 1851 lecture on women's rights. He returned them "torn up, with an insulting letter, saying he would not read them and asking Mrs. Rose where her bravery would be on her death-bed." "A woman who ventured to speak against slavery in the slave States is little likely to quail on her death-bed before the bogey pictures of a Christian god or a Christian devil," commented the London *Freethinker*, which published this piece. The *Investigator* echoed these sentiments. Many Christians continued to assume that atheists could be converted on their deathbeds. Hypatia Bradlaugh Bonner later reported that "Mrs. Rose had greatly dreaded that during her last illness she would be invaded by religious persons who might make her unsay the convictions of her whole life when her brain was weakened by illness and she did not know what she was doing," so she arranged for Hypatia to be with her "when she fell ill."[7]

Before then, however, two writers depicted Ernestine Rose's last years. In February 1889, Henrietta Muller, a wealthy English feminist who founded and edited the *Women's Penny Paper*—"The only Paper in the World Conducted, Written, Printed and Published by Women"—visited Rose's home in London. She found Rose lonely and depressed, sitting in her chair near a portrait of William. "Our lives were as one," Rose told Muller; "he rejoiced in my work, and gladly furnished the means for my journeys and lectures." Muller said she would like to read some of Rose's speeches. Rose replied, "I have destroyed nearly all the newspaper reports lately, thinking no one would care to see them." Her hired attendant, Miss Byrne, confirmed that "it is only quite lately that whole bags full of papers have been torn up." Muller "could not help regretting that we might never" again hear that "still sonorous voice" on an English platform. Before Muller departed, "three or four sparrows hopped down on the balcony close to the window, and Mrs. Rose called for a plate of crumbled bread and fed them. A kindly smile beamed on her face as she watched these birds, who were evidently her daily pensioners and little companions. 'There is a sick one,' she said, 'who is always fed by two others.'" When Muller left, Rose gave her "a hearty, sisterly shake of the hand."[8]

The second portrait comes from later in 1889, when Joseph Mazzini Wheeler visited "two veteran freethinkers" in Brighton. George Jacob Holyoake had moved there and Rose stayed near him for a few months each year. "She suffers much, and is only able to go out and enjoy the sea-air by means of a bath-chair," Wheeler reported. "But she still retains her keen interest in all Liberal movements, and her fine face is lighted up when she speaks of America, of which she is proud to own herself a citizen, and recalls the memories of the days when her voice was a trumpet-call to the soldiers of freedom." Wheeler found her "seated at the window; beside her was a chair, upon which was a pile of coppers ready to give to any musician or needy person who may pass. . . . [T]he poor bless her wherever she goes, for she is ever mindful of others, and her chief pleasure is in ministering to their wants."[9]

Both Muller and Wheeler found Ernestine Rose lonely and depressed because of the recent deaths of close friends. Alice Bradlaugh, her most frequent visitor, died prematurely of typhoid in 1888, at thirty-two. Horace Seaver fell mortally ill early in 1889 and died on August 21 at seventy-nine. A tribute to him mentioned that "he was pleased to receive remembrances from his old friend Mrs. Rose." "It is impossible for me to describe to you my grief and sorrow when I heard that our dear friend Horace Seaver had died," Rose wrote Josiah Mendum in October, "and how sorry I was and am for you to have lost your fifty years' companion and friend." She added that she would have written sooner but for her health, and she contributed $25 for a monument to commemorate Seaver. It was the last letter she was able to write.[10] More losses followed. Josiah Mendum died at eighty, on January 11, 1891. His son Ernest Mendum wrote in the *Investigator* that "the closest friendship existed between this brave and noble woman and those two brave and noble men, Horace Seaver and Josiah P. Mendum, as long as they lived." Less than three weeks later, on January 30, Charles Bradlaugh died at fifty-eight. Three thousand mourners, including Mohandas Gandhi, attended his funeral, which was silent at Bradlaugh's request. "It was a great blow to" Ernestine Rose "when my father died," Hypatia Bradlaugh Bonner wrote; "she had always counted upon him to do her the last services at the graveside, and when I went to see her in the years before his death, at parting, she rarely omitted to say: 'Give my love to dear father, and tell him I hope the time will soon come when he will take charge of me.'"[11]

Ernestine Rose herself died a year and a half later at eighty-two. Bradlaugh Bonner was sent for but reached Brighton "too late to see Mrs. Rose alive." However, "she was fortunate in having a kind and able doctor"—Washington Epps—"and a devoted attendant"—Miss Byrne—both of whom attended her funeral on August 8 at Highgate Cemetery where she was buried in William's grave.[12] "I have lost another true and valued friend, and the world has lost a good citizen," Bradlaugh Bonner wrote in her obituary for the *National Reformer*. George Jacob Holyoake, "who spoke by the desire of Mrs. Rose," delivered the eulogy to "many" mourners "who either knew and admired Mrs. Rose personally or honored her for the work she had done." "It is no longer necessary for me to live," he quoted her as saying; "I can do nothing now. But I have lived." William Rose's "regard for his wife exceeded anything of the kind I have ever known," Holyoake declared, "and her affection for him was such that though she had numerous personal friends in . . . America, she would never leave England, where her husband lay buried. Her desire was to be in the same grave, and today, in this spot, her desire is fulfilled."[13]

Ernestine Rose wrote her will in 1890. She left her "gold watch with chain and key as worn by me" to Ernest Mendum, her namesake. She left the rest of her estate to descendants of her father's family by his second wife, which implies that she communicated with her Polish relatives, although she never wrote about this. All her personal effects except her watch went to her London "niece," Jeannette Morgenstern Pulvermacher. The rest of her property was divided equally between Pulvermacher and her two sisters, Ernestine Morgenstern Radjewski of Berlin and Bertha Morgenstern Sigismund of New York. These three women were actually Rose's half-nieces, the children of her half-sister, her father's second wife's daughter. This legacy, as well as one descendant being named "Ernestine," means that Rose had some contact with her family, but not a great deal. Pulvermacher actually died in 1890, and so her daughter, Anna Pulvermacher Allinson, inherited. She attended Rose's funeral, but she and her family, the Allinsons, never met Ernestine Rose. When Yuri Suhl, Rose's first biographer, visited them in London in the 1940s, they had only dim memories of a portrait of Rose that used to hang in their front hall. A few months after Rose's funeral, a London free-thought newspaper suggested that she had wanted to leave her estate to "the furtherance of her views," but her executors, Philip S. and Philip M. Justice, "had refused to act for her if she did so." However, "she left her property exactly as she wished," Holyoake wrote, and "there was less of it than was commonly supposed, she having sunk a considerable portion of it in an annuity some years ago."[14]

A number of other tributes to Rose appeared after her death. One that would have especially pleased her was made by Lillie Devereux Blake, a US feminist and freethinker from the next generation. Blake had heard Rose speak in 1874 "when she was an old lady and in frail health, but she thrilled the audience by the electric force of her words, and her dark eyes flashed as her voice rose in the fiery earnestness of her eloquence." After Rose's death, Blake declared that "the liberal laws which we now live under are due to the tireless exertions of this gifted woman and never ought the women of New York to forget the debt of gratitude they owe to Ernestine L. Rose."[15]

However, they did forget, as did almost everyone else. "I doubt whether one American Jew in ten thousand has ever heard of her," Henry Lewis wrote in a 1927 article on Rose. "In vain you will search for her in the files of old Jewish newspapers and periodicals, in any existing history of the Jews in America or in the fat tomes of the *Jewish Encyclopedia*."[16] As a Jew, as an atheist, as a woman and a foreigner, Ernestine Rose did not fit into the early-twentieth-century narrative of US history. In 1871, the *Boston Investigator* predicted—correctly, as it turned out—that Ernestine Rose would be appreciated "in about a hundred years." The renewed women's liberation movement of the 1970s revived women's history; black history and Jewish Studies also contributed to restoring her life.

Ernestine Rose wrote hardly anything about her personal life and kept little documentation of her career because she thought it would interest no one. She was wrong. She ardently put her principles into practice. At a time when respectable women were supposed to remain in their homes, she petitioned and lectured, toured and wrote. She embodied female equality in both her everyday life and her political activism. She was a true pioneer, working for the ideals of racial equality, feminism, free thought, and internationalism. Today, progress has certainly been made in some of the causes she championed, but it remains incomplete. Equal human rights still are not available to many women and minorities throughout the United States. Immigration—the arrival of "foreigners" like Ernestine Rose—remains controversial. The resurgence of fundamentalist religions with their patriarchal foundations has given Rose's nineteenth-century struggles for free thought renewed importance. A 2012 Gallup Poll found that more Americans would vote for blacks, Jews, women, gays, and Muslims than for atheists. But it also showed that more than half of all Americans, 54 percent, would vote for an atheist for president, compared to only 18 percent in 1958.[17] As Ernestine Rose would have said, "The world moves."

Notes

INTRODUCTION

1. *The Proceedings of the National Woman's Rights Convention Held at Worcester, October 15th and 16th, 1851* (New York: Fowler & Wells, 1852): 32; Paulina W. Davis, *A History of the National Woman's Rights Movement* (New York: Journeymen Printers' Co-operative Association, 1871): 19.

2. For some of the proceedings of the 1850 meeting and reactions to it, see John F. McClymer, *This High and Holy Moment: The First National Woman's Rights Convention, Worcester, 1850* (New York: Harcourt, Brace, 1999); *The Call to the Second National Woman's Rights Convention*, Women's Rights National Historical Park, Seneca Falls, NY.

3. On women's public speaking generally, see Karlyn Kohrs Campbell, *Man Can Not Speak for Her: A Critical Study of Feminist Rhetoric with Texts* (New York: Praeger, 1989), vol. 1: 10–11. For a specific example, see the "Pastoral Letter of the Congregational Ministers of Massachusetts," [directed against the Grimké sisters' anti-slavery speaking tour], reprinted in *The Liberator*, August 11, 1837; *Proceedings . . . 1851*: 102; Ernestine Rose, Letter to Susan B. Anthony, 1877, in Paula Doress-Worters, ed., *Mistress of Herself: Speeches and Letters of Ernestine L. Rose, Early Women's Rights Leader* (New York: Feminist Press, 2008): 348.

4. *Boston Investigator*, January 19, 1881: 5. The German reporter was Ottilie Assing, writing in 1858. Christoph Lohmann, ed., trans., intro., *Radical Passions: Ottilie Assing's Reports from America and Letters to Frederick Douglass* (New York: Peter Lang, 1999): 114; Jenny P. d'Héricourt, "Madame Rose," *Revue Philosophique et Religieuse* (Paris: Bureaux de la Revue, 1856), vol. 5: 129. For an English translation of this article, which I occasionally depart from, see "Madame Rose: A Life of Ernestine Rose as told to Jenny P. d'Héricourt," *Journal of Women's History*, vol. 15, #1 (2003): 183–201, Introduction by Paula Doress-Worters, trans. Jane Pincus, Mei Mei Ellerman, Ingrid Kisliuk, Erica Harth, and Allan J. Worters, with Karen Offen.

5. Editorial, *Worcester Daily Spy*, October 24, 1850; Joseph Barker in *The Reasoner*, November 2, 1856: vol. XXI, #544, 139; John White Chadwick, ed., *A Life for Liberty: Anti-Slavery and Other Letters of Sallie Holley* (New York: G. Putnam's Sons, 1899): 127.

6. Ernestine Rose, Speech, Worcester, 1851, in Doress-Worters, *Mistress of Herself*: 92–94.

7. Ernestine Rose, Speech, Worcester, 1851, in Doress-Worters, *Mistress of Herself*: 94, 97–98.

8. Ernestine Rose, Speech, Worcester, 1851, in Doress-Worters, *Mistress of Herself*: 100.

9. Ernestine Rose, Speech, Worcester, 1851, in Doress-Worters, *Mistress of Herself*: 101–103.

10. *Albany Register* from Elizabeth Cady Stanton, Susan B. Anthony, and Matilda Joslyn Gage, eds., *History of Woman Suffrage*, vol. 1: *1848–1861* (New York: Fowler & Wells, 1881): 606; for Anthony, see Stanton, Anthony, and Gage, *History of Woman Suffrage*, I: 100.

11. Jean-Jacques Rousseau, *Emile*, trans. Barbara Foxley (London: Everyman's Library, 1974 [1762]): 370.

12. *The Proceedings of the Woman's Rights Convention Held at Worcester, October 23rd and 24th, 1850* (Boston: Prentiss & Sawyer, 1851): 7.

13. Sara A. Underwood, *Heroines of Free Thought* (New York: C. P. Somerby, 1876): 268.

14. Underwood, *Heroines of Free Thought*: 269.

15. Ernestine L. Rose, Speech, *Proceedings of the Woman's Rights Convention held at the Broadway Tabernacle, in the City of New York, on Tues. & Wed., Sept. 6th & 7th, 1853* (New York: Fowler & Wells, 1853): 4–5.

16. Ernestine L. Rose, Speech at the New England Anti-Slavery Convention, in Doress-Worters, *Heroines of Free Thought*: 192; Ernestine L. Rose, Speech at the First Anniversary of the American Equal Rights Association, in Doress-Worters, *Mistress of Herself*: 336.

17. *Proceedings of the Meeting of the Loyal Women of the Republic, held in New York, May 14, 1863* (New York: Phair & Co., 1863): 27; *The Liberator*, May 29, 1862: 3; Farewell Letter of Mrs. Rose, in Doress-Worters, *Mistress of Herself*: 208.

18. Chadwick, *A Life for Liberty*: 127; Ernestine L. Rose, Third National Woman's Rights Convention, 1852, in Doress-Worters, *Mistress of Herself*: 127; Ernestine L. Rose, "The Social Problem," *Boston Investigator*, February 10, 1869: 3.

19. L. E. Barnard, "Ernestine L. Rose," in Stanton, Anthony, and Gage, *History of Woman Suffrage*, I: 95–100; Jenny P. d'Héricourt, "Madame Rose": 129–139; Bonnie S. Anderson, *Joyous Greetings: The First International Women's Movement, 1830–1860* (New York: Oxford University Press, 2000); Underwood's chapter on Rose is in her *Heroines of Free Thought*: 255–281.

CHAPTER 1

1. Ernestine L. Rose, Speech at the Third National Woman's Rights Convention, Syracuse, 1852, in Paula Doress-Worters, ed., *Mistress of Herself: Speeches and Letters*

of *Ernestine L. Rose, Early Women's Rights Leader* (New York: Feminist Press, 2008): 121.

2. The files of the Piótrkow Jewish community from 1808 to 1853, which are in Polish, are currently housed in the Łódź Archives. The Polish researcher Violetta Wiernicka scoured these holdings looking for Rose's birth certificate or her parents' marriage registration, but in vain.

3. There are three contemporary biographies of Rose: Lemuel E. Barnard's "Ernestine L. Rose," first published in *The Liberator*, May 16, 1856, but widely reprinted in Elizabeth Cady Stanton, Susan B. Anthony, and Matilda Joslyn Gage, eds., *History of Woman Suffrage* (reprint Salem, NH: Ayer Publishers, 1985), vol. 1: *1848–1861* [1881]: 95–100, with later additions by Susan B. Anthony. Thanks to Professor Reginald H. Pitts, SUNY–Old Westbury, and the Western Reserve Society in Cleveland for helping me to identify the person always previously called "L. E. Barnard," as Lemuel E. Barnard, a progressive lecturer and activist. Second to be written was Jenny P. d'Héricourt's "Madame Rose," in *La Revue Philosophique et Religieuse* (Paris: Bureaux de la Revue, 1856), vol. 5: 129–139. This piece was translated by a committee under the editorship of Paula Doress-Worters as "Madame Rose: A Life of Ernestine L. Rose as told to Jenny P. d'Héricourt," *Journal of Women's History*, vol. 15, #1 (2003): 183–201. I have occasionally found this translation either too literal or incorrect and so have used my own. Third was Sara A. Underwood's "Ernestine L. Rose," in her *Heroines of Free Thought* (New York: C. P. Somerby, 1876): 255–281. Underwood met Rose in 1874. This book is available online from the Schlesinger Library at Radcliffe College.

4. Thanks to Professor Robert Shapiro, Judaic Studies Department, Brooklyn College, for help with this section. See also Shaul Stampfer, "Gender Differentiation and Education of the Jewish Woman in Nineteenth-Century Eastern Europe," *Polin: Studies in Polish Jewry*, vol. 7 (1992): 65.

5. The phrase "I was a rebel at the age of five," is used by Yuri Suhl, Rose's first modern biographer, as the epigraph to his book on her. Suhl gave no reference for it. Yuri Suhl, *Ernestine L. Rose: Women's Rights Pioneer*, 2nd ed. (New York: Biblio Press, 1990 [1959]): 1. The closest I have been able to find for it is from the *New York Herald*'s article on the 1858 Eighth National Woman's Rights Convention in New York City, May 14, 1858: 3, which reads, "She had known what it was to rebel since she was five years old." Since newspapers usually put first-person remarks ("I") into the third person ("she"), this is the most likely source for the quotation. (This quotation is not in the Convention's *Proceedings*.) For leaving the school, d'Héricourt, "Madame Rose": 131.

6. Rachel Biale, *Women and Jewish Law: An Exploration of Women's Issues in Halakhic Sources* (New York: Schocken Books, 1984): 35–36; "Anyone who teaches his daughter Torah taught her *tiflut* (usually translated as indecency or frivolity)," cited in Stampfer, "Gender Differentiation": 64; Moshe Rosman, "The History of Jewish Women in Early Modern Poland," in ChaeRan Freeze, Paula Hyman, and Antony

Polonsky, eds., *Jewish Women in Eastern Europe, Polin: Studies in Polish Jewry,* vol. 18 (2005): 35.

7. D'Héricourt, "Madame Rose": 131; Rose, *New York Herald,* May 14, 1858: 3; Barnard, "Ernestine L. Rose": 95.

8. Ernestine L. Rose, Speech at the Second National Woman's Rights Convention, Worcester, MA, 1851, in Doress-Worters, *Mistress of Herself:* 99; Ernestine L. Rose, *Proceedings of the Woman's Rights Convention, West Chester, Pennsylvania,* 1852, in Stanton, Anthony, and Gage, eds., *History of Woman Suffrage,* vol. 1: 357; Ernestine L. Rose, Letter, *Boston Investigator,* February 17, 1864, in Doress-Worters, *Mistress of Herself:* 317.

9. D'Héricourt, "Madame Rose": 131; Underwood, "Ernestine L. Rose": 260.

10. Thanks to Toba, Josef, and Gina Singer for help with this point. Cited in Lucy Stone's obituary for Ernestine Rose, *Woman's Journal,* September 1892; d'Héricourt, "Madame Rose": 131–132.

11. Barnard, "Ernestine L. Rose": 95–96; www.piotrkowtrybunalski.friko.pl/ciekawostki/krolowa for "Ernestyna Heretyczka." Thanks to Agnieszka Klimek for bringing this website to my attention. Ernestine L. Rose, *Proceedings of the Woman's Rights Convention held at Syracuse, September 8th, 9th, & 10th, 1852* (Syracuse, NY: J. E. Masters, 1852): 85–86.

12. Ernestine L. Rose, Letter, *Boston Investigator,* March 10, 1864, in Doress-Worters, *Mistress of Herself:* 315. On Polish Judaism, see Raphael Mahler, *Hasidim and the Jewish Enlightenment: Their Confrontation in Galicia and Poland in the First Half of the Nineteenth Century,* trans. Aaron and Jenny Machlowitz, Eugene Orenstein (Philadelphia: Jewish Publication Society of America, 1985): 245ff; Glenn Dynner, *Men of Silk: The Hasidic Conquest of Polish Jewish Society* (New York: Oxford University Press, 2006): 228–229; Gershon David Hundert, *Jews in Poland-Lithuania in the Eighteenth Century: A Genealogy of Modernity* (Berkeley: University of California Press, 2006): 239.

13. D'Héricourt, "Madame Rose": 132; d'Héricourt, *Boston Investigator,* December 8, 1869: 2; Barnard, "Ernestine L. Rose": 96; Underwood, "Ernestine L. Rose": 261–262. Underwood states that Ernestine's mother died years earlier, but d'Héricourt and Barnard agree that her mother died when Ernestine was fifteen. This is Ernestine's only mention of her mother.

14. D'Héricourt, "Madame Rose": 132; Pu'ah Rakowska, cited in ChaeRan Y. Freeze, *Jewish Marriage and Divorce in Imperial Russia* (Hanover, NH: University Press of New England, 2002): 14.

15. Israel Bartel, *The Jews of Eastern Europe 1772–1881,* trans. Chaya Naor (Philadelphia: University of Pennsylvania Press, 2005): 14–17; Paul R. Mendes-Flohr and Jehuda Reinharz, eds., *The Jew in the Modern World: A Documentary History* (New York: Oxford University Press, 1980): 516; Julian K. Janczak, "Ludnosc," ["Population"] in Bogdan Baranowski, ed., *Dzieje Piotrków a Trybunalskiego [Historical Events of Piótrkow Trybunalski]* (Łódź: Wydawnictwo

Lodzkie, 1989): 246. Thanks to Violetta Wiernicka for this citation. On shtetls then, see Michał Galas, "Inter-Religious Contacts in the Shtetl: Proposals for Future Research," and Adam Teller, "The Shtetl as an Arena for Polish-Jewish Integration in the Eighteenth Century," in *The Shtetl: Myth and Reality, Polin: Studies in Polish Jewry*, vol. 17 (2004): 29, 36, 42.

16. Ernestine L. Rose, Speech at the 1855 New England Anti-Slavery Convention, in Doress-Worters, *Mistress of Herself*: 188; d'Héricourt, "Madame Rose": 135.

17. When Napoleon ruled France, he reversed some minor laws about the Jews (like rabbis would not be paid by the state), but these changes had all been done away with by the 1830s. Thanks to Nadia Malinovich for help with this point. Ben Giladi, ed., *A Tale of One City: Piotrkow Trybunalski* (New York: Shengold, 1991): 37; Rose's speech at the May 28, 1844, Social Reform Convention in Boston, cited in *The Phalanx*, vol. 1, #13, June 29, 1844; Oskar Flatt, *Opis Piótrkowa Trybunalskiego pod wzgledem historycznum i statystycznym [Piótrkow Trybunalski's Historical and Statistical Development]* (Warsaw, 1850): 16. Thanks to Violetta Wiernicka for this citation.

18. D'Héricourt, "Madame Rose": 132–133.

19. Thanks to Małgorzata Witecka, archivist of the Polish Archives in Warsaw, and Agnieszka Klimek for helping me to research the records of the Kalisz court.

20. Ernestine L. Rose, Speech, *Proceedings of the National Woman's Rights Convention, held at Cleveland, Ohio on Oct. 5th, 6th and 7th, 1853* (Cleveland: Grey, Beardsley, Spear, 1854): 104; Ernestine L. Rose, *A Defence of Atheism* (Boston: J. P. Mendum, 1889 [1861]): 24; Ernestine L. Rose, Speech, *Proceedings of the Tenth National Woman's Rights Convention, held at the Cooper Institute, New York City, May 10th and 11th, 1860* (Boston: Yerrinton & Garrison, 1860): 53–54; Rose, *Proceedings . . . Cleveland*: 104. The quotation is from Plato's *Apology*.

21. Underwood, "Ernestine L. Rose": 263–264; d'Héricourt, "Madame Rose": 133; d'Héricourt, *Boston Investigator*, December 8, 1869: 2.

22. "Letters from Mrs. Ernestine L. Rose, No. I," *Boston Investigator*, July 30, 1856: 1; Underwood, "Ernestine L. Rose": 280; Ernestine L. Rose, Letter to the *Albany Daily State Register* in Doress-Worters, *Mistress of Herself*: 168.

23. For the Hasidic nature of the Warsaw Jewish community, see the Dynner and Hundert citations in footnote 12, this chapter. The Jewish Enlightenment is known as "Haskalah." Steven M. Lowenstein, *The Berlin Jewish Community: Enlightenment, Family, and Crisis, 1770–1830* (New York: Oxford University Press, 1994): 34ff.; David Sorkin, *The Transformation of German Jewry, 1780–1840* (New York: Oxford University Press): 57–58; Matt Erlin, *Berlin's Forgotten Future: City, History, and Enlightenment in Eighteenth-Century Germany* (Chapel Hill: University of North Carolina Press, 2004): 30; Freeze, *Jewish Marriage and Divorce*: 43.

24. Winfried Löschburg, *A History of Travel*, trans. Ruth Michaelis-Jena and Patrick Murray (Leipzig: Edition Leipzig, 1979): 126ff, 138. Also see www.shtetlinks.jewishgenorg/lyakhovich/stagecoach.html.

25. Löschburg, *A History of Travel*: 113, 117, 137–138; Freeze, *Jewish Marriage and Divorce*: 67; Thomas Hodgskin, *Travels in the North of Germany* (New York: Augustus M. Kelley, 1969 [1820]), vol. 1: 61.

26. John Torpey, *The Invention of the Passport: Surveillance, Citizenship and the State* (Cambridge UK: Cambridge University Press, 2000): 62–63; Andreas Fahrmeir, "Governments and Forgers: Passports in Nineteenth-Century Europe," in Jane Caplan and John Torpey, eds., *Documenting Individual Identity: The Development of State Practices in the Modern World* (Princeton, NJ: Princeton University Press, 2001): 219–220.

27. D'Héricourt, "Madame Rose": 133. Throughout this section, d'Héricourt calls Potowska "Madamoiselle Susmond." She may have used this more Germanic-sounding last name to make her entry easier.

28. On the lack of records, 75 percent of which were destroyed in 1943, private communication from Thomas Breitfeld, Director, Geheimes Staatsarchiv Preussischer Kulturbesitz, February 18, 2011; for research on this section, thanks to Amy Hackett and Dana Strohscheer. On Friedrich Wilhelm III, private communication from Professor Dr. Thomas Stamm-Kuhlmann, Ernst-Moritz-Arndt Universität Greifswald, April 26, 2011; Thomas Stamm-Kuhlmann, "Restoration Prussia," in Philip G. Dwyer, ed., *Modern Prussian History 1830–1947* (Harlow, Essex, UK: Pearson Education, 2001): 50; Paul and Gisela Habermann, *Friedrich Wilhelm III: König von Preussen im Blick wohlwollender Zeitzeugen* (Schernfeld: SH-Verlag, 1990): 56ff., 96–97.

29. D'Héricourt, "Madame Rose": 133. When I queried H-German about this interchange, Mark Lause of the University of Cincinnati replied, "Where my research has crossed the path of Ernestine Rose . . . I've found nothing to indicate that she exaggerated her activities and importance." I agree and have assumed that she told the truth about this encounter.

30. Her only mention of Berlin was in the context of "*espionage*" in Paris: "Our arrival and stay was in the Paris papers, and from them copied into the Berlin, and very likely all German papers. It was mentioned in the Berlin papers that we would come to Berlin." "Letters from Mrs. Ernestine L. Rose, No. IX," *Boston Investigator*, November 26, 1856: 1. Rose sent six long letters to the *Boston Investigator* from Berlin during this stay.

31. Erlin, *Berlin's Forgotten Future*: 51–52, 117; Hodgskin, *Travels in the North of Germany*, vol. 1: 78–79.

32. Lowenstein, *The Berlin Jewish Community*: 59, 104–105, 177; Michael A. Meyer, *German-Jewish History in Modern Times*, vol. 2: *Emancipation and Acculturation 1780–1871* (New York: Columbia University Press, 1997): 151–152, 201ff.; Robert Darnton, *The Case for Books: Past, Present, and Future* (New York: Public Affairs, 2009): 201; d'Héricourt, "Madame Rose": 133.

33. D'Héricourt, "Madame Rose": 133; Meyer, *German-Jewish History in Modern Times*: 199–200; Sorkin, *The Transformation of German Jewry*: 69–70, 79, 104;

Ernestine L. Rose, Speech at the 1853 Anniversary of West Indian Emancipation, in Doress-Worters, *Mistress of Herself*: 152.

34. D'Héricourt, "Madame Rose": 133; *The Beacon*, March 31, 1838. *The Beacon's* pagination changed every few years and so is not provided.

35. D'Héricourt, "Madame Rose": 134; d'Héricourt, *Boston Investigator*, December 8, 1856: 1; Barnard, "Ernestine L. Rose": 96; Underwood, "Ernestine L. Rose": 264. Barnard writes that "In Hague [*sic*], she became acquainted with a very distressing case of a poor sailor, the father of four children, whose wife had been imprisoned for an alleged crime of which he insisted she was innocent. Inquiring into the case Mlle. Potoski [*sic*] drew up a petition which she personally presented to the King of Holland and had the satisfaction of seeing the poor woman restored to her family." The king was Willem I. Neither the archivist, H. J. de Muij-Flenike, nor a Dutch researcher, Regina Bruijn-Boot, could find this petition in the Dutch National Archives.

36. Philip Mansel, *Paris between Empires: Monarchy and Revolution 1814–1852* (New York: St. Martin's Press, 2001), *passim*; "Letters from Mrs. Ernestine L. Rose, No. V," *Boston Investigator*, October 8, 1856: 1.

37. "Letters from Mrs. Ernestine L. Rose, No. X," *Boston Investigator*, December 3, 1856: 1; "Letters from Mrs. Ernestine L. Rose, No. V," *Boston Investigator*, October 8, 1856: 1.

38. Pamela M. Pilbeam, *The 1830 Revolution in France* (London: Macmillan, 1991): 60–64; "Letters from Mrs. Ernestine L. Rose, No. VI," *Boston Investigator*, October 15, 1856: 1; Mansel, *Paris between Empires*: 248.

39. Mansel, *Paris between Empires*: 259; Pilbeam, *The 1830 Revolution*: 82ff.; "Letters from Mrs. Ernestine L. Rose, No. VI," *Boston Investigator,* October 15, 1856: 1; Barnard, "Ernestine L. Rose": 96; John M. Merriman, ed., *1830 in France* (New York: New Viewpoints, 1975): 4–5; "Letters from Mrs. Ernestine L. Rose, No. IX," *Boston Investigator,* November 26, 1856: 1.

40. Jósef Straszéwicz, *The Life of Countess Emily Plater*, trans. J. K. Salomoński (New York: James Linen, 1843), *passim*. Plater joined up with the main Polish army and commanded a regular army regiment until her death from illness in December 1831; d'Héricourt, "Madame Rose": 134.

41. Ernestine L. Rose, Speech at the 1850 Thomas Paine Celebration, in Doress-Worters, *Mistress of Herself*: 75.

42. Underwood, "Ernestine L. Rose": [268,] 265.

CHAPTER 2

1. Jenny P. d'Héricourt, "Madame Rose," *La Revue Philosophique et Religieuse* (Paris: Bureaux de la Revue, 1856), vol. 5: 134.

2. Passports were not introduced in Britain until 1837. John Torpey, *The Invention of the Passport: Surveillance, Citizenship and the State* (Cambridge, UK: Cambridge

University Press, 2000): 68; Jerry White, *London in the Nineteenth Century: A Human Awful Wonder of God* (London: Vintage Books, 2007): 101–102; Todd M. Endelman, *The Jews of Britain, 1656–2000* (Berkeley: University of California Press, 2001), *passim*. English Jews still suffered some restrictions, like not being able to run for Parliament, but their situation was better there than in most of Europe.

3. *The London Journal of Flora Tristan (Promenades dan Londres)*, trans. Jean Hawkes (London: Virago Press, 1982 [1840, 1842]): 17; Frederick Von Raumer, *England in 1835: Letters Written to Friends in Germany*, trans. Sarah Austin and H. E. Lloyd (Philadelphia: Carey, Lea, and Blanchard, 1836): 28–29.

4. "Letters from Mrs. Ernestine L. Rose, No. II," *Boston Investigator*, August 6, 1856: 1; H. D. Rogers, "Transatlantic Correspondence," *Boston Investigator*, September 21, 1832: 1.

5. Ernestine L. Rose, quoted in Elizabeth Cady Stanton, Susan B. Anthony, and Matilda Joslyn Gage, eds., *History of Woman Suffrage* (Salem, NH: Ayer Co., 1985), vol. 2, *1861–1876* [1881]: 397; d'Héricourt, "Madame Rose": 134.

6. Von Raumer, *England in 1835*: 130. In 1856, Rose complained that "The sun never rises clear on London." "Letters from Mrs. Ernestine L. Rose, No. IV," *Boston Investigator*, August 20, 1856: 1; Malwida von Meysenbug, *Memoiren einer Idealistin*, 2 vols. (Berlin: Schuster & Loeffler, 1881), vol. 1: 329. Also see Christine L. Corton, *London Fog: The Biography* (Cambridge, MA: Harvard University Press, 2015).

7. D'Héricourt, "Madame Rose": 134; Lemuel E. Barnard, "Ernestine L. Rose," in Stanton, Anthony, and Gage, eds., *History of Woman Suffrage*, vol. 1: 96; Diane Newton and Jonathan Lumby, *The Grosvenors of Eaton* (Eccleston, UK: Jennet, 2002), *passim*; "Grosvenor, Richard, second marquess of Westminster (1795–1869)," *Oxford Dictionary of National Biography*.

8. Material on Grosvenor House, which was demolished in the early twentieth century and bore no resemblence to the current Grosvenor House Hotel, is drawn from "Old Grosvenor House," ch. XIII, *Survey of London*, vol. 40: *The Grosvenor Estate in Mayfair*, Part Two: *The Buildings* (1980) in British History Online. In 1856, Ernestine Rose told Lemuel Barnard that "she became acquainted with Lord Grosvenor and family, with Frances Farrar, sister of Oliver Farrar, M.P., the Miss Leeds, and others of the nobility." Few traces of these people's lives remain. Oliver Farrar, a London lawyer, was neither a member of Parliament nor of the nobility. His sister Frances never married and lived to be ninety-three. The "Miss Leeds" cannot be found. Barnard, "Ernestine L. Rose": 96.

9. David E. Swift, *Joseph John Gurney: Banker, Reformer, and Quaker* (Middletown CT: Wesleyan University Press, 1962): 7, 35, 106–107, 209–210.

10. Elise A. Haighton in Theodore Stanton, ed., *The Woman Question in Europe* (New York: G. Putnam's Sons, 1884): footnote, 167; June Rose, *Elizabeth Fry* (New York: St. Martin's Press, 1980): 79 and *passim*.

11. Robert Owen, "Character and Environment: A Prison Experience," in A. L. Morton, *The Life and Ideas of Robert Owen* (New York: International Publishers, 1969): 78–80.

12. Ernestine L. Rose, Speech, *Proceedings of the Free Convention, held at Rutland, Vt., July* [sic. although the convention actually took place in June] *the 25th, 26th, and 27th, 1858* (Boston: J. B. Yerrinton and Son, 1858): 31. In this 1858 speech, Rose referred to a prison visit of 1843. Barnard, "Ernestine L. Rose": 96.

13. For a brief summary of Owen's life, see G. D. H. Cole, "Robert Owen and Owenism," in *Persons and Periods: Studies* (London: Macmillan, 1938): 196–215; *The Life of Robert Owen by Himself* (London: G. Bell & Sons, 1920 [1857–58]): 81.

14. *The Life of Robert Owen by Himself*: 102–103; Ernestine L. Rose, Speech at Robert Owen's Birthday Celebration, 1853, in Paula Doress-Worters, ed., *Mistress of Herself: Speeches and Letters of Ernestine L. Rose, Early Women's Rights Leader* (New York: Feminist Press, 2008): 132–133.

15. Robert Dale Owen, *Threading My Way: An Autobiography* (New York: Augustus M. Kelley, 1967 [1874]): 115; *The Beacon*, December 23, 1837: 60–61.

16. *The Life of Robert Owen by Himself*: 126; Cole, "Robert Owen and Owenism": 200; Ernestine L. Rose, Speech, in *Report of the Proceedings of the Festival in Commemoration of the Centenary Birthday of Robert Owen, the Philanthropist, Held at Freemasons' Hall, London, May 16, 1871* (London: E. Truelove, 1871): 20.

17. For the complete Declaration and reactions to it, see Albert Post, *Popular Freethought in America, 1825–1850* (New York: Columbia University Press, 1943): 32–33.

18. Robert Owen, *A Catechism of the New View of Society*, cited in Morton, *The Life and Ideas of Robert Owen*: 198–199.

19. Robert Owen, Statement, March 30, 1834, cited in Morton, *The Life and Ideas of Robert Owen*: 196; Owen's 1835 *Lectures on the Marriages of the Priesthood in the Old Immoral World* summarized these views which had been expressed earlier. This policy did not extend to Quaker or Jewish marriages.

20. Lucretia Mott to Richard and Hannah Webb, February 25, 1842, Manuscript Division, Anti-Slavery Collection, Boston Public Library, Ms. A.1.2, vol. 12.2: 34, page 7 of the letter; Barbara Taylor, *Eve and the New Jerusalem: Socialism and Feminism in the Nineteenth Century* [Great Britain] (New York: Pantheon, 1983): 184; Frances Trollope, *Domestic Manners of the Americans* (London: Folio Society, 1974 [1832]): 127; Ernestine Rose, Centenary Birthday Speech: 20.

21. Ernestine L. Rose, Speech at the Seventh National Woman's Rights Convention, 1856, in Doress-Worters, *Mistress of Herself*: 232.

22. Edward Royle, *Modern Britain: A Social History, 1750–2010*, 3rd ed. (London: Bloomsbury Academic, 2012): 146; *Proceedings of the Second Co-operative Congress, held in Birmingham, October 4, 5, and 6, 1831 and composed of delegates from the co-operative societies of Great Britain and Ireland* (John and James Powell, 1831): 10, 11, 17.

23. D'Héricourt, "Madame Rose": 134; Ernestine Rose, Centenary Birthday Speech: 20–21.

24. Morton, *The Life and Ideas of Robert Owen*: 99; for "Dear and Respected Father," Rose's April 14, 1845, letter to Owen, for "your Daughter," Rose's December, 1844 letter to Owen, both in Doress-Worters, *Mistress of Herself*: 67–68; Lemuel E. Barnard, "Ernestine L. Rose," *Boston Investigator*, July 9, 1856: 3; Jenny P. d'Héricourt, "Mrs. Ernestine L. Rose," *Boston Investigator*, December 8, 1869: 2. No known writings by Owen about Potowska exist.

25. Robert Owen, *A New View of Society* [1813], in Morton, *The Life and Ideas of Robert Owen*: 23–24; Ernestine L. Rose, Speech at Robert Owen's Birthday Celebration, 1853, in Doress-Worters, *Mistress of Herself*: 133; Robert Owen, *The New Moral World*, February 6, 1836, vol. 2, #67: 115–116.

26. "The Grand National Consolidated Trade Union Manifesto," reprinted in William L. Sachse, ed., *English History in the Making: Readings from the Sources since 1689* (Waltham, MA: Ginn-Blaisdell, 1970), vol. 2: 87; Robert Owen, Statement, March 30, 1834, cited in Morton, *The Life and Ideas of Robert Owen*: 196.

27. J. F. C. Harrison, *Robert Owen and the Owenites in Britain and America: The Quest for the New Moral World* (London: Routledge & Kegan Paul, 1969): 76, 249–250; Taylor, *Eve and the New Jerusalem*: 116–117; Morris U. Schappes, "Ernestine L. Rose: Her Address on the Anniversary of West Indian Emancipation," *Journal of Negro History*, vol. 34, #3 (July 1949): 355, fn. 14; *Manual of the Association of all Classes of all Nations*, No. 2 (London, 1836): 30; Ernestine L. Rose, Speech at Robert Owen's Birthday Celebration, 1853, in Doress-Worters, *Mistress of Herself*: 133.

28. Thomas Hirst, *Report of the Third Congress of Delegates from Co-operative Societies of Great Britain and Ireland held in London April 23rd to 30th 1832 under the presidency of Robert Owen* (no publication information given): 38; Taylor, *Eve and the New Jerusalem*: 57, 95, 218; *The Crisis*, May 18, 1833, vol. 2, #14: 146; *Proceedings of the Second Co-operative Congress*: 17.

29. Mrs. E. Little, "What Are the Rights of Women?" *Ladies Wreath* 2 (1848–49): 133; the other two citations in Anna Clark, *The Struggle for the Breeches: Gender and the Making of the British Working Class* (Berkeley: University of California Press, 1995): 199; "Kate" [Catherine Watkins, later Barmby], "An Appeal to Women," *The New Moral World*, August 15, 1835 vol. 1, #42: 335; Clark, *The Struggle for the Breeches*: 252–253.

30. Taylor, *Eve and the New Jerusalem*: 135, 80, 60, 56. The female member of the GNCTU board was Anna Wheeler. Ernestine L. Rose, Centenary Birthday Speech: 20.

31. *The Crisis*, April 21, 1832, vol. 1, #2: 8; *The Crisis*, June 15, 1833, vol. 2, #23: 132.

32. Eliza Macauley, *The Crisis*, July 7, 1833, vol. 1, #18: 66. For more on Macauley, see Taylor, *Eve and the New Jerusalem*: 71–74. For Rose in New York, *The Beacon*, December 23, 1837; Mary Leman Grimstone, *The New Moral World*, January 24, 1835, vol. 1, #13: 101; Mary Leman Grimstone, *The New Moral World*, February 21, 1835, vol. 1, #17: 134–135; d'Héricourt, "Madame Rose": 129.

33. *The Crisis*, August 25, 1832, vol. 1, #25: 99; Taylor, *Eve and the New Jerusalem*: 153, 128; "Pastoral Letter of the Congregational Ministers of Massachusetts," 1837, in Ruth Barnes Moynihan, Cynthia Russett, and Laurie Crumpacker, eds., *Second to None: A Documentary History of American Women* (Lincoln: University of Nebraska Press, 1993), vol. 1: *From the Sixteenth Century to 1865*: 252; *American Quarterly Review*, 1837, cited in Valerie Kossew Pichanick, *Harriet Martineau: The Woman and Her Work, 1802–76* (Ann Arbor: University of Michigan Press, 1980): 100.

34. Moncure D. Conway, cited in Sara A. Underwood, "Ernestine L. Rose," in *Heroines of Free Thought* (New York: C. Sowerby, 1876): 265; d'Héricourt, "Madame Rose": 134. For more on women and domestic labor in Co-operation, see Taylor, *Eve and the New Jerusalem*, ch. 7 for Britain, and Carol A. Kolmerten, *Women in Utopia: The Ideology of Gender in the American Owenite Communities* (Bloomington: University of Indiana Press, 1990).

35. Taylor, *Eve and the New Jerusalem*: 139, 217; *Proceedings of the Second Co-operative Congress*: 107. Ernestine Rose wrote, "I am as fond of dancing as ever" in 1865, when she was fifty-five, in a letter to the *Boston Investigator*, February 15, 1865: 2; Harrison, *Robert Owen and the Owenites*: 216–218.

36. Private communication from Todd Endelman; Stanton, Anthony, and Gage, eds., *History of Woman Suffrage*, vol. 1: 300; W. E. Rose, Letter to Robert Owen, September 31 [*sic*], 1845, #1389, Owen Archives, Co-operative College, Holyoake House, Manchester, England. The version printed in Doress-Worters, *Mistress of Herself*: 71 has been considerably cleaned up. For the Roses' singing, Thomas Paine Celebration, 1840, in Doress-Worters, *Mistress of Herself*: 60; d'Héricourt, "Madame Rose": 138–139; Ernestine L. Rose, *Proceedings of the Free Convention*: 61.

37. Richard William Leopold, *Robert Dale Owen: A Biography* (Cambridge, MA: Harvard University Press, 1940): 110–111; d'Héricourt, "Madame Rose": 134; private communication from Rebecca Probert.

38. Cited in Ronald George Garnett, *Co-operation and the Owenite Socialist Communities in Britain, 1825–1845* (Manchester, UK: Manchester University Press, 1972): 162, footnote 66.

39. Cited in Harrison, *Robert Owen and the Owenites*: 55; Ernestine Rose, Letter to *Albany Register*, 1854, in Doress-Worters, *Mistress of Herself*: 168.

40. J. B. Matrat, *Practical Emigration to the United States of North America Systematized*, *The New Moral World*, March 26, 1836, vol. 2, #74: 172–174, and *The New Moral World*, April 2, 1836, vol. 2, #75: 183–184; *The New Moral World*, May 14, 1836, vol. 2, #81: 230; d'Héricourt, "Madame Rose": 134–135.

CHAPTER 3

1. Cited in Edwin G. Burrows and Mike Wallace, *Gotham: A History of New York City to 1898* (New York: Oxford University Press, 1999): 45; London information from

Jerry White, *London in the Nineteenth Century: A Human Awful Wonder of God* (London: Vintage Books, 2007): 67–80; Burrows and Wallace, *Gotham*: 450. For a map of New York City in 1838, see *www.hypercities.com*.

2. A[sa] Greene, *A Glance at New York Embracing the City Government, Theatres, Hotels, Churches, Mobs, Monopolies, Learned Professions, Newspapers, Rogues, Dandies, Fires and Firemen, Water and Other Liquors, &c. &c.* (New York: A. Greene, 1 Beekman Street, 1837), epigraph.

3. Burrows and Wallace, *Gotham*, 469; Frances Trollope, *Domestic Manners of the Americans* (London: Folio Society, 1974 [1832]): 248; Robert Ernst, *Immigrant Life in New York City 1825—1863* (New York: King's Crown Press, Columbia University, 1949): 23.

4. Thanks to Deborah Dash Moore and Howard Rock for help with the size of the Jewish population then; the cartoon, "The Times," by Edward Williams Clay and Henry R. Robinson, is available on Wikipedia under File: The times panic 1837.jpg; Greene, *A Glance*: 12–13.

5. Ernestine L. Rose, "Speech at the New England Anti-Slavery Convention," 1855, in Paula Doress-Worters, ed., *Mistress of Herself: Speeches and Letters of Ernestine L. Rose, Early Women's Rights Leader* (New York: Feminist Press, 2008): 188; Greene, *A Glance*: 219.

6. Jane Wheeler, "Clothing of the 1830s," *www.connorprairie.org*; *The Beacon*, December 23, 1837. In her 1856 description of Rose, d'Héricourt wrote that she did not "hide" her hair. Jenny P. d'Héricourt, "Madame Rose," *La Revue Philosophique et Religieuse* (Paris: Bureaux de la Revue, 1856), vol. 5: 129.

7. J. F. C. Harrison, *Robert Owen and the Owenites in Britain and America: The Quest for the New Moral World* (London: Routledge & Kegan Paul, 1969): 3; Frank Thistlethwaite, *America and the Atlantic Community: Anglo-American Aspects, 1790–1850* (New York: Harper & Row, 1959): 59–60; the merchant was John Pintard, cited in Ernst, *Immigrant Life*: 23.

8. "Overflowing houses," Benjamin Offen, quoted in Albert Post, *Popular Freethought in America, 1825–1850* (New York: Columbia University Press, 1943): 90; Greene, *A Glance*: 47. The Tammany Hall Society had existed since the late eighteenth century; its new home on East 14th Street was built in 1830.

9. Post, *Popular Freethought*: 129–130; see *The Beacon*, November 19, 1842, for a list of Herttell's writings; cited in Norma Basch, *In the Eyes of the Law: Women, Marriage, and Property in Nineteenth-Century New York* (Ithaca, NY: Cornell University Press, 1982): 66; Ernestine L. Rose, Letter to Susan B. Anthony, 1877, in Doress-Worters, *Mistress of Herself*: 348. For one example of Rose referring back to her petitioning, see the *New York Times*, May 14, 1869.

10. Ernestine L. Rose, Speech, *Proceedings of the Free Convention, held at Rutland, Vt., July* [*sic*, although the convention actually took place in June] *the 25th, 26th, and 27th, 1858* (Boston: J. B. Yerrinton and Son, 1858): 31; *The Beacon*, March 16, 1839, on Offen; *The Beacon*, June 3, 1837, on the debate.

11. *The Beacon*, June 3, 1837, October 14, 1837; *Boston Investigator*, August 6, 1845: 3; *The Beacon*, March 31, 1838. For some other "Polish lady" references, see *The Beacon*, August 5, 1837, September 9, 1837, October 7, 21, 28, 1837, and December 23, 1837. Today, Frankfort Street lies under the entrance to the Brooklyn Bridge. The Roses lived in fifteen homes during their thirty-three years in New York. None of them still existed in 1939–40, when the Works Progress Administration (WPA) did a photographic survey of Manhattan. Thanks to Jahongir Usmanov for help with this point.

12. *The Beacon*, June 3, 1837, August 5, 1837, December 23, 1837, March 31, 1838.

13. *The Beacon*, June 3, 1837; Trollope, *Domestic Manners*: 75; de Tocqueville cited in Celia Morris Eckhardt, *Fanny Wright: Rebel in America* (Cambridge MA: Harvard University Press, 1984): 170.

14. "Red Harlot of Infidelity" from the 1836 *Advocate of Moral Reform*, cited in Lori D. Ginzberg, "'The Hearts of Your Readers Will Shudder': Fanny Wright, Infidelity, and American Freethought," *American Quarterly*, vol. 46, #2 (June, 1994): 195; "crazy, atheistical woman" from the 1829 *Commercial Advertiser* cited in Ginzberg, "'The Hearts of Your Readers Will Shudder'": 203–204.

15. *The Beacon*, December 23, 1837. This scene is also discussed in Chapter 2, this volume.

16. On Kneeland's conviction, see Stephan Papa, *The Last Man Jailed for Blasphemy* (Franklin, NC: Trillium Books, 1998); Ernestine L. Rose, Letter, *Boston Investigator*, May 27, 1885: 4; *The Beacon*, December 23, 1837; cited in Post, *Popular Freethought*: 203–205, 208–209; cited in Ginzberg, "'The Hearts of Your Readers Will Shudder'": 207.

17. Cited in Mary Ryan, *Women in Public: Between Banners and Ballots, 1825–1880* (Baltimore, MD: Johns Hopkins University Press, 1990): 27; cited in Ginzberg, "'The Hearts of Your Readers Will Shudder'": 203. For the biblical verses about Lot's daughters, see *Genesis* 19: 30–38. Cited in Post, *Popular Freethought*: 79.

18. *Connecticut Courant*, February 9, 1839: 1.

19. *The Beacon*, January 26, 1839; Robert Dale Owen, Letter, *Boston Investigator*, May 5, 1837: 3; Ernestine Louise Rose, Letter to Robert Owen, December, 1844, #1344, Owen Archives, Co-operative College, Holyoake House, Manchester, England. The version printed in Doress-Worters, *Mistress of Herself*: 65–67, has been considerably cleaned up. Ernestine L. Rose, Letter to the *Boston Investigator*, 1860, in Doress-Worters, *Mistress of Herself*, 258. See Doress-Worters, *Mistress of Herself*: 260–261, for Rose's expansion of these remarks at the Tenth National Woman's Rights Convention in May 1860.

20. *The Beacon*, January 26, 1837, February 22, 1843, July 1, 1843, August 10, 1844, March 29, 1845; Thomas Paine, *The Age of Reason*, ed. Philip Sheldon Foner (New York: Citadel Press, 1974): 50ff; Twain cited in Walter Woll, *Thomas Paine: Motives for Rebellion* (Frankfurt am Main: Peter Lang, 1992): 197; Ernestine L. Rose, Letter, *Boston Investigator*, February 15, 1865: 2.

21. Kenneth W. Burchell, "Birthday Party Politics: The Thomas Paine Birthday Celebrations and the Origins of American Democratic Reform," in Ronald F. King and Elsie Begler, eds., *Thomas Paine: Common Sense for the Modern Era* (San Diego, CA: San Diego State University Press, 2007): 174–189, *passim*; Ernestine L. Rose, Letter, *Boston Investigator*, February 9, 1881: 2.

22. *Boston Investigator*, February 19, 1840, excerpted in Doress-Worters, *Mistress of Herself*: 59–61.

23. For AACAN and Masquerier, Gregory Claeys, "Lewis Masquerier and the Later Development of American Owenism, 1835–1845," *Labor History*, vol. 29, #2 (Spring 1988): 238, gives a list of the US branch's members; for Masquerier as Rose's friend, Ernestine L. Rose, Letter, *Boston Investigator*, February 9, 1881: 2; Sara A. Underwood, "Ernestine Rose," in *Heroines of Free Thought* (New York: C. Sowerby, 1876): 265; d'Héricourt, "Madame Rose": 139; Carol Kolmerten, *The American Life of Ernestine L. Rose* (Syracuse, NY: Syracuse University Press, 1999): 38, fn. 1; *Proceedings of the Woman's Rights Convention held at West Chester, Pa. [sic], June 2nd and 3rd, 1852* (Philadelphia: Merrihew and Thomson, 1852): 18; Ernestine L. Rose, Letter to Robert Owen, in Doress-Worters, *Mistress of Herself*: 66.

24. In 1881, Rose listed friends who accompanied her to the Paine banquets as "Francis Pares, Osborn, Thomas, James and Alfred Thompson, Oliver White, Dr. Hull, Mr. Vale, Mr. Webb, Benjamin Walker, Robert Walker, Mr. Payon, Mr. Masquerier, and many others." Ernestine L. Rose, Letter, *Boston Investigator*, February 9, 1881: 2; for J. P. Mendum, Obituary, *Boston Investigator*, January 21, 1891: 1–2; for James Thompson, Ernestine L. Rose, Letter, *Boston Investigator*, February 8, 1871: 2; for William Wright, Ernestine L. Rose, Letter, *Boston Investigator*, June 3, 1874: 2; the unidentified person signed his letter "W. W.," but wrote after William Wright had died. Letter, *Boston Investigator*, August 14, 1878: 3.

25. *Herald of Freedom* (Concord, NH), November 3, 1843.

26. *The Working Man's Advocate*, July 20, 1844: 4; John Humphrey Noyes, *History of American Socialisms* (Philadelphia: J. Lippincott, 1870): 163–166; for Rose's Boston lectures, *Boston Investigator*, March 27, 1844, April 3, 1844; Linck C. Johnson, "Reforming the Reformers: Emerson, Thoreau, and the Sunday Lectures at Amory Hall, Boston," *ESQ* (1991): 241, which mentions Rose's talk there on "Social Reform"; Mrs. Rose, "Social Re-Organization," *The Communitist*, October 2, 1844. Doress-Worters, *Mistress of Herself*, gives an exerpt from this three-hour speech: 62–64.

27. Noyes, *History of American Socialisms*: 177–179; Ernestine L. Rose, Letter to Robert Owen, December, 1844 in Doress-Worters, *Mistress of Herself*: 65–66.

28. "Mrs. Rose, Social Lecturer," *Boston Investigator*, March 27, 1844: 3.

29. Post, *Popular Freethought*: 100–101, 125, 160–161, 50–51; Claeys, "Lewis Masquerier": 235–236; Barbara Taylor, *Eve and the New Jerusalem: Socialism and Feminism in the Nineteenth Century* [Great Britain] (New York: Pantheon,

1983): 249, 258–259; Harrison, *Robert Owen and the Owenites*: 191–192. A lone, small Owenite commune managed to survive in Wales until the 1850s.

30. *Boston Investigator*, May 14, 1845: 1. The complete convention proceedings were published in this issue and that of May 28, 1845: 1. They were also reprinted as *The Meteor of Light, containing the Minutes of the Proceedings of the Infidel Convention, held in the City of New York, May 4th, 5th, and 6th, 1845* (Boston: J. P. Mendum, 1845).

31. The European delegates were Robert Owen (England) and Henry Schroeder (Germany). The other women were Laurinda Brunsen (New York), Hannah Allen (New York), Ruth Brettelle (New Jersey), Eliza Smith (Pennsylvania), and Mrs. Otis Hinckley [*sic*] (Indiana). *Boston Investigator*, May 14, 1845: 1; Burrows and Wallace, *Gotham*: 735–736.

32. This debate was not reprinted in the *Boston Investigator* and was only partially provided in the *Meteor of Light*. It appears in *The Beacon*, June 1, 1845: 191. Thanks to Marcia Gallo for help with the point about "queer."

33. Cited in Post, *Popular Freethought*: 169.

34. Mrs. Rose, Speech at the New England Social Reform Society Convention, 1844, in Doress-Worters, *Mistress of Herself*: 63–64.

35. Cited in A. L. Morton, *The Life and Ideas of Robert Owen* (New York: International Publishers, 1969): 63.

36. *Proceedings of the Free Convention*: 30.

37. D'Héricourt, "Madame Rose": 130; *Herald of Freedom*, November 3, 1843; Mrs. Rose, Speech at the New England Social Reform Society Convention (which should not be confused with the New England Moral Reform Society, created to "reform" prostitutes), 1844, in Doress-Worters, *Mistress of Herself*: 63.

CHAPTER 4

1. *New York Herald*, May 14, 1858: 3. Although the word "feminism" did not exist until the late nineteenth century, its meaning is appropriate for the early women's rights movement as well. On this subject, see Bonnie S. Anderson, *Joyous Greetings: The First International Women's Movement, 1830–1860* (New York: Oxford University Press, 2000): 3, and Karen M. Offen, "On the French Origin of the Words *Feminism* and *Feminist*," *Feminist Issues*, vol. 8, #2 (Fall 1988): 45–51; Ernestine Rose, from the *Albany Argus*, March 4, 1854, cited in Elizabeth Cady Stanton, Susan B. Anthony, and Matilda Joslyn Gage, eds., *History of Woman Suffrage* (Reprint Salem, NH: Ayer and Co., 1985), vol. 1: *1848–1861* [1881]: 607.

2. Paulina W. Davis, *A History of the National Woman's Rights Movement* (Reprint New York: Source Books, 1970 [1871]): 11; William E. Rose, Letter to Robert Owen, 1845, in Paula Doress-Worters, ed., *Mistress of Herself: Speeches and Letters of Ernestine L. Rose, Early Women's Rights Leader* (New York: Feminist Press, 2008): 71; *Boston Investigator*, October 8, 1845: 3, October 15, 1845: 3, July 29,

1846: 3, August 26, 1846: 1, December 23, 1846: 3. For this gendered treatment of tuberculosis in the period, see Sheila M. Rothman, *Living in the Shadow of Death: Tuberculosis and the Social Experience of Illness in America* (Baltimore, MD: Johns Hopkins University Press, 1995), parts I and II.

3. *Boston Investigator*, July 29, 1846: 3, writing about events at the end of March that year; Stanton, Anthony, and Gage, *History of Woman Suffrage*, vol. 3, *1876–1885* [1886]: 515.

4. For Royall, Annie Laurie Gaylor, ed., *Women without Superstition: "No Gods—No Masters": Selected Writings of Women Freethinkers of the Nineteenth and Twentieth Centuries* (Madison, WI: Freedom from Religion Foundation, 1997): 23–32, and Cynthia Earman, "An Uncommon Scold," *Treasure Talk*, Library of Congress, January 2001; for Anthony, *The Selected Papers of Elizabeth Cady Stanton and Susan B. Anthony,* vol. 1: *In the School of Anti-Slavery 1840–1866*, ed. Ann D. Gordon (New Brunswick, NJ: Rutgers University Press, 1997): 265–266. Any abbreviations and misspellings in Anthony's diary have been preserved here.

5. The friend was Moncure D. Conway; the advertisements cannot be found. Cited in Sara A. Underwood, "Ernestine L. Rose," in *Heroines of Free Thought* (New York: C. Somerby, 1876): 270–271.

6. Ernestine L. Rose, Speech at the Anniversary of the West Indian Emancipation, 1853, in Doress-Worters, *Mistress of Herself*: 151.

7. US and British anti-slavery women gathered tens of thousands of names on abolitionist petitions. The US Congress passed the "Gag Rules" from 1836 to 1844 to prevent these petitions from even being presented.

8. Rose was the only woman in a group that included Emerson and Thoreau. She spoke on "Social Reform." Linck C. Johnson, "Reforming the Reformers: Emerson, Thoreau, and the Sunday Lectures at Amory Hall, Boston," *ESQ* 37 (1991): 235–289.

9. Cited in Julie Roy Jeffrey, "Permeable Boundaries: Abolitionist Women and Separate Spheres," *Journal of the Early Republic*, vol. 21 (Spring 2001): 89; Foster cited in Anna M. Speicher, *The Religious World of Antislavery Women: Spirituality in the Lives of Five Abolitionist Lecturers* (Syracuse, NY: Syracuse University Press, 2000): 89; Angelina Grimké cited in Katherine Du Pre Lumpkin, *The Emancipation of Angelina Grimké* (Chapel Hill: University of North Carolina Press, 1974): 107; Abby Kelley cited in Blanche Glassman Hersh, *The Slavery of Sex: Feminist-Abolitionists in America* (Urbana: University of Illinois Press, 1978): 34.

10. Ernestine L. Rose, Speech at the Anniversary of the West Indian Emancipation, 1853, in Doress-Worters, *Mistress of Herself*: 149–150.

11. Albert Post, *Popular Free Thought in America 1825–1850* (New York: Columbia University Press, 1943): 208; cited in Gregory Claeys, "Lewis Masquerier and the Later Development of American Owenism, 1835–1845," *Labor History*, vol. 29, #2 (Spring 1988): 234; cited in Oliver Johnson, *William Lloyd Garrison and His Times* (Boston: B. B. Russell, 1879): 79. Thanks to Harriet Alonso for supplying this quotation.

12. Nancy A. Hewitt, "Feminist Frequencies: Regenerating the Wave Metaphor," *Feminist Studies*, vol. 38, #3 (Fall 2012): 669–670; Julia Wilbur Papers, Box 3: Diaries, 1844–1865, Quaker History Collection, Haverford College, Haverford, PA, November 30, 1853; William C. Nell to Amy Post, November 10, 1857, in *William Cooper Nell, Selected Writings 1832–1874*, ed. Dorothy Porter Wesley and Constance Porter Uzelac (Baltimore, MD: Black Classics Press, 2002): 496. Thanks to Nancy Hewitt for sending me the Wilbur and Nell documents.

13. Lucretia Mott to Richard and Hannah Webb, May 14, 1849, in *Selected Letters of Lucretia Coffin Mott*, ed. Beverly Wilson Palmer (Urbana: University of Illinois Press, 2002): 185; Lucretia Mott, Sermon at the Unitarian Church, Brooklyn, November 24, 1867, in Dana Greene, ed., *Lucretia Mott: Her Complete Speeches and Sermons* (New York: Edwin Mellon, 1980): 300–301; Lucretia Mott to Elizabeth Cady Stanton, March 16, 1855, in *Selected Letters*: 236; Ernestine L. Rose, Speech at the Fourth National Woman's Rights Convention, 1853, in Doress-Worters, *Mistress of Herself*: 162.

14. Cited in Dorothy Sterling, *Ahead of Her Time: Abby Kelley and the Politics of Antislavery* (New York: W.W. Norton, 1991): 138, 142, 384.

15. Cited in the *Boston Investigator*, September 5, 1849: 3; Kelley Foster cited in Sterling, *Ahead of Her Time*: 253.

16. Cited in *William Lloyd Garrison 1805–1879: The Story of His Life Told by His Children* (Boston: Houghton Mifflin, 1894), vol. 3: 281, 297; *The Liberator*, May 17, 1850: 2.

17. Philip S. Foner, ed., *Frederick Douglass on Women's Rights* (New York: Da Capo Press, 1992 [1976]): 158, 167, 18. For Rose's active support of black women's voting rights, see Chapter 7 in this volume.

18. For New York State, see Carole Shammas, "Re-Assessing the Married Women's Property Acts," *Journal of Women's History*, vol. 6, #1 (Spring 1994): 14; for Rose, "Woman's Rights," 1860, in Doress-Worters, *Mistress of Herself*: 259.

19. Davis, *History*: 11, footnote; E. C. S. [Elizabeth Cady Stanton], "Reminiscences of Paulina Wright Davis," in Stanton, Anthony, and Gage, *History of Woman Suffrage*, vol. 1: 283; Paulina Wright, Letter to Abby Kelley, December 25, 1842, in Sterling, *Ahead of Her Time*: 160. For Davis's anatomy lectures, see the Paulina Wright Davis Papers, Vassar College Library, Folder 46. No biography of Davis currently exists. The best summary of her life is Sarah Henry Lederman's piece on her for Wikipedia.

20. Paulina Wright Davis in *The Una*, April 1854, vol. 2, #4: 243; Davis, *History*: 11–12, 19.

21. Elizabeth Cady Stanton, Scrapbooks, Vassar College Library; Elizabeth Cady Stanton, *Eighty Years and More: Reminiscences 1815–1897* (Reprint New York: Schocken Books, 1971 [1898]): 150.

22. Stanton, Anthony, and Gage, *History of Woman Suffrage*, vol. 1: 422. For Stanton's life in these years, see Elisabeth Griffith, *In Her Own Right: The Life of Elizabeth Cady Stanton* (New York: Oxford University Press, 1984), ch. 3, and Lori D. Ginzberg, *Elizabeth Cady Stanton: An American Life* (New York: Hill and Wang,

2009), ch. 2. Thanks to Carol Faulkner for information on Mott and Stanton's meetings.

23. For the proceedings of these two conventions, see the Library of Congress website, www.loc.gov.

24. Only the Motts and one other participant lived more than forty miles away, and all three were then visiting relatives in the region. For distances traveled, Judith Wellman, "The Seneca Falls Women's Rights Convention: A Study of Social Networks," *Journal of Women's History*, vol. 3, #1 (Spring 1991): 14; for Douglass's editorial, Stanton, Anthony, and Gage, *History of Woman Suffrage*, vol. 1: 74–75; for the *New York Herald*, Stanton, Anthony, and Gage, *History of Woman Suffrage*, vol. 1: 805. For the importance of the Seneca Falls convention, Judith Wellman, *The Road to Seneca Falls: Elizabeth Cady Stanton and the First Woman's Rights Convention* (Urbana: University of Illinois Press, 2004), 10–11.

25. Ernestine L. Rose, Speech at the Fourth National Woman's Rights Convention, 1853, in Doress-Worters, *Mistress of Herself*: 158.

26. Abner Kneeland died in 1844, Benjamin Offen in 1848, and Thomas Herttell in 1849; *Boston Investigator*, February 16, 1848: 1. I have been unable to discover the author, title, or provenance of this poem. Rose used it in an 1847 letter she wrote to the Boston Infidel Relief Society and at the 1849 Paine Dinner. *Boston Investigator*, December 1, 1847: 3; Doress-Worters, *Mistress of Herself* : 73–74; toast to Rose made at the 1850 Paine dinner, in Doress-Worters, *Mistress of Herself* : 75; for the other toasts, *The Beacon*, February 8, 1840: 92.

27. *Boston Investigator*, February 21, 1849: 1. This passage is not included in Doress-Worters's edited version of Rose's speech (*Mistress of Herself*). *Boston Investigator*, February 2, 1850: 1; Ernestine L. Rose, Speech at the Thomas Paine Celebration, 1850, in Doress-Worters, *Mistress of Herself*: 75, 77. After the brief 1848 Polish uprising against Russia failed, Bem fought for Hungary against Austria.

28. Ernestine L. Rose, Paine Speech, 1850, in Doress-Worters, *Mistress of Herself*: 78. Jagiello information drawn from Ellen C. Clayton, *Female Warriors: Memorials of Female Valour and Heroism from the Mythological Ages to the Present*, 2 vols. (London: Tinsley Bros., 1879), vol. 2: 105–107. Thanks to Agnieszka Klimek for help with Jagiello, whose last name is often misspelled "Jagella" or "Jagello." Ernestine Rose, Speech, *Proceedings of the Woman's Rights Convention Held at Worcester October 23 and 24, 1850* (Boston: Prentiss & Sawyer, 1851): 15.

29. *The Liberator*, June 7, 1850: 3. Despite the committee, Davis ended up doing all the work herself. Davis, *History*: 12–13; John F. McClymer, *This High and Holy Moment: The First National Woman's Rights Convention, Worcester, 1850* (New York: Harcourt Brace, 1999): 67–68.

30. McClymer, *This High and Holy Moment*: 67–69; *Proceedings . . . 1850*: 7, 9, 20, 46, 51, 53. The second speaker was Abby Price, from the Christian commune of Hopedale.

31. The first phrases in this sentence are from Rose's speech at the Eighth National Woman's Rights Convention in 1858, used at the beginning of this chapter. *New York Herald*, May 14, 1858: 3. The last phrase contrasts free thought as "of more importance even than the one that has so long lain at my heart, the rights of woman." Ernestine L. Rose, Speech at the Hartford Bible Convention, 1853, in Doress-Worters, *Mistress of Herself*: 136.

32. Ernestine Rose, Resolution and Speech, National Woman's Rights Convention, 1850, from the *New York Tribune*, October 25, 1850, reprinted in Doress-Worters, *Mistress of Herself*: 81–82; *Proceedings . . . 1850*: 14; the newspaper was the Boston *Chronotype*; McClymer, *This High and Holy Moment*: 104.

33. *Proceedings . . . 1850*: 15; Rose's speech as reported in the Boston *Daily Mail*, reprinted in McClymer, *This High and Holy Moment*: 119.

34. *Proceedings . . . 1850*: 15, 16, 17; *New-York Tribune*, October 26, 1850, reprinted in McClymer, *This High and Holy Moment*: 140, 148; *Proceedings . . . 1850*: 19–20. The other committees were the Central Committee, the Committee on Education, the Committee on Industrial Avocations, the Committee on Social Relations, and the Committee of Publication. All were headed by women except the Committee on Industrial Avocations.

35. Harriot K. Hunt, M.D., *Glances and Glimpses: Or Fifty Years Social, including Twenty Years Professional Life* (Reprint New York: Source Book Press, 1970 [1856]): 252; for the *Tribune*, Doress-Worters *Mistress of Herself*: 81; for the *Daily Mail*, McClymer, *This High and Holy Moment*: 107.

36. Cited in McClymer, *This High and Holy Moment*: 154–155, 157.

37. For the participants, Stanton, Anthony, and Gage, *History of Woman Suffrage*, vol. 1: 824–825; for the Committees, *Proceedings . . . 1850*: 19; Susan B. Anthony cited in *Elizabeth Cady Stanton/Susan B. Anthony: Correspondence, Writings, Speeches*, ed. and intro. Ellen Carol DuBois (New York: Schocken Books, 1981): 243.

38. Ernestine L. Rose, Speech at the Second National Woman's Rights Convention, 1851, in Doress-Worters, *Mistress of Herself*: 98, 102.

CHAPTER 5

1. Ernestine Rose, "Woman's Rights," 1860, in Paula Doress-Worters, ed., *Mistress of Herself: Speeches and Letters of Ernestine L. Rose, Early Women's Rights Leader* (New York: Feminist Press, 2008): 258–259.

2. She probably traveled through Connecticut, Delaware, Illinois, Indiana, Iowa, Kentucky, Maine, Maryland, Massachusetts, Michigan, Missouri, New Hampshire, New Jersey, New York, North Carolina, Ohio, Pennsylvania, Rhode Island, South Carolina, Tennessee, Vermont, Virginia, and Wisconsin. She did not visit Alabama, Arkansas, California, Florida, Louisiana, Mississippi, or Texas. L[emuel] E. Barnard, "Ernestine L. Rose," *The Liberator*, May 16, 1856, reprinted with later additions by Susan B. Anthony in Elizabeth Cady Stanton, Susan B. Anthony, and

Matilda Joslyn Gage, eds., *History of Woman Suffrage* (Reprint Salem, NH: Ayer, 1985 [1881]), vol. 1, *1848–1861*: 97; Jenny P. d'Héricourt, "Madame Rose," (*La Revue Philosophique et Religieuse*), 1856, vol. 5: 135; Farewell Letter of Mrs. Rose, 1856, in Doress-Worters, *Mistress of Herself*: 209.

3. For the schedule Anthony set up, which called for two lectures a day from January 5 to 26, see *Selected Papers of Elizabeth Cady Stanton and Susan B. Anthony,* vol. 1, *In the School of Anti-Slavery 1840–1866,* ed. Ann D. Gordon (New Brunswick, NJ: Rutgers University Press, 1997): 291; for one instance of Anthony being called "Napoleon," a frequently used nickname, see Antoinette Brown in *The Liberator,* October 14, 1855; Ernestine Rose, Taunton correspondence with Charles H. Plummer, 1854–55, Alma Lutz Collection, Vassar College Archives; *Albany State Register,* February 17, 1855, reprinted in *The Liberator,* March 9, 1855.

4. *The Liberator,* March 16, 1855, March 23, 1855, May 25, 1855; Ernestine L. Rose, Speech at the New England Anti-Slavery Convention, 1855, in Doress-Worters, *Mistress of Herself*: 187–193; *The Liberator,* June 1, 1855; Ernestine L. Rose, Letter, written July 25, 1855, published in the *Boston Investigator,* August 1, 1855: 1; *New York Tribune,* July 30, 1855: 1; *The Liberator,* September 14, 1855; *Boston Investigator,* September 19, 1855: 1 and September 26, 1855: 1. The baby's last name was Lyons.

5. Mrs. E. L. Rose, Letter, 1855, in Doress-Worters, *Mistress of Herself*: 194–196; the Proceedings of the Sixth National Woman's Rights Convention appeared in the *New-York Daily Times,* October 23 and 24, 1855; for the Indiana Convention, Stanton, Anthony, and Gage, *History of Woman Suffrage,* vol. 1: 307; *Boston Investigator,* December 12, 1855: 1, 4, December 19, 1855: 4, December 26, 1855: 2.

6. D'Héricourt, "Madame Rose": 139; *Boston Investigator,* February 16, 1859: 1; Ernestine L. Rose, Letter to Charles H. Plummer, January 29, 1855, Vassar College Archives; *Boston Investigator,* Classified advertisement, December 22, 1852: 3. This ad ran throughout the fall of 1852, as well as in 1853 and '54; *Boston Investigator,* Classified advertisement, June 27, 1860: 8, as well as in a number of other issues. *Proceedings of the Woman's Rights Convention held at Syracuse, September 8th, 9th, and 10th, 1852* (Syracuse, NY: J. E. Masters, 1852): 96; *Proceedings of the Presentation to the Honorable Robert Dale Owen of a Silver Pitcher, on behalf of the Women of Indiana, on the 28th Day of May, 1851* (New Albany [IN]: 1851): 4; Martha Wright to Lucretia Mott, March 29, 1855, citing Anthony, in the Garrison Family Papers, Massachusetts Historical Society; Susan B. Anthony in Stanton, Anthony, and Gage, *History of Woman Suffrage,* vol. 1: 98.

7. D'Héricourt, "Madame Rose": 138–139. In describing Rose's pleasure in cooking, d'Héricourt uses an obsolete French idiom, "*chanter sa marmite, comme disent les bonnes femmes.*" Thanks to Claudette Fillard for help with the translation. For more on housework, see Susan Strasser, *Never Done: A History of American Housework* (New York: Pantheon, 1982). On moving, Ernestine Rose, Speech, Tenth National Woman's Rights Convention, 1860, in Doress-Worters, *Mistress of Herself*: 283.

8. *Boston Investigator*, December 5, 1855: 1. William sometimes had male friends stay with him when Ernestine was on the road. One mentioned was S. C. Chandler. Ernestine L. Rose, Letter, 1858 in Doress-Worters, *Mistress of Herself*: 245; *Proceedings of the Woman's Rights Convention, Held at the Broadway Tabernacle, in the City of New York, on Tuesday and Wednesday, Sept. 6th and 7th, 1853* (New York: Fowler and Wells, 1853): 47. In her biography of Ernestine Rose, Carol Kolmerten argues that being called "Mrs. Rose" meant she was an outsider in the women's movement. But this was common usage in the mid-nineteenth century. Anthony and Stanton were each other's best friends for over fifty years, but they remained "Susan" and "Mrs. Stanton" to each other until the end. Carol A. Kolmerten, *The American Life of Ernestine L. Rose* (Syracuse, NY: Syracuse University Press, 1999): 78. Remarks against single women from the *New York Herald*, 1853, cited in Sylvia D. Hoffert, *When Hens Crow: The Woman's Rights Movement in Antebellum America* (Bloomington: Indiana University Press, 1995): 97.

9. *Bangor Jeffersonian*, December 25, 1855, reprinted in *The Liberator*, January 4, 1856: 4. For this subject in general, see Gayle V. Fischer, *Pantaloons and Power: Nineteenth-Century Dress Reform in the United States* (Kent, OH: Kent State University Press, 2001); "The Champions of Woman's Suffrage," *Harper's Bazar*, June 12, 1869: 385.

10. Ernestine L. Rose, Letters to Charles H. Plummer, Alma Lutz Collection, Vassar College Archives; Edwin G. Burrows and Mike Wallace, *Gotham: A History of New York City to 1898* (New York: Oxford University Press, 1999): 655–656; Ernestine L. Rose, Letter, 1853, in Doress-Worters, *Mistress of Herself*: 145.

11. Susan B. Anthony Diary in *Selected Papers of Elizabeth Cady Stanton and Susan B. Anthony*, vol. 1: 294–295, any misspellings or abbreviations are reproduced as written; Joseph Barker, Sheffield Lecture, printed in George Jacob Holyoake's *The Reasoner*, vol. 21, #54, November 2, 1856: 139.

12. From the *Ohio Democrat*, reprinted in the *Boston Investigator*, March 3, 1852: 2; praise for her "argumentative power" from the *New York Herald*, September 12, 1852. For one example of an audience calling for Rose to speak, see the *New York Tribune*, May 13, 1859: 5, reporting on the Ninth National Woman's Rights Convention. The female reporter's comment is in the *Boston Investigator*, May 20, 1860: 1. The reporter published anonymously but was Ada Clare, who wrote for Henry Clapp's *Saturday Press*. Sherry Ceniza, *Walt Whitman and 19th-Century Women Reformers* (Tuscaloosa: University of Alabama Press, 1998): 146.

13. Blanche Glassman Hersh, *The Slavery of Sex: Feminist-Abolitionists in America* (Urbana: University of Illinois Press, 1978): 193–194; Ernestine L. Rose, Speech, *Proceedings of the National Woman's Rights Convention held at Cleveland, Ohio, on Wednesday, Thursday, and Friday, October 5th, 6th, and 7th, 1853* (Cleveland: Gray, Beardsley, Spear, 1854): 33. Rose used nearly identical words at the Fifth National Convention the following year in Philadelphia, in Doress-Worters, *Mistress of Herself*: 179–180, and at the Seventh National in New York

in 1856, in Doress-Worters, *Mistress of Herself*: 226; Ernestine L. Rose, Testimony before New York State Assembly Committee, 1855, in Doress-Worters, *Mistress of Herself*: 185; Ernestine L. Rose, Speech, *Proceedings . . . Cleveland*: 36; for the same argument, also see Ernestine L. Rose, Speech, *Proceedings of the Tenth National Woman's Rights Convention, held at the Cooper Institute, New York City, May 10th and 11th, 1860* (Boston: Yerrinton & Garrison, 1860): 52.

14. For an early petition Rose distributed asking for the vote, see *The Liberator*, January 24, 1851: 6; for the speech cited, Ernestine L. Rose, Speech, Seventh National Woman's Rights Convention, 1856, in Doress-Worters, *Mistress of Herself*: 232; for one example of her refusal to promise how women would use their rights, *Proceedings . . . Cleveland*: 33; Ernestine L. Rose, Speech, Second National Woman's Rights Convention, 1851, in Doress-Worters, *Mistress of Herself*: 92; Ernestine L. Rose, Reviews of Horace Mann's Two Lectures, 1852, in Doress-Worters, *Mistress of Herself*: 109; Ernestine L. Rose, Speech, New England Anti-Slavery Convention, 1855, in Doress-Worters, *Mistress of Herself*: 190.

15. Ernestine L. Rose, Speech, Fourth National Woman's Rights Convention, 1853, in Doress-Worters, *Mistress of Herself*: 158; *New York Herald*, May 14, 1858: 3; Ernestine L. Rose, Speech at the Anniversary of West Indian Emancipation, 1853, in Doress-Worters, *Mistress of Herself*: 148; Ernestine L. Rose, Speech, *Proceedings . . . New York . . . 1853*: 52; Ernestine L. Rose, Speech at the Third National Woman's Rights Convention, 1852, in Doress-Worters, *Mistress of Herself*: 122.

16. Ernestine L. Rose, Reviews of Horace Mann's Two Lectures, in Doress-Worters, *Mistress of Herself*: 111; Ernestine L. Rose, Letter to Joseph Barker, *Boston Investigator*, December 12, 1855: 1.

17. Ernestine L. Rose, Third National Woman's Rights Convention, 1852, in Doress-Worters, *Mistress of Herself*, 127. In 1849, Lucretia Mott gave a similar speech rebutting the critic Richard Henry Dana's lecture arguing that demands for women's rights "unsexed" women. Her "Discourse on Woman," like Rose's 1851 Worcester speech, was published as a tract and widely distributed by the women's movement.

18. *Proceedings . . . Syracuse*: 78–87; for Rose's comments: 85–86.

19. For Mott's introduction of Rose, which is incorrect in Doress-Worters, *Mistress of Herself*: 121, see *Proceedings . . . Syracuse*: 63; for Rose's reply, Doress-Worters, *Mistress of Herself*: 121; for "hen-picked," which was not included in the original *Proceedings*, see *The Liberator*, October 8, 1852: 4; for Brown's feelings for Rose, see her letter of December 19, 1850, where she wrote Lucy Stone from New York City, "If I knew where Mrs. Rose was I would call on her, shall perhaps find her out," cited in *Friends and Sisters: Letters between Lucy Stone and Antoinette Brown Blackwell, 1846–93*, ed. Carol Lasser and Marlene Deahl Merrill (Urbana: University of Illinois Press, 1987): 98. For Rose's other remarks at the convention, Doress-Worters, *Mistress of Herself*: 123, 125–126.

20. For one example of a woman's statement of religious belief, see *Syracuse . . . Proceedings*: 89; for "neither Greek nor Jew," *Galatians* 3:28; for Eve, *Genesis* 3:16;

for an extended account of the biblical argument for women's rights, Lucretia Mott, "Discourse on Woman," in *Lucretia Mott: Her Complete Speeches and Sermons*, ed. Dana Greene (New York: Edwin Mellon Press, 1980): 145ff.; for the hymn, *Proceedings . . . Syracuse*: 97; *Proceedings . . . Cleveland*: 150–170, 185–187; Stanton, Anthony and Gage, *History of Woman Suffrage*, vol. 1: 144; for the Philadelphia Convention, the only proceedings are in *The Liberator*, January 12, 1855: 4. Thanks to Carol Faulkner for help with Grew.

21. Solomon from *Ecclesiastes* 3:1; for one use of this quotation, see *Proceedings . . . Cleveland*: 23; Ernestine Rose, Third National Woman's Rights Convention, 1852, in Doress-Worters, *Mistress of Herself*: 130; Ernestine Rose, Hartford Bible Convention, in Doress-Worters, *Mistress of Herself*: 141. Rose quoted from *John* 3:19.

22. Ernestine L. Rose, Speech, Hartford Bible Convention, in Doress-Worters, *Mistress of Herself*: 144, 137; Ernestine L. Rose, Speech, *Proceedings of the Hartford Bible Convention* (New York: Partridge & Britten, 1854): 330–331. These proceedings are online at https//archive.org/details/proceedingsforharoohart. *William Lloyd Garrison 1805–1879: The Story of His Life Told by His Children* (Boston: Houghton Mifflin, 1894), vol. 3: 385; for the Bangor article and Rose's replies to it, Doress-Worters, *Mistress of Herself*: 197–199; Ella Gibbons, Letter, *Boston Investigator*, June 12, 1889: 3; for Anthony, Yuri Suhl Collection, Box 3, Folder 17, Howard Gotlieb Archives, Boston University; for Rose's attempts to organize other Bible Conventions, which she did with Joseph Barker, Horace Seaver, J. Mendum, J. M. Beckett, and the German freethinker Augustus Theodore Stamm, see the *Boston Investigator*, October 11, 1854: 1, December 12, 1855: 4, and December 19, 1855: 4.

23. *Proceedings . . . New York . . . 1853*: 47, 53, 77, 88; New York *Express* quoted in *The Liberator*, September 16, 1853: 4.

24. *Proceedings . . . New York . . . 1853*: 89, 90, 95; Anneke cited in Gerhard K. Friesen, "A Letter from M. F. Anneke: A Forgotten German-American Pioneer in Women's Rights," *Journal of German-American Studies*, vol. 12, #1 (1977): 38; "Farewell Letter of Mrs. Rose," 1856, in Doress-Worters, *Mistress of Herself*: 209.

25. For Anneke's life, see Susan L. Piepke, *Mathilde Franziska Anneke (1817–1884): The Works and Life of a German-American Activist including English Translations of "Woman in Conflict with Society" and "Broken Chains"* (New York: Peter Lang, 2006), and Maria Wagner, *Mathilde Franziska Anneke in Selbstzeugnissen und Dokumenten* (Frankfurt am Main: Fischer Taschenbuch, 1980). Quotation on religion cited in Piepke, *Mathilde Franziska Anneke*: 35, 31; on Rose, Anneke's *Deutscher Frauen = Zeitung [German Women's Newspaper]*, October 15, 1852: 53. Rose's speech is on pp. 53–55. Although this newspaper ran for two and a half years, this is the only surviving copy and is at the American Antiquarian Society, Worcester, Massachusetts. For Rose speaking to German-American women, Friesen, "A Letter from M. F. Anneke": 39; Anneke's comment on meeting Rose again in 1869 in Wagner, *Mathilde Franziska Anneke*: 346–347. Anneke used the German word "Streiterin," a female fighter for a cause, which I have translated as

"campaigner." Thanks to Jörg Thurow and the German Women's History Study Group for help with this translation.

26. Ernestine L. Rose, Speech, Fourth National Woman's Rights Convention, 1853, in Doress-Worters, *Mistress of Herself*: 159–162.

27. Sallie Holley, *A Life for Liberty: Anti-Slavery and Other Letters of Sallie Holley*, ed. John White Chadwick (New York: G. Putnam's Sons, 1899): 127.

28. Ceniza, *Walt Whitman*: 140, 101; Walt Whitman, *Notebooks and Unpublished Prose Manuscripts* (New York: New York University Press, 1984), vol. 1: 344; Horace Traubel, *With Walt Whitman in Camden* (Carbondale: Southern Illinois Press, 1982), vol. 6: *September 15, 1889—July 6, 1890*: 322–323, vol. 7: *July 7, 1890—February 10, 1891*: 258–259. In his papers at Boston University, Box 4, Folder 4, Yuri Suhl says that Rose's favorite line from Whitman was "I am the poet of the woman the same as the man," from his *Leaves of Grass*, but gives no source for this. I have not found any comment from Rose about Whitman.

29. Hersh, *The Slavery of Sex*: 108. On the anti-alcohol movement and feminism, see Ian Tyrrell, "Women and Temperance in Antebellum America, 1830–1860," in *Civil War History*, vol. 28, #2 (June, 1982): 128–152; Ernestine L. Rose, "Causes of Social Evils: Slavery, Intemperance, and War," *Boston Investigator*, January 25, 1854: 3; "Letters from Mrs. Ernestine L. Rose, No. X," *Boston Investigator*, December 3, 1856: 1. On the split between German immigrants and Americans on the issue of alcohol, see Michaela Bank, *"Women of Two Countries": German-American Women, Women's Rights and Nativism* (New York: Berghahn Books, 2012), *passim*.

30. The Washington Theatre was also known as Carusi's Saloon. Susan B. Anthony Diary, March 21, 1854, *Selected Papers of Elizabeth Cady Stanton and Susan B. Anthony*, vol. 1: 265; Susan B. Anthony Diary, March 24, 1854, in Doress-Worters, *Mistress of Herself*: 170; Susan B. Anthony Diary, March 28, 1854, *Selected Papers of Elizabeth Cady Stanton and Susan B. Anthony*, 270; Susan B. Anthony Diary, April 2, 1854 in Doress-Worters, *Mistress of Herself*: 172.

31. *The Selected Papers of Elizabeth Cady Stanton and Susan B. Anthony*, vol. 1: 268–269. Doress-Worters, *Mistress of Herself*: 172–174, gives the wrong date for this exchange and cuts parts of it. *Proceedings . . . New York . . . 1853*: 90; *Proceedings of the Seventh National Woman's Rights Convention, held in New York City, at the Broadway Tabernacle, on Tuesday and Wednesday, Nov. 25th and 26th, 1856* (New York: Edwin O. Jenkins, 1856): 19. On Phillips, see James Brewer Stewart, *Wendell Phillips: Liberty's Hero* (Baton Rouge: Louisiana State University Press, 1986).

32. *Proceedings . . . Syracuse*: 20; Stanton, Anthony, and Gage, *History of Woman Suffrage*, vol. 1: 650; *New York Tribune*, reprinted in *The Liberator*, November 3, 1854: 4; for one example of Rose being called "exotic," see the *Albany Register*, March 6, 1854, in Doress-Worters, *Mistress of Herself*: 162; for a parody of Rose's accent, the *Buffalo Commercial Advertiser*, reprinted in *The Liberator*, October 21, 1853. For Stone, Andrea Moore Kerr, *Lucy Stone: Speaking Out for Equality* (New Brunswick, NJ: Rutgers University Press, 1992), especially p. 50 for her impact on

audiences and the Higginson quotation. For the other quotations about her, Sally G. McMillan, *Lucy Stone: An Unapologetic Life* (New York: Oxford University Press, 2015): x, 20, 76–78, 80; and Joelle Million, *Woman's Voice, Woman's Place: Lucy Stone and the Birth of the Woman's Rights Movement* (Westport, CT: Praeger, 2003): 96.

33. Lucy Stone to Susan B. Anthony, November 2, 1855, *Stanton and Anthony Papers*, microfilm, reel 8, frames 298–309; Lucy Stone to Susan B. Anthony, March 24, 1859, Blackwell Family Papers, Library of Congress, http://lcweb2.loc.gov/service/mss/eadxmlmss/eadpdfmss/1998/ms998003.pdf. Thanks to Ann D. Gordon for sending me these letters. *Boston Investigator*, March 10, 1886: 6.

34. Susan B. Anthony Diary, April 9, 1854, *Selected Papers of Elizabeth Cady Stanton and Susan B. Anthony*, vol. 1: 269, any misspellings or abbreviations are reproduced as written. The hymn's lyrics, written by Stephen Greenleaf Bulfinch, went

> *All men are equal in their birth,*
> *Heirs of the earth and skies;*
> *All men are equal when that earth*
> *Fades from their dying eyes.*
>
> *God meets the throngs who pay their vows*
> *In courts that hands have made,*
> *And hears the worshiper who bows*
> *Beneath the plantain shade.*
>
> *'Tis man alone who difference sees*
> *And speaks of high and low*
> *And worships these, and tramples those*
> *While the same path they go.*
>
> *On, then, to the glorious field!*
> *He who dies his life shall save;*
> *God himself shall be our shield,*
> *He shall bless and crown the brave.*

Anthony copied the third verse into her diary, so she probably gave that one to Rose; Susan B. Anthony Diary, April 9, 1854, *Selected Papers of Elizabeth Cady Stanton and Susan B. Anthony*, vol. 1: 269–270.

35. Ernestine L. Rose, Speech, Worcester, 1851, in Doress-Worters, *Mistress of Herself*: 103; *Proceedings . . . New York . . . 1853*: 64; Farewell Letter of Mrs. Rose, in Doress-Worters, *Mistress of Herself*: 208.

36. *Boston Investigator*, October 11, 1854: 3; *The Lily*, November 1, 1854; Anthony cited in Dale McGowan, ed., *Voices of Unbelief: Documents from Atheists and Agnostics* (Santa Barbara, CA: ABC-CLIO, 2012): 85; *The Liberator*, January 12, 1855: 4. The *Proceedings* of this convention were not published separately, but appear in this edition of *The Liberator*.

37. *The Liberator*, January 12, 1855: 4; Stamm came from Homburg in Hessen and received an M.D. degree from the University of Pennsylvania in 1855. *Boston Investigator*, October 11, 1854: 1, December 12, 1855: 4, December 19, 1855: 4. For Finch, see Rose's letter on his death, *Boston Investigator*, April 17, 1857: 2. For Assing, Maria Wagner, *Was Die Deutschen aus Amerika berichteten 1828–1865* (Stuttgart: Hans-Dieter Heinz Akademischer Verlag, 1985); Christopher Lohmann, ed., *Radical Passion: Ottilie Assing's Reports from America and Letters to Frederick Douglass* (New York: Peter Lang, 1999): 82. For Assing's life, Maria Diedrich, *Love across Color Lines: Ottilie Assing and Frederick Douglass* (New York: Hill & Wang, 1999).

38. For one instance of Rose's use of Paine's motto, see her speech at the 1851 Paine dinner, *Boston Investigator*, February 12, 1851: 1; *Proceedings . . . New York . . . 1853*: 84, 87.

39. Ernestine L. Rose, Speech at the 1852 Thomas Paine Celebration, *Boston Investigator*, February 11, 1852: 1; Ernestine L. Rose, Speech at the 1855 Thomas Paine Celebration, in Doress-Worters, *Mistress of Herself*: 182.

40. Farewell Letter of Mrs. Rose, in Doress-Worters, *Mistress of Herself*: 208.

CHAPTER 6

1. *Boston Investigator*, July 7, 1858: 2 for the weather; *Proceedings of the Free Convention, held at Rutland, Vt., July* [*sic*, although the convention took place on these dates in June, not July] *25th, 26th, and 27th, 1858* (Boston: J. B. Yerrinton and Son, 1858): 11, https://archive.org/details/proceedingoffreoofreerich.

2. *Proceedings . . . Free*: 120; on the Davises, see Ann Braude, *Radical Spirits: Spiritualism and Women's Rights in Nineteenth-Century America* (Boston: Beacon Press, 1989), passim.

3. "Moral Lunatics" from the Portland, Maine, *Advertiser* and *Burlington Free Press* cited in Thomas L. Altherr, "A Convention of 'Moral Lunatics': The Rutland, Vermont Free Convention of 1858," *Vermont History* 69 (Symposium Supplement), 2001: 90, 101; *New York Times*, June 29, 1858; *New York Tribune*, reprinted in *The Liberator*, July 9, 1858; *New York Times*, June 29, 1858.

4. Henry David Thoreau, *Civil Disobedience*, part 2 (1849). Thanks to Claudette Fillard for suggesting this reference. Susan B. Anthony, Letter to Mr. Garrison, in Paula Doress-Worters, ed., *Mistress of Herself: Speeches and Letters of Ernestine L. Rose, Early Women's Rights Leader* (New York: Feminist Press, 2008): 178.

5. Ernestine L. Rose, Farewell Letter, in Doress-Worters, *Mistress of Herself*: 208–209. This was not the famous portrait of Paine done by John Wesley Jarvis in 1805, which hangs in the Smithsonian. Jarvis suffered a stroke in 1834, so Rose's painting was most likely a copy done by his son, the painter Charles Wesley Jarvis. J. M. Wheeler to Moncure D. Conway in *The Freethinker*, vol. 17, part 2, October 3, 1897: 637. The source of the Roses' extra income is unclear, but a few years later, they had invested in Boston and Chicago properties. See Chapter 8 for more detail.

6. For information on Lemuel Barnard, thanks to Reginald H. Pitts, State University of New York at Old Westbury and the Western Reserve Historical Society in Cleveland. Barnard published as "L. E. Barnard," so in women's history circles, his gender was in doubt. His piece on Rose was first published in his new magazine *Excelsior, or the Reformer's Companion* early in 1856. Information on the *Excelsior* from *The Criterion: Literary and Critical Journal*, vol. 1, #13 (1856): 201. This original version of Barnard's article was reprinted in *The Liberator*, May 16, 1856, and the *Boston Investigator*, July 9, 1856: 4. The better known version, from Elizabeth Cady Stanton, Susan B. Anthony, and Matilda Joslyn Gage, eds., *History of Woman Suffrage* (Reprint Salem NH: Ayer Publishers, 1985 [1881]), vol. 1, *1848–1861*: 95–100, diverges from the original in the middle of Barnard's second-to-last paragraph, where Susan B. Anthony changed the sentence "for twenty-four years a public speaker" to "for fifty years a public speaker." She then added four pages of her own reminiscences and an 1877 letter from Rose. That version eliminates Barnard's last paragraph, which I cite.

7. "Letters from Mrs. Ernestine L. Rose, No. I," *Boston Investigator*, July 30, 1856: 1.

8. *The Reasoner*, June 1, 1856, vol. 20, #522: 170; *The Reasoner*, June 8, 1856, vol. 20, #523: 181–182.

9. "Letters from Mrs. Ernestine L. Rose, No. II," in Doress-Worters, *Mistress of Herself*: 211–212; "Letter from Mrs. Rose," *Boston Investigator*, November 26, 1856: 1. Also see George Jacob Holyoake, Letter to Robert Owen, #2606, Co-operative College, Holyoake House, Manchester, England, where Holyoake informs Owen that Rose wants to see him again before she leaves.

10. By the time Rose visited the Crystal Palace, it had been moved from Hyde Park to Sydenham, a London suburb. It still housed important exhibitions. "Letters from Mrs. Ernestine L. Rose, No. II," *Boston Investigator*, August 6, 1856: 1; "Letters from Mrs. Ernestine L. Rose, No. III," *Boston Investigator*, August 13, 1856: 1; "Letters from Mrs. Ernestine L. Rose, No. IV," *Boston Investigator*, August 20, 1856: 1.

11. *Mary Howitt: An Autobiography*, ed. Margaret Howitt (London: Wm. Isbister, 1889), 2 vols., vol. 2: 69; Ernestine L. Rose, Speech, Seventh National Woman's Rights Convention, in Doress-Worters, *Mistress of Herself*: 223–234.

12. For Barbara Leigh Smith, see Sheila R. Herstein, *A Mid-Victorian Feminist: Barbara Leigh Smith Bodichon* (New Haven, CT: Yale University Press, 1985), especially ch. 3, "First Attempts: An Educational Experiment and the Married Women's Property Campaign." For that campaign, Rebecca Probert, "Family Law Reform and the Women's Movement in England and Wales, 1830–1914," in Stephan Meder and Christoph-Eric Mecke, eds., *Family Law in Early Women's Rights Debates: Western Europe and the United States in the Nineteenth and Early Twentieth Centuries* (Köln: Böhlau Verlag, 2012): 184–185; for Parkes, Emma Lowndes, *Turning Victorian Ladies into Women: The Life of Bessie Rayner Parkes 1829–1925* (Palo Alto, CA: Academica Press, 2012); [Bessie Rayner Parkes], *Remarks on the Education of Girls* (London: John Chapman, 1854): 12, 20; for Fox, Brenda Colloms, "Fox, Eliza

Florence Bridell (1823/4–1903)," *Oxford Dictionary of National Biography*, online edition, October 2009.

13. Ernestine Rose, Speech, Seventh National Woman's Rights Convention, in Doress-Worters, *Mistress of Herself*: 224, and *The Woman's Rights Almanac for 1858, Containing Facts, Statistics, Arguments, Records and Progress, and Proofs of the Need of It* (Worcester, MA: Z. Baker; Boston: R. F. Walcott): 21. I have corrected the spelling of Deroin's name, which Americans often mangled. For confirmation of Rose's description of Deroin, see Adrien Ranvier, "Une Féministe de 1848: Jeanne Deroin," *La Révolution de 1848: Bulletin de la Société d'histoire de la révolution de 1848*, 4 (1907–1908): 495.

14. Thanks to Claire Moses for helping to identify Lemonnier, whose name the *Boston Investigator* spelled as "Lemourier." Rose wrote in longhand and was not a perfect speller; her editors probably did not know French, so foreign names were often distorted: the "Champs Élysées" becomes the "Champs Ulysses" twice in their pages. Rose also mentioned Charles Lemaire and Felix Etienne, whom I have been unable to identify. "Letters from Mrs. Ernestine L. Rose, No. IX," *Boston Investigator*, November 26, 1856: 1; Madame D'Héricourt, "What M. Proudhon Thinks of Women," *The Reasoner*, vol. 22, #562, March 8, 1857, 1. Bessie Rayner Parkes translated some of d'Héricourt's pieces into English and Holyoake published them.

15. "Letters from Mrs. Ernestine L. Rose, No. IX," *Boston Investigator*, November 26, 1856: 1. For d'Héricourt's life, Karen Offen, "A Nineteenth-Century French Feminist Rediscovered: Jenny P. d'Héricourt 1809–1875," *Signs: Journal of Women in Culture and Society*, vol. 13, #1 (Autumn, 1987): 144–158; for Mikhailov, Richard Stites, "M. L. Mikhailov and the Emergence of the Woman Question in Russia," *Canadian Slavic Studies*, vol. 3, #2 (Summer, 1969): 178–199; d'Héricourt published her pieces in the radical Turin journal *La Ragione* (*Reason*).

16. For d'Héricourt's use of "biography" to describe her piece, Jenny P. d'Héricourt, "Mrs. Ernestine L. Rose," *Boston Investigator*, December 8, 1869: 2; for the quotation about Rose, Jenny P. d'Héricourt, "Madame Rose," *Revue Philosophique et Religieuse*, vol. 5, 1856: 136. The 1869 *Investigator* piece is a shortened, English version of d'Héricourt's original 1856 article. For an English translation of this article, which I sometimes depart from, see Paula Doress-Worters, ed., "Madame Rose: A Life of Ernestine L. Rose as told to Jenny P. d'Héricourt," *Journal of Women's History*, vol. 15, #1 (2003): 183–201; Jenny P. d'Héricourt, "La Bible et La Question des Femmes," *Revue Philosophique et Religieuse*, vol. 6, August 1, 1857: 16–34.

17. D'Héricourt, "Madame Rose": 129–130.

18. D'Héricourt, "Madame Rose": 135, 137–138.

19. "Letters from Mrs. Ernestine L. Rose, No. XI," *Boston Investigator*, December 3, 1856: 1. In this letter, Rose mentions visiting [any misspellings are preserved throughout] Lyons, Geneva, Chamberry, Basle, Strasborg, Badenbaden, Heidelberg, Frankfort, Coblentz, Cologne, Berlin, Dresden, Prague, Vienna, Trieste, Venice, Milan, Turin, Genoa, Leghorn, Florence, Rome, Naples, Pompei, Mt. Vesuvius, and Marseilles;

"Letter from Mrs. Rose," *Boston Investigator*, November 26, 1856: 2; "Letters from Mrs. Ernestine L. Rose, No. XI," in Doress-Worters, *Mistress of Herself*, 220; "Farewell Letter of Mrs. Rose," in Doress-Worters, *Mistress of Herself*, 209; "Letter from Mrs. Rose," *Boston Investigator*, November 26, 1856: 2.

20. Ernestine L. Rose, Speech, Seventh National Woman's Rights Convention, in Doress-Worters, *Mistress of Herself*, 222; *Proceedings of the Seventh National Woman's Rights Convention, held in New York City at the Broadway Tabernacle on Tuesday and Wednesday, November 25 and 26, 1856* (New York: Edward O. Jenkins, 1856): 13.

21. Ernestine L. Rose, Speech, Seventh National Woman's Rights Convention, in Doress-Worters, *Mistress of Herself*, 228–229, 234–235.

22. Ernestine L. Rose, Speech, Fourth National, 1853, in Doress-Worters, *Mistress of Herself*, 159–160; Ernestine L. Rose, Speech, Seventh National, 1856, in Doress-Worters, *Mistress of Herself*, 230.

23. Ernestine L. Rose, Speech, Fourth National, 1853, in Doress-Worters, *Mistress of Herself*, 160. Richard Carlile's *Every Woman's Book: or What Is Love? Containing the Most Important Instructions for the Prudent Regulation of the Principles of Love and the Number of the Family* was published in London; Robert Dale Owen's *Moral Physiology: or a Brief and Plain Treatment of the Population Question* came out in New York. It was the first contraceptive tract published in the United States. Charles Knowlton's guide to contraception, *Fruits of Philosophy or, the Private Companion of Young Married People*, appeared in the United States in 1832 and stayed in print for many years, but Rose never met him. Angus McLaren, *Birth Control in Nineteenth-Century England* (New York: Holmes & Meier, 1978): 52, 56–57; Janet Farrell Brodie, *Contraception and Abortion in Nineteenth-Century America* (Ithaca, NY: Cornell University Press, 1994): 181–182.

24. Brodie, *Contraception and Abortion*: 123–124; the *New York Times* denunciation of Dale Owen was reprinted in *The Beacon*, October 21, 1839; on Wright, Edwin G. Burrows and Mike Wallace, *Gotham: A History of New York City to 1898* (New York: Oxford University Press, 1999): 511, and Lori D. Ginzberg, "'The Hearts of Your Readers Will Shudder': Fanny Wright, Infidelity and American Freethought," *American Quarterly*, vol. 46, #2 (June 1994): 195, 196.

25. *Proceedings . . . Free*: 54, 60–61.

26. Ernestine L. Rose, Letter to the Editor, June 29, 1858, in Doress-Worters, *Mistress of Herself*, 244–245. The *Times* published her letter on July 2, 1858, and referred to it in their July 3 edition; the letter was also printed in the *Boston Investigator*. *Boston Investigator*, November 10, 1869: 3, November 17, 1869: 5, January 19, 1870: 1, 4.

27. *Boston Investigator*, November 17, 1869: 5. The article was signed "Montgarnier," almost certainly a pseudonym. I have been unable to discover his real identity. Montgarnier had published articles in the *Investigator* since 1839.

28. The first quotation is from Moncure D. Conway, who visited Modern Times and later became a friend of Rose's; the second is from Andrews. Both cited in Madeleine B. Stern, *The Pantarch: A Biography of Stephen Pearl Andrews* (Austin: University

of Texas Press, 1968): 85, 83; *New York Herald, May* 14, 1858: 3. This is the fullest account of this convention, whose proceedings were not published.

29. Wright cited in Carol Faulkner, *Lucretia Mott's Heresy: Abolition and Women's Rights in Nineteenth-Century America* (Philadelphia: University of Pennsylvania Press, 2011): 158; Beverly Wilson Palmer, ed., *Selected Letters of Lucretia Coffin Mott* (Urbana: University of Illinois Press, 2002): 261; Ernestine Rose, Speech, Second Anniversary of the American Equal Rights Association, *New York Times*, May 14, 1869.

30. Rose's mention of "ecclesiastical" law-givers refers to the fact that high officials of the Church of England automatically had seats in the House of Lords. Ernestine L. Rose, Letter to the Editor, in Doress-Worters, *Mistress of Herself*, 239.

31. For these statements and the ensuing debate between Greeley, Dale Owen, and Andrews, see Taylor Stoehr, *Free Love in America: A Documentary History* (New York: AMS Press, 1979): 228–244; Elizabeth Cady Stanton to Martha Coffin Wright, cited in Lori D. Ginzberg, *Elizabeth Cady Stanton: An American Life* (New York: Hill and Wang, 2009): 100; Stanton and Blackwell's speeches are given in Doress-Worters, *Mistress of Herself*, 266–279.

32. Ernestine L. Rose, Speech, Tenth National, in Doress-Worters, *Mistress of Herself*, 280–283.

33. Susan B. Anthony, Diary, April 14, 1854, in *The Selected Papers of Elizabeth Cady Stanton and Susan B. Anthony,* vol. 1: *In the School of Anti-Slavery 1840–1866,* ed. Ann D. Gordon (New Brunswick, NJ: Rutgers University Press, 1997): 271; on spiritualism and women, see Braude, *Radical Spirits*, especially p. 3; Ernestine L. Rose, Letter on Religion, *Boston Investigator*, August 25, 1858: 1; Ernestine L. Rose, Letter on Spiritualism, *Boston Investigator*, October 13, 1858: 1.

34. Ernestine L. Rose, Speech, Seventh National, in Doress-Worters, *Mistress of Herself*, 225; Lucretia Mott to Lucy Stone, July 1, 1857, in Palmer, *Mott Letters*: 259. Thanks to Gunja SenGupta for help with Anniversary Week. For Grimké, Anna M. Speicher, *The Religious World of Antislavery Women: Spirituality in the Lives of Five Abolitionist Lecturers* (Syracuse, NY: University of Syracuse Press, 2000): 139, and the *New York Herald*, May 14, 1858: 3.

35. *New York Tribune*, May 13, 1859: 5 for the audience calling for Rose; [Ada Clare], "Woman's Rights," *Boston Investigator*, May 30, 1860: 3. Clare went on to praise Rose's delivery when she spoke after this "dreary" speech; *Boston Investigator*, May 1, 1861: 4. *The Liberator*, April 19, 1861. The Annual Anti-Slavery Meeting was also canceled the week before it would have taken place. *The Liberator*, April 26, 1861.

36. *Minutes of the Infidel Convention, held in the City of Philadelphia, September 7th & 8th, 1857* (Philadelphia: Published by the Central Committee, 1858): 3, 36; Rose also wrote a letter to the group in 1859, *Boston Investigator*, November 23, 1859: 1; for her participation in the 1860 convention, see the *Boston Investigator*, October 31, 1860: 1, and November 7, 1860: 1.

37. Ernestine L. Rose, Letter, *Boston Investigator*, November 4, 1857: 1; "Mrs. Rose," *Boston Investigator*, May 26, 1858: 1; for Paine Banquet attendance figures, see the *Boston Investigator* for February 17, 1858: 2, February 16, 1859: 3, 4, February 15, 1860: 1, and February 20, 1861: 3; Ernestine L. Rose, Thomas Paine Speech 1859, in Doress-Worters, *Mistress of Herself*, 247. For Rose's other mentions of the Mortara Case, see the *Boston Investigator*, February 15, 1860: 3, and Doress-Worters, *Mistress of Herself*, 292 for 1861.

38. Ernestine L. Rose, Speech at the 1857 Thomas Paine Dinner, *Boston Investigator*, February 18, 1857: 1; Ernestine L. Rose, Letter, December 14, 1859, in Doress-Worters, *Mistress of Herself*, 250; Ernestine L. Rose, Speech at the New England Anti-Slavery Convention, in Doress-Worters, *Mistress of Herself*, 192.

39. *The Liberator*, October 5, 1860, February 15, 1861; *Boston Investigator*, March 13, 1861: 1; Ernestine L. Rose, Thomas Paine Speech 1861, in Doress-Worters, *Mistress of Herself*, 294.

CHAPTER 7

1. Ernestine L. Rose, "The World Moves!" *Boston Investigator*, August 29, 1860: 3.

2. *A Defence of Atheism: Being a Lecture Delivered in Mercantile Hall, Boston, April 10, 1861, by Mrs. Ernestine L. Rose* (Boston: J. P. Mendum, Investigator Office, 1889). This work was published in 1861, 1881, and 1889; the third edition is the most widely available. The *Boston Investigator* advertised *A Defence of Atheism* and sold it for 5¢ for many years.

3. Rose, *Defence of Atheism*: 4–6, 18.

4. Rose, *Defence of Atheism*: 8–12.

5. Rose, *Defence of Atheism*: 13–15, 18–19.

6. Mazzini asserted this in the presence of Garibaldi, who replied, "I am an atheist. Have I then no sense of duty?" "Ah," replied Mazzini, "You imbibed a sense of duty with your mother's milk." This anecdote, reported by G. J. Holyoake, is cited in Priscilla Robertson, *Revolutions of 1848: A Social History* (Princeton, NJ: Princeton University Press, 1952): 366. Rose, *Defence of Atheism*: 19–22. The friend was the English editor J. M. Wheeler, writing Rose's obituary in his *Freethinker*, August 14, 1892, six weeks after she gave him her book.

7. Cited in Sherry H. Penney and James D. Livingston, *A Very Dangerous Woman: Martha Wright and Women's Rights* (Amherst: University of Massachusetts Press, 2004): 136; Lucretia Mott to Martha Wright, November 3, 1858, Mott MSS, Box 2, Lucretia Mott Papers, Friends Historical Library, Swarthmore College; Lucretia Mott to Mary Hussey Earle, February 20, 1863, *Selected Letters of Lucretia Coffin Mott*, ed. Beverly Wilson Palmer (Urbana: University of Illinois Press, 2002): 330, 333; Lucretia Mott to Martha Wright, September 5, 1855, *Mott Letters*: 244. The phrase "the mad-dog cry of 'atheist,'" used frequently in this period, came from the hideous execution of the atheist Lucilio Vanini in 1619 in Toulouse. Just before his

death, the executioner pulled out his tongue with a pair of pincers. Vanini's howl became interpreted as demonstrating that atheists were really animals rather than humans.

8. Ernestine L. Rose, "Toast for the Committee of the Paine Celebration," in Paula Doress-Worters, ed., *Mistress of Herself: Speeches and Letters of Ernestine L. Rose, Early Women's Rights Leader* (New York: Feminist Press, 2008): 302. The *Boston Investigator* originally misprinted "cancer" as "curse," which Doress-Worters reprints. Rose wrote correcting the error: "I have no more belief in the efficacy of a curse to do harm than in the efficacy of religion, from which it sprang, to do good." *Boston Investigator*, February 12, 1862: 5; Letter from C. T., *Boston Investigator*, March 3, 1862: 5. Ward Howe's lyrics were published in the *Atlantic Monthly* in February 1862.

9. *Boston Investigator*, June 4, 1862: 2, June 25, 1862: 2, June 10, 1863: 2; *The Liberator*, November 24, 1854; Ernestine L. Rose, Letter, *Boston Investigator*, September 26, 1855: 1. After Barker returned to England, he denounced his former colleagues as having "immoral habits" and "licentiousness of life," but never mentioned Rose again. *The Life of Joseph Barker Written by Himself*, ed. John Thomas Barker (London: Hodder & Stoughton, 1880): 314–315.

10. Susan B. Anthony to Elizabeth Cady Stanton, December 23, 1860, in *The Selected Papers of Elizabeth Cady Stanton and Susan B. Anthony*, vol. 1: *In the School of Anti-Slavery 1840–1866*, ed. Ann D. Gordon (New Brunswick, NJ: Rutgers University Press, 1997): 452; *The Liberator*, February 15, 1861. Also see Rose's follow-up letter on this mêlée, published in the *Boston Investigator*, March 13, 1861: 3, and *The Liberator*, March 22, 1861; *The Liberator*, March 16, 1862.

11. James M. McPherson, *Battle Cry of Freedom: The Civil War Era* (New York: Oxford University Press, 1988), *passim*; *The Liberator*, May 29, 1862: 3, August 15, 1862.

12. For the Woman's National Loyal League, which was also called the National Woman's Loyal League or the Women's Loyal League, see Wendy Hamand Venet, *Neither Ballots nor Bullets: Women Abolitionists and the Civil War* (Charlottesville: University Press of Virginia, 1991), ch. 5, and *Proceedings of the Meeting of the Loyal Women of the Republic, held in New York, May 14, 1863* (New York: Phair & Co., 1863).

13. *Proceedings . . . Loyal Women*: 21–22, 27–28.

14. *Proceedings . . . Loyal Women*: 42–48.

15. *Proceedings . . . Loyal Women*: 49, 53–54, iii, 11, 32. For more examples of Christian diction, see 6–7, 9–10, 11, 16, 33, 39, 56–57, 60, 65, 69–71. The only other speaker who did not express some religious sentiments was Lucy N. Coleman, who was hissed for saying "the God of Heaven—if such exists" and hissed again for declaring "I would willingly stand on the battle-field." *Proceedings . . . Loyal Women*: 25. For the amendment, Evelyn A. Kirkley, *Rational Mothers and Infidel Gentlemen: Gender and American Atheism 1865–1915* (Syracuse, NY: Syracuse University Press, 2000): 6–7; *New York Herald*, May 15, 1863.

16. McPherson, *Battle Cry of Freedom*: 609–611; Edwin G. Burrows and Mike Wallace, *Gotham: A History of New York City to 1898* (New York: Oxford University Press, 1999): 888–895.

17. Paine cited in Louis Harap, *The Image of the Jew in American Literature: From Early Republic to Mass Immigration* (Philadelphia, PA: Jewish Publication Society of America, 1974): 24.

18. *Boston Investigator*, January 16, 1856: 1. The acrostic was submitted by a Maine man who used the pseudonym "Cosmopolite." Any comment Rose may have made about it no longer exists. For Seaver's life, see the *Horace Seaver Memorial* (Boston: J. P. Mendum, 1889), which is available online at https://archive.org/details/horace-seavermem000bost. For Rose raising money for Seaver, *Boston Investigator*, March 4, 1858: 3, and repeated in a number of subsequent issues; *Boston Investigator*, May 5, 1858: 2, for Seaver's thanks. "Philo-Spinoza" wrote for the *Investigator* for more than thirty years. His real name remains unknown. His pseudonym combines the name of Philo Judaeus, a Hellenistic Greek Jew who criticized literal interpretations of the Bible, with that of the seventeenth-century Dutch Jewish philosopher Baruch Spinoza, condemned by the Jewish community as a heretic for his unorthodox views.

19. Bertram Korn, *American Jewry and the Civil War* (New York: Atheneum, 1970): 1–2; Harap, *The Image of the Jew*: 11, 7, 5; *Boston Investigator*, August 27, 1862: 3, December 3, 1862: 2.

20. Hasia R. Diner, *A Time for Gathering: The Second Migration 1820–1880* (Baltimore, MD: Johns Hopkins University Press, 1992), *Jewish People in America* series, vol. 2: 186. For a detailed discussion of Grant's order and its ramifications, see Korn, *American Jewry*, ch. 6, "Exodus 1862": 121–155; for the newspapers, Korn, *American Jewry*: 161. Seaver's first two antisemitic editorials appeared in the *Boston Investigator*, August 19, 1863, and September 23, 1863. This third one, published October 28, 1863, is reprinted in Doress-Worters, *Mistress of Herself*: 311–313.

21. Ernestine L. Rose, Letter, January 29, 1864, in Doress-Worters, *Mistress of Herself*: 313–315, 317–318. Doress-Worters prints Rose's letters as Seaver divided them; I discuss them as a whole. The antisemitic letter was written by John W. Cole, a Connecticut merchant, *Boston Investigator*, January 20, 1864: 5. Frances Trollope, *Domestic Matters of the Americans* (London: Folio Society, 1974 [1832]): 224; Ernestine L. Rose, "Encouraging Letter," *Boston Investigator*, February 24, 1864: 5.

22. For Rose, Doress-Worters, *Mistress of Herself*: 326; for Seaver, Doress-Worters, *Mistress of Herself*: 316, 319; for Rose's supporter, William Wood, "The Jewish God and the Editor," *Boston Investigator*, May 18, 1864: 2.

23. For Seaver, Doress-Worters, *Mistress of Herself*: 321; for Rose, Doress-Worters, *Mistress of Herself*: 325–326. For Seaver accusing Rose of "scolding," *Boston Investigator*, March 9, 1864: 2. For Seaver's replies to Rose's letters, which Doress-Worters edits severely, see the *Boston Investigator*, March 2, 1864: 2; March 9, 1864: 2; March 16, 1864: 2; April 6, 1864: 3, and April 13, 1864: 2. For Rose's last

letter, Doress-Worters, *Mistress of Herself*: 330; for Seaver's, Doress-Worters, *Mistress of Herself*: 333.

24. *Boston Investigator*, March 30, 1864: 4, April 20, 1864: 3; Philo-Spinoza, "Moses and the Prophets," *Boston Investigator*, June 1, 1864: 3; Wood, *Boston Investigator*, May 18, 1864: 2; *The Jewish Record*, vol. 3, #22, February 19, 1864: 2. *The Jewish Record* became *The Hebrew Leader* in 1865.

25. *Boston Investigator*, February 20, 1867: 4.

26. Burrows and Wallace, *Gotham*: 902–905; *New York World*, April 20, 1865.

27. Ida Husted Harper, *Life and Work of Susan B. Anthony* (Indianapolis, IN: Bowen-Merrill, 1898–1908), vol. 1: 237–238; *New York Tribune*, May 13, 1864; Rose wrote to J. M. Beckett, the Bostonian who invited her to the Infidel Convention, on January 13, 1865. Beckett gave the letter to Horace Seaver, who published it with his account of the proceedings. *Boston Investigator*, February 15, 1865: 1.

28. Lucretia Mott to Martha Wright, September 8, 1857, *Mott Letters*: 261; *Boston Investigator*, March 23, 1859: 3; *The Revolution*, June 17, 1869; Sara A. Underwood, *Heroines of Free Thought* (New York: C. Somerby, 1876): 273.

29. Little is known about Sara Underwood, who also produced a book on spirit writing. She was married to B[enjamin] F[ranklin] Underwood, who also worked for the *Investigator* as a free-thought lecturer and journalist. Sara Underwood's *Heroines of Free Thought* included Manon Roland, Mary Wollstonecraft Godwin, George Sand, Harriet Martineau, Frances Wright d'Arusmont, Emma Martin, Margaret Reynolds Chappellsmith, Frances Power Cobbe, and George Eliot as well as Ernestine Rose. Rose was the only American among them, although she lived in England when the book was published. I have not been able to identify "Old Mother." For Slenker, who met Rose and began writing for the *Investigator* in 1867 with a piece on "Why Are There So Few Women Infidels?" see Annie Laurie Gaylor, ed., *Women without Superstition "No Gods, No Masters": The Collected Writings of Women Freethinkers of the Nineteenth and Twentieth Centuries* (Madison, WI: Freedom from Religion Foundation, 1997): 237–241. For Dickinson, see J. Matthew Gallman, *America's Joan of Arc: The Life of Anna E. Dickinson* (New York: Oxford University Press, 2006).

30. Sara A. Underwood, "New York Anniversaries," *Boston Investigator*, May 27, 1868: 2. Underwood described Stanton as looking and acting like an ancient Roman matron; she found her face had "a certain masculine character." She thought Rose "more benignant and womanly."

31. Underwood, *Heroines of Free Thought*: 267. For Stanton's life, see Lori D. Ginzberg, *Elizabeth Cady Stanton: An American Life* (New York: Hill and Wang, 2009), and Elisabeth Griffith, *In Her Own Right: The Life of Elizabeth Cady Stanton* (New York: Oxford University Press, 1984).

32. Ernestine L. Rose, "Speech at the First Anniversary of the American Equal Rights Association," May 10, 1867, in Doress-Worters, *Mistress of Herself*: 336; *Proceedings*

of the Eleventh National Woman's Rights Convention, Held at the Church of the Puritans, New York, May 10, 1866 (New York: Robert J. Johnston, 1866): 2.

33. *Proceedings ... Eleventh*: 19–20, 40, 43; *Proceedings of the First Anniversary of the American Equal Rights Association held at the Church of the Puritans, New York, May 9 and 10, 1867* (New York: Robert J. Johnston, 1867): 77–80.

34. Faye E. Dudden, *Fighting Chance: The Struggle over Woman Suffrage and Black Suffrage in Reconstruction America* (New York: Oxford University Press, 2011): 88–95; Philip S. Foner, ed., *Frederick Douglass on Women's Rights* (New York: Da Capo Press, 1992 [1976]): 79–80; Elizabeth Cady Stanton, letter to the *National Anti-Slavery Standard*, December 26, 1865, reprinted in Elizabeth Cady Stanton, Susan B. Anthony, and Matilda Joslyn Gage, eds., *History of Woman Suffrage* (Salem, NH: Ayer, 1985 [1881]), vol. 2, *1861–1876*: 94–95; Dudden, *Fighting Chance*: 88; Stanton, Anthony, and Gage, *History of Woman Suffrage*, vol. 2: 322, footnote. Others who opposed Amendment 14 according to Stanton and Anthony included Martha Wright, the free black Robert Purvis, minister Olympia Brown, Josephine Griffing, the white reformer Parker Pillsbury, Matilda Joslyn Gage, Susan B. Anthony, and Clarina Howard Nichols, as well as Rose, Mott, Davis, and Stanton.

35. Ernestine L. Rose, "Speech at the First Anniversary of the American Equal Rights Association," in Doress-Worters, *Mistress of Herself*: 334–336; *Proceedings ... First Anniversary of AERA*: 20, 53.

36. *The Revolution*, November 26, 1868. The portraits were gifts from J. P. Mendum, Rose's friend and the *Boston Investigator*'s publisher. The long article about the Jews was written by a Californian identified only as "Exit." The Jewish *Messenger* rebuked *The Revolution*'s editors for publishing it; Stanton replied that the *Messenger* was harder on Jewish women than *The Revolution*. *The Revolution*, March 11, 1869, April 8, 1869; Ginzberg, *Elizabeth Cady Stanton*: 135–136; Kathi Kern, *Mrs. Stanton's Bible* (Ithaca, NY: Cornell University Press, 2001): 208–209.

37. Stanton, Anthony, and Gage, *History of Woman Suffrage*, vol. 2: 353. Stanton repeated this remark a number of times, often changing the names of the women mentioned. For some examples, see *The Revolution*, December 24, 1868; *The Selected Papers of Elizabeth Cady Stanton and Susan B. Anthony*, vol. 2, *Against an Aristocracy of Sex 1866–1873*, ed. Ann D. Gordon (New Brunswick, NJ: Rutgers University Press, 1997): 196, 198, n. 1; Dudden, *Fighting Chance*: 169; Ernestine L. Rose, Speech, 1869 Anniversary Meeting of the Equal Rights Association, in Stanton, Anthony, and Gage, *History of Woman Suffrage*, vol. 2: 397.

38. Underwood, *Heroines of Free Thought*: 256–258, 280–281. On the Universal Peace Union, see Merle Curti, *Peace or War: The American Struggle 1636–1936* (New York: W.W. Norton, 1936): 77. Ernestine Rose also attended the Universal Peace Union New York meeting in May 1869, where only thirteen others participated. *New York World*, May 15, 1869. For more on Rose and pacifism, see Chapter 8, this volume.

39. Ernestine L. Rose, "Authoresses to the Rescue," written December 20, 1868, published in *The Revolution*, January 21, 1869, and the *Boston Investigator*, February 2, 1869: 2; Ernestine L. Rose, "The Social Problem," written January 3, 1869, published in the *Boston Investigator*, February 10, 1869: 3, and *The Revolution*, April 15, 1869.

40. Ernestine L. Rose, "Letter to the National Woman Suffrage Convention," Doress-Worters, *Mistress of Herself*: 343–344. For the complete letter, see *The Revolution*, January 28, 1869.

41. "The Working Woman's Association," *The Revolution*, January 14, 1869; *New York Times*, January 9, 1869: 8.

42. The proceedings of this convention were not published. The accounts in the *New York Times* and the *New York Tribune* are much fuller than that given in the *History of Woman Suffrage*, vol. 2, and I have relied primarily on them. *New York Times*, May 13, 1869; Stanton, Anthony, and Gage, *History of Woman Suffrage*, vol. 2: 378–382; *New York Times*, May 14, 1869; Stanton, Anthony, and Gage, *History of Woman Suffrage*, vol. 2: 389–391; *New York Times*, May 14, 1869; Stanton, Anthony, and Gage, *History of Woman Suffrage*, vol. 2: 392–397; Jenny P. d'Héricourt, "Ernestine L. Rose," *The Agitator*, June 25, 1869. Anneke and d'Héricourt's speeches were translated into English by Stanton's cousin, Elizabeth Smith Miller. *New York Times*, May 14, 1869; *New York Tribune*, May 14, 1869; Stanton, Anthony, and Gage, *History of Woman Suffrage*, vol. 2: 396–398.

43. "Ernestine Rose Has Sailed for Europe," *Boston Investigator*, June 16, 1869: 5; Lucretia Mott to Susan B. Anthony, June 6, 1869, in Palmer, *Selected Letters of Lucretia Coffin Mott*: 417; a copy of Rose's citizenship document is in the Yuri Suhl Papers, Box 15, Howard Gotlieb Archives, Boston University.

44. Stanton, Anthony, and Gage, *History of Woman Suffrage*, vol. 2: 406, 427–428; *New York Times*, May 19, 1869; *The Revolution*, May 27, 1869; *Boston Investigator*, June 30, 1869: 5.

45. *Boston Investigator*, June 16, 1869: 5; Harper, *Susan B. Anthony*, vol. 1: 329; Stanton and Anthony Papers, Microfilm, Anthony Diary, May 18, 1870, reel 2.

CHAPTER 8

1. Laura Curtis Bullard, "Mrs. Ernestine L. Rose in England," *The Revolution*, July 13, 1871; Ernestine L. Rose, Letter, *Boston Investigator*, September 15, 1869: 2. Since Rose sent handwritten letters, editors often misread her script, so Luxeuil became "Luxenill." The French historian Françoise Basch corrected this error in her *Rebelles Américaines au XIXe Siècle: Mariage, amour libre et politique* (Paris: Méridiens Klincksieck, 1990): 131, footnote 15. (The book deals with Ernestine Rose and Victoria Woodhull.)

2. Ernestine L. Rose, Letter, *Boston Investigator*, September 15, 1869: 2; D'Héricourt's piece on Rose was published in the Chicago-based women's rights newspaper *The*

Agitator on June 25, 1869, and reprinted in the *Boston Investigator*, December 8, 1869: 2. Doggett had written for *The Agitator*; she also helped found the Chicago branch of Sorosis and was elected to the Academy of Science there for her work in botany. For Doggett, see *Letters of William Lloyd Garrison*, vol. 5: *Let the Oppressed Go Free 1861–1867*, ed. Walter M. Merrill and Louis Rachames (Cambridge, MA: Belknap Press, 1979): 335, footnote 2; Kate N. Doggett, Letter from Lisbon, *The Revolution*, March 3, 1870: 135.

3. Ernestine L. Rose, Letter, *Boston Investigator*, July 20, 1870: 2. Both names were seriously distorted by the *Investigator*. Richer, identified because Rose stated he edited a "Women's Rights paper," became "Lion Banjoue" and Léodile Champseix was called "Marie Champsex." Champseix wrote as a woman but used the male pseudonym André Léo, the names of her twin sons. She first corresponded with US feminists in 1869.

4. Ernestine L. Rose, Letter, *Boston Investigator*, February 8, 1871: 2; Paulina W. Davis, *A History of the National Woman's Rights Movement for Twenty Years* (New York: Journeymen Printers' Co-operative Association, 1871): 10, 19; Paulina Wright Davis Papers, Vassar College, 1872, and Folder 12, Travel Diary.

5. Ernestine L. Rose, Letter, *Boston Investigator*, February 8, 1871: 2; Wikipedia entry for James Thompson; Ernestine L. Rose, Letter, *Boston Investigator*, February 9, 1881: 2.

6. *The National Reformer*, March 9, 1873, November 2, 1873; Elizabeth Crawford, *The Women's Suffrage Movement: A Reference Guide 1866–1928* [Great Britain] (London: UCL Press, 1999): 213; *The Revolution*, March 9, 1871.

7. Crawford, *The Women's Suffrage Movement*: 260. *The National Reformer*, the *Boston Investigator*, and *The Revolution* all published accounts of Rose's speech; I have used the fullest one, which is from *The Revolution*, July 13, 1871.

8. *National Reformer*, May 7, 1871, reprinted in the *Boston Investigator*, May 24, 1871.

9. For a chart of this and other radical families, see Crawford, *The Women's Suffrage Movement*: 768; for Ashworth, 20–21.

10. For one early piece championing Bradlaugh, see the *Boston Investigator*, December 7, 1864: 2; Warren Sylvester Smith, *The London Heretics 1870–1914* (New York: Dodd, Mead, 1968): 38ff; Shaw cited in Susan Budd, *Varieties of Unbelief: Atheists and Agnostics in English Society 1850–1960* (London: Heineman, 1977): 43.

11. *The Times* [London], June 25, 1880, cited in Anne Taylor, *Annie Besant: A Biography* (New York: Oxford University Press, 1992): 150; Hypatia Bradlaugh Bonner, "Ernestine L. Rose," *National Reformer*, August 14, 1892.

12. Mary Elizabeth Burtis, *Moncure Conway 1831–1907* (New Brunswick, NJ: Rutgers University Press, 1952): 178. For Conway's openness to free thought, see Burtis, *Moncure Conway*: 132, and Smith, *The London Heretics*: 105, 113; *Boston Investigator*, July 5, 1871: 6.

13. *Report of the Proceedings of the Festival in Commemoration of the Centenary Birthday of ROBERT OWEN, the Philanthropist, held at Freemasons Hall, London, May 16, 1871* (London: E. Truelove, 1871): 20–21; *Boston Investigator*, July 5, 1871: 6; September 6, 1871: 6; August 28, 1872: 5.

14. *Report of . . . Centenary Birthday of ROBERT OWEN*: 21; "Mrs. Ernestine L. Rose in England," *The Revolution*, July 13, 1871; Ernestine L. Rose, Letter to Susan B. Anthony, July 4, 1876, in Paula Doress-Worters, ed., *Mistress of Herself: Speeches and Letters of Ernestine L. Rose, Early Women's Rights Leader* (New York: Feminist Press, 2008): 346; Ernestine L. Rose, Letter, written December 27, 1870, *Boston Investigator*, February 8, 1871: 2; since Rose's letters had to cross the Atlantic by ship, they were written weeks before they could be published.

15. Ernestine L. Rose, Letter, *Boston Investigator*, August 23, 1871: 6; *National Reformer*, November 2, 1873; Ernestine L. Rose, Letter, *Boston Investigator*, February 9, 1876: 1.

16. Ernestine L. Rose, Letter, *Boston Investigator*, October 21, 1874: 4; Ernestine L. Rose, Letter to Susan B. Anthony, July 4, 1876, in Doress-Worters, *Mistress of Herself*: 346; "Mrs. Ernestine L. Rose," *Boston Investigator*, June 30, 1886: 4.

17. Ernestine L. Rose, Letter, *Boston Investigator*, August 8, 1877: 2. The *Freethinker's* editor was G. W. Foote. Smith, *The London Heretics*: 62–66.

18. *Report of a General Conference of Liberal Thinkers, for the "Discussion of Matters Pertaining to the Religious Needs of Our Time, and the Methods of Meeting Them" Held June 13th & 14th at South Place Chapel, Finsbury, London* (London: Trübner & Co., 1878): 28. Available online at https://books.google.com/books?id=gFM-AAAAYAA. Hereafter called *Liberal Thinkers*; Thomas Wentworth Higginson, "An English Heretic. Charles Bradlaugh," *Boston Investigator*, August 21, 1872: 3; Smith, *The London Heretics*: 38.

19. Maurice J. Quinlan, *Victorian Prelude: A History of English Manners 1700–1830*: 46, 54, 165, 208, 213. In addition, pubs were closed throughout Britain, except in London. *Boston Investigator*, April 20, 1870: 5.

20. "Our London Letter," *Boston Investigator*, written February 15, 1873, published April 2, 1873: 2; Ernestine L. Rose, Letter, *Boston Investigator*, October 21, 1874: 1. P. A. Taylor's given names were Peter Alfred, but he was usually referred to as P. A.; Mentia Taylor's full first name was Clementia, but she never used it. Mentia Taylor attended Ernestine Rose's funeral; P. A. Taylor died in 1891, the year before Rose.

21. Alcott cited in Elizabeth Crawford, "Taylor [née Doughty], Clementia," Oxford Dictionary of National Biography, www.oxforddnb.com/. For the Taylors, see Crawford, *The Women's Suffrage Movement*: 673–677, and Wikipedia entry on Peter Alfred Taylor. "Open evenings" from *The Revolution*, January 19, 1871.

22. Ernestine L. Rose, *Owen Centenary*: 21. Rose also praised Thomas Henry Huxley, the freethinking biologist known as "Darwin's bulldog." Crawford, *The Women's Suffrage Movement*: 351.

23. On the Contagious Diseases Acts and the campaign to repeal them, Christine Bolt, *The Women's Movements in the United States and Britain from the 1790s to the 1920s*

(Amherst: University of Massachusetts Press, 1993): 127–132. Thanks to Susan Pedersen for help with this section.

24. Membership in the House of Lords then descended only through the male line; the House of Commons was also all-male, elected only by men. Gladstone cited in Patricia Hollis, *Women in Public 1850–1900: Documents of the Victorian Women's Movement* (London: George Allen & Unwin, 1979): 320; Lady Amberley cited in Philippa Levine, *Victorian Feminism 1850–1900* (Tallahassee: Florida State University Press, 1987): 76; Queen Victoria cited in Crawford, *The Women's Suffrage Movement*: 10; Beresford Hope cited in Hollis, *Women in Public 1850–1900*: 306.

25. Cited in the *Boston Investigator*, June 5, 1872: 6; for Priscilla Bright McLaren, Crawford, *The Women's Suffrage Movement*: 400–404. In addition, Crawford writes about four women present at Rose's first Edinburgh speech. They were Rosaline Masson: 390; Flora Stevenson: 655; Jane Taylour: 683; and Eliza Wigham: 708.

26. Rose gave three speeches in Edinburgh, the long one I have quoted from on January 27, published in *The Daily Review* (Edinburgh), January 28, 1873. The *Review* printed her remarks in the third person ("she"); I have changed them back to the first person ("I"), which she would have used. Her second Edinburgh speech was made on January 29, the third on January 30. Both appeared in *The Daily Review*, January 31, 1873. Her first Edinburgh speech was reprinted in the *Boston Investigator*, February 26, 1873: 3.

27. Elizabeth Cady Stanton, Susan B. Anthony, and Matilda Joslyn Gage, eds., *History of Woman Suffrage*, vol. 2, *1861–1876* (New York: Fowler & Wells, 1881): 534; *The Selected Papers of Elizabeth Cady Stanton and Susan B. Anthony* (New Brunswick, NJ: Rutgers University Press, 1997), ed. Ann D. Gordon, vol. 2, *Against an Aristocracy of Sex 1866–1873*: 363, note 3; *The Revolution*, November 4, 1869; February 17, 1870; August 4, 1870; September 8, 1870; Davis, *History*: 6; Elizabeth Cady Stanton and Susan B. Anthony Papers, ed. Ann D. Gordon, Microfilm, Reel 18, frames 858, 865; Ernestine L. Rose, Letter to Susan B. Anthony, July 4, 1876; Stanton, Anthony, and Gage, *History of Woman Suffrage*, vol. 2: 50–51.

28. *National Reformer*, March 9, 1873; *Boston Investigator*, July 20, 1870: 6; March 22, 1871: 6; February 11, 1874: 4; February 14, 1877: 3.

29. *Boston Investigator*, July 20, 1870: 6; February 8, 1871: 2; August 21, 1871: 6. Rose made five speeches in 1871, three in 1872, as well as attending a women's peace conference in London, and four speeches in 1873. *Boston Investigator*, July 23, 1873: 6.

30. *Boston Investigator*, November 17, 1873: 6; November 26, 1873: 6.

31. Stanton, Anthony, and Gage, *History of Woman Suffrage*, vol. 2: 534; *Boston Investigator*, January 14, 1874: 2. Stansfeld also championed Italian nationalism. He attended William Rose's funeral in 1882. *National Reformer*, February 15, 1874, written January 20, 1874.

32. The editors of the *History of Woman Suffrage* did not print the proceedings of this convention. The fullest account of it, which I have used, is from the *New York Times*,

May 15, 1874: 8, and May 16, 1874: 8. The speaker preceding Rose was Octavius B. Frothingham, a radical clergyman.

33. *Boston Investigator*, April 26, 1871: 6; February 26, 1873: 3; July 15, 1874: 2; July 29, 1874: 2; February 10, 1875: 3; April 28, 1875, for the new masthead; February 9, 1876: 1; November 21, 1877: 6; November 28, 1877: 6; December 6, 1876: 6 for Anthony. For Rose's donations in the late 1870s, see the *Boston Investigator*, February 9, 1876: 1; May 24, 1876: 1; August 2, 1876: 5; February 2, 1877: 5; November 22, 1877: 5; January 2, 1878: 5; June 12, 1878: 5; March 5, 1879: 3.

34. *Boston Investigator*, December 23, 1874: 2, written November 14; February 10, 1875: 3, written on Ernestine Rose's birthday, January 13; April 14, 1875: 2, written March 20; *National Reformer*, October 10, 1875, reprinted in the *Boston Investigator*, November 3, 1875: 5.

35. *Boston Investigator*, February 21, 1877: 2, written January 12. Rose misspelled Yorkshire place names here, which the *Investigator* reproduced. So "Elkley" is really "Ilkley" and "Harrowgate" is "Harrogate." Holyoake was referring back to 1845 and wrote that his observation was made "more than thirty years later." George Jacob Holyoake, *The History of Co-operation*, revised and completed, 2 vols. (New York: E. Dutton, 1906), vol. 2: 463.

36. Thanks to my friend, John Graney, MD, for trying to diagnose her. Ernestine L. Rose, Letter, *Boston Investigator*, February 8, 1871: 3; Ernestine L. Rose, Letter to Susan B. Anthony, Stanton, Anthony, and Gage, *History of Woman Suffrage*, vol. 2: 50; Ernestine L. Rose, Letter, *Boston Investigator*, August 8, 1877: 2, written July 8; Ernestine L. Rose, Letter to Mrs. Moncure Conway, May 9, 1879, University of Michigan Special Collections; Ernestine L. Rose, Letter, *Boston Investigator*, August 8, 1877: 2, written July 8.

37. *Liberal Thinkers*: 3; Smith, *The London Heretics*: 115; Ernestine Rose, *Liberal Thinkers*: 26. Rose was echoing the French revolutionary Manon Roland's comment just before she was guillotined: "O Liberty! What crimes are committed in thy name." Ernestine Rose, *Liberal Thinkers*: 27. For Voysey, who then opened a "theistic church" in London and became a hero to both Conway and many liberal Anglicans, see Smith, *The London Heretics*: 127–129; for his decision not to return the second day because of Rose's remarks, Burtis, *Moncure Conway*: 171.

38. Ernestine Rose, *Liberal Thinkers*: 27; Arthur J. Nethercot, *The First Five Lives of Annie Besant* (London: Rupert Hart-Davies, 1961): 69–70, 73, 77; *National Reformer*, October 10, 1875; Nethercot, *The First Five Lives of Annie Besant*: 128–136; Taylor, *Annie Besant*: 109, 127, 135.

39. Ernestine Rose, *Liberal Thinkers*: 27. For Higginson, *The Magnificent Activist: The Writings of Thomas Wentworth Higginson (1823–1911)*, ed. Howard N. Meyer (New York: Da Capo Press, 2000), for the *Worcester Call*: 13; Thomas Wentworth Higginson, *Liberal Thinkers*: 28–31; Ernestine Rose and Thomas Wentworth Higginson, *Liberal Thinkers*: 31. I have been unable to identify the quotation she used.

40. *Liberal Thinkers*: 49, 43. The speaker was Johnston Russell of Limerick. Ernestine Rose, *Liberal Thinkers*: 62–63; *Unitarian Herald* cited in the *Boston Investigator*, July 31, 1878: 3; Ernestine Rose, *Liberal Thinkers*: 74, 77.

41. Burtis, *Moncure Conway*: 172–173; Stanton and Anthony Papers, Microfilm, Reel 20, frame 317; Ernestine Rose, Letter, *Boston Investigator*, December 25, 1878: 2; *Congrès International des Sociétés des Amis de la Paix, tenu à Paris les 26e, 27e, 29e et 30e Septembre, et le 1e Octobre 1878* (Paris: Imprimerie Nationale, 1880): 36. Hereafter *Amis de la Paix*. Thanks to Sandi Cooper for letting me read her copy of the proceedings. Merle Curti, *Peace or War: The American Struggle 1636–1936* (New York: W.W. Norton, 1936): 86; Charles Lemonnier, *Les États-Unis d'Europe* (Paris: Librairie de la Bibliothèque Démocratique, 1872); Lemonnier published the bilingual monthly "Les États Unis d'Europe—Die Vereinigten Staaten von Europa," until 1889; *Autobiography, Memories and Experiences of Moncure Daniel Conway*, 2 vols. (Boston: Houghton, Mifflin, 1904), vol. 2: 284; *Boston Investigator*, July 31, 1872: 6; April 9, 1873: 4.

42. Ernestine Rose, *Amis de la Paix*: 36; *Amis de la Paix*: 58, 89, 99, 142. The Frenchwoman who proposed the resolution was Eugénie Niboyet; other women who spoke were Léonie Rouzade, Hubertine Auclert, Julia Ward Howe, and Mrs. Henry Richard.

43. Sara A. Underwood, *Heroines of Free Thought* (New York: C. Somerby, 1876): 259; D. M. Bennett, *The World's Sages, Infidels and Thinkers* (New York: Liberal and Scientific Publishing House, 1876): 949; Elmina D. Slenker, Letter, *Boston Investigator*, December 4, 1878: 5. For Slenker, see Annie Laurie Gaylor, ed., *Women without Superstition "No Gods—No Masters": The Collected Writings of Women Freethinkers of the Nineteenth and Twentieth Centuries* (Madison, WI: Freedom from Religion Foundation, 1997): 237–242; Ernestine L. Rose, Letter to Susan B. Anthony, January 9, 1877, in Doress-Worters, *Mistress of Herself*: 347. Dale Owen wrote very little, saying "as to Ernestine L. Rose, I think it probable that you know more of her than I do." Stanton, Anthony, and Gage, *History of Woman Suffrage*, vol. 1: 292–293; for Barnard: 95–100; Stanton and Anthony Papers, Microfilm, Reel 20, frame 634; *Boston Investigator*, February 14, 1877: 3; February 7, 1877: 4.

44. *Boston Investigator*, December 25, 1878: 2, written November 26. The Comstock Law's prohibition of birth control information remained in effect until 1915, when Margaret Sanger contested it. In 1887, Elmina D. Slenker, then sixty, was jailed for "mailing private, sealed letters giving advice on sex and marriage." Gaylor, *Women without Superstition*: 401, 237. Rose wrote that the short piece she quoted in the December 25 letter came from "a satirical journal, edited by my old friend, Fritz Jemit, called *Der Guckkasten* [the show-box]." Neither I nor some German researchers have been able to identify the editor or the journal. Reprinted from the Manchester *Women's Suffrage Journal* in the *Boston Investigator*, March 10, 1880: 4, written January 31, 1880; Rose actually wrote two letters to Stanton, one on May 15, 1880, which is reprinted in Doress-Worters, *Mistress of Herself*: 351, and a

second one with slight changes on May 17, which she asked Stanton to use. Chicago Historical Society/Chicago History Museum.

45. Ernestine L. Rose, Letter to Mrs. Moncure Conway, May 9, 1879, University of Michigan Special Collections; Walter Arnstein, *The Bradlaugh Case: Atheism, Sex, and Politics among the Late Victorians* (Columbia: University of Missouri Press, 1983): 50; Stanton, Anthony, and Gage, *History of Woman Suffrage*, vol. 2, footnote: 842–843; Arnstein, *The Bradlaugh Case*: 75.

46. Kate Field, "Mr. Bradlaugh's Great Speech," *New York Tribune*, July 25, 1880; member of Parliament cited in Arnstein, *The Bradlaugh Case*: 110.

47. Taylor, *Annie Besant*: 92ff.; Arthur Bonner and Charles Bradlaugh Bonner, *Hypatia Bradlaugh Bonner: The Story of Her Life* (London: Watts, 1942): 30; Alice Bradlaugh, *Oxford Dictionary of National Biography;* Edward Royle, *Radicals, Secularists and Republicans: Popular Freethought in Britain 1866–1915* (Manchester, UK: Manchester University Press, 1980): 118.

48. From the *Boston Investigator*, February 22, 1882, in Doress-Worters, *Mistress of Herself*: 355–356; *National Reformer*, February 5, 1882; Doress-Worters, *Mistress of Herself*: 356. The elder daughter, Alice, was "Miss Bradlaugh," while her younger sister was "Miss Hypatia Bradlaugh."

49. Letter from Sarah Hull Haddock, whom I have not been able to identify, to Madam Anneke, Box 5, Folder 7, Anneke Papers, Wisconsin Historical Society. Thanks to Carol Faulkner for sending me this letter. Hypatia Bradlaugh Bonner, "Mrs. Ernestine L. Rose," *National Reformer*, August 14, 1892.

EPILOGUE

1. Anthony's diary entry for March 22, 1883, in Ida Husted Harper, *Life and Work of Susan B. Anthony*, 3 vols. (Indianapolis, IN: Bowen-Merrill, 1898–1908), vol. 2: 553–554; Stanton and Anthony Papers, Microfilm, Reel 22, frames 1009, 1011; Stanton's diary entry from December 15, 1882, in Theodore Stanton and Harriot Stanton Blatch, eds., *Elizabeth Cady Stanton as Revealed in Her Letters, Diary and Reminiscences*, 2 vols. (New York: Harper & Bros., 1922), vol. 2: 201.

2. Anthony cited in Harper, *Life and Work of Susan B. Anthony*, vol. 2: 554; Miss Jeannie Armstrong, "Mrs. E. L. Rose, &c.," *Boston Investigator*, December 16, 1885: 2. Anne Taylor, *Annie Besant: A Biography* (New York: Oxford University Press, 1992): 157–158. The decision to reject Besant and Bradlaugh from University College, London, Britain's first secular college, was made by a "Lady Superintendent" and upheld by the College Council, which gave no reason for its decision. Hypatia Bradlaugh Bonner, "Mrs. Ernestine L. Rose," *National Reformer*, August 14, 1892.

3. Stanton and Blatch, *Elizabeth Cady Stanton*, vol. 2: 201; Stanton and Anthony Papers, Microfilm, Reel 20, frames 1010, 1011; Elizabeth Cady Stanton, *Eighty Years and More: Reminiscences 1815–1897* (reprint, New York: Schocken Books, 1971 [1898]): 366.

4. The *National Reformer* printed her 1860 speech on divorce, July 23, 1882; the *Boston Investigator* printed *A Defence of Atheism*, November 2, 1881: 1, and her 1851 Worcester speech, March 17, 1886: 1. In addition, advertisements for these speeches appeared weekly in the *Boston Investigator* until Rose's death in August 1892. Her Worcester Speech was also excerpted in the International Council of Women's "Conference of the Pioneers" in 1888, *Report of the International Council of Women* (Washington, DC: Spring 1888), "Conference of the Pioneers," Stanton and Anthony Papers, Microfilm, Reel 26, frame 332; the *Boston Investigator* printed her 1883 Edinburgh speech, February 2, 1887: 1. For Ernestine Rose Nock, the *Boston Investigator*, January 17, 1883: 2; January 31, 1883, 2. For tributes to Rose, *Boston Investigator*, June 6, 1883: 3, November 7, 1883: 2; December 19, 1883: 4; May 27, 1885, 2; July 22, 1885: 2; August 26, 1885: 5; December 9, 1885: 2; December 16, 1885: 2; March 10, 1886: 6; March 17, 1886: 6; April 28, 1886: 5; June 30, 1886: 4; December 22, 1886: 4; January 26, 1887: 6; February 23, 1887: 2; March 16, 1887: 4; June 15, 1887: 6; August 10, 1887: 3; October 19, 1887: 3; December 28, 1887: 6; January 18, 1888: 1; April 25, 1888: 2; June 6, 1888: 6; June 13, 1888: 6; July 11, 1888: 6; July 18, 1888: 2; December 5, 1888: 4; January 30, 1889: 6; February 13, 1889: 3; April 10, 1889: 4; May 1, 1889: 2; May 22, 1889: 6; June 12, 1889: 6; June 19, 1889: 6; October 9, 1889: 2; November 26, 1890: 3; June 17, 1891: 2. For Ernestine Rose's Letters, sometimes included in tribute articles: *Boston Investigator*, December 19, 1883: 4; May 27, 1885: 2; June 24, 1885: 5; June 30, 1886: 4; March 6, 1889: 6; November 6, 1889: 6. For Rose's letters about the *Boston Investigator*, *Boston Investigator*, June 30, 1886: 4; *National Reformer*, January 13, 1889.

5. For Robert Ingersoll, who became a colonel in the Union Army during the Civil War, see Susan Jacoby, *Freethinkers: A History of American Secularism* (New York: Henry Holt, 2004), ch. 6, "The Great Agnostic and the Golden Age of Freethought": 149–185; Jeannie Armstrong, "Mrs. E. L. Rose, &c.," *Boston Investigator*, December 16, 1885: 2; "Mrs. Ernestine L. Rose," *Boston Investigator*, June 24, 1885: 5; "A Pleasant Occasion," *Boston Investigator*, December 9, 1885: 2.

6. Ernestine L. Rose, Letter to Rev. Edward F. Strickland, August 30, 1887, American Jewish Archives, Cincinnati. Rose's letter implies that she knew Strickland's "dear wife." His collection ended up in the Schlesinger Library at Radcliffe College, Cambridge, MA and contains the only photograph of her that remains. It is used on this book's cover and is its first illustration. Thanks to Ann D. Gordon for help in identifying Strickland. J. M. Wheeler, "Rose (Ernestine Louise)," in his *Biographical Dictionary of Freethinkers of All Ages and Nations* (London: Progressive Publishing, 1889); Elmina D. Slenker, "Eminent Women: Ernestine L. Rose," *The Truth Seeker*, August 31, 1889. Her article on Rose was the second (following one on Frances Wright) in a series of ten women.

7. "Mrs. Ernestine L. Rose," *Boston Investigator*, October 19, 1887: 3; in rebuttal to an 1882 London penny pamphlet, *Death's Test on Christians and Infidels—Echoes from Seventy Death Beds*, which argued that freethinkers would convert, *The Freethinker*

published R[euben] May, ed., *Death's Test or Christian Lies about Dying Infidels* (London: Freethought Publishing Co., 1882); Hypatia Bradlaugh, "Mrs. Ernestine L. Rose," *National Reformer*, August 14, 1892.

8. *Women's Penny Paper*, February 2, 1889: 1. Muller used the pseudonym "Helena B. Temple." For her life, see Elizabeth Crawford, *The Women's Suffrage Movement: A Reference Guide 1866–1928* [Great Britain] (London: UCL Press, 1999): 428–430. Sara A. Underwood used much of this article for a piece on Rose in the "Women's Department" of the Chicago *Religio-Philosophical Journal*, which the *Boston Investigator* reprinted on May 1, 1889: 2.

9. "A Note from Mr. Holyoake," *Boston Investigator*, June 19, 1889: 6; Joseph Mazzini Wheeler, "A Visit to Two Veteran Freethinkers in England," *Boston Investigator*, October 9, 1889: 2.

10. *Boston Investigator*, August 28, 1889: 4, 6; October 2, 1889: 6; Ernestine L. Rose, Letter, *Boston Investigator*, November 6, 1889: 6, written October 21.

11. "Obituaries—Mrs. Ernestine L. Rose," *Boston Investigator*, August 17, 1892: 6; Charles Bradlaugh, Wikipedia entry; Hypatia Bradlaugh Bonner, *Boston Investigator*, February 25, 1891: 6; Hypatia Bradlaugh Bonner, "Mrs. Ernestine L. Rose," *National Reformer*, August 14, 1892.

12. For a portrait of Washington Epps, MD, see Sir Lawrence Alma-Tadema's 1885 painting in the Museum of Art, Pittsburgh, PA. Epps witnessed Rose's will. For a list of those who attended Rose's funeral, Hypatia Bradlaugh Bonner, "Mrs. Ernestine L. Rose," *National Reformer*, August 14, 1892: 107, and George Jacob Holyoake, "Eulogy for Ernestine Rose," August 8, 1892, in Paula Doress-Worters, ed., *Mistress of Herself: Speeches and Letters of Ernestine L. Rose, Early Women's Rights Leader* (New York: Feminist Press, 2008): 357.

13. Holyoake, "Eulogy," in Doress-Worters, *Mistress of Herself*: 358; Hypatia Bradlaugh Bonner, "Mrs. Ernestine L. Rose," *National Reformer*, August 14, 1892; "Funeral of Mrs. Ernestine L. Rose," *London Daily News*, August 9, 1892, reprinted in the *Boston Investigator* and Doress-Worters, *Mistress of Herself*: 357–358.

14. "Last Will and Testament of Ernestine Louise Rose," reprinted in Yuri Suhl, *Ernestine L. Rose: Women's Rights Pioneer*, 2nd ed. (New York: Biblio Press, 1990): 289–290; Yuri Suhl Papers, Howard Gotlieb Archival Center, Boston University. Rose's stepmother's name and that of her daughter remain unknown; the daughter did marry a man whose last name was Morgenstern. G. J. Holyoake, "The Late Mrs. Rose," *Boston Investigator*, January 11, 1893: 6, reprinted from the London *Freethinker*.

15. For the other tributes, see L[ucy] S[tone], *Women's Journal*, August 13, 1892; J. M. Wheeler, *Freethinker*, August 14, 1892; J. H. Cook, "A Tribute to Ernestine L. Rose," *Boston Investigator*, September 7, 1892: 3; "In Memory of Mrs. Ernestine L. Rose," *New York Tribune*, October 13, 1892; Susan B. Anthony, *Minutes of the Suffrage Convention*, January 16, 1893, in Elizabeth Cady Stanton, Susan B. Anthony, and Matilda Joslyn Gage, eds., *History of Woman Suffrage* (Reprint, Salem, NH: Ayer,

1985): vol. 1, 100, 1902 edition; Elizabeth Cady Stanton, "Tribute to Ernestine Rose," January 16, 1893, 25th Annual Convention of the National American Woman Suffrage Association, in Doress-Worters, *Mistress of Herself*: 359–360; Samuel Putnam, *400 Years of Freethought* (New York: Truth Seeker, 1894): 216, 495, 795; "Ernestine L. Rose, a Reminiscence from Lillie Devereux Blake," *Boston Investigator*, November 26, 1890: 3. Blake's words about New York State women and Rose are cited without notes in Suhl, *Ernestine L. Rose*: 275. For Blake's life, see Grace Farrell, *Lillie Devereux Blake: Retracing a Life Erased* (Amherst: University of Massachusetts Press, 2002).

16. Henry Lewis, "Ernestine Rose: First Jewish Advocate of Women's Rights," *Forward*, June 19, 1927.

17. *Boston Investigator*, March 22, 1871: 6; according to a 2012 Gallup Poll, 96 percent of Americans would vote for a black for president, 95 percent for a woman, 94 percent for a Catholic, 92 percent for a Hispanic, 91 percent for a Jew, 80 percent for a Mormon, 68 percent for a gay or lesbian, 58 percent for a Muslim, and 54 percent for an atheist.

Selected Bibliography

MANUSCRIPT AND ARCHIVAL SOURCES

Boston University, Howard Gotlieb Archives
    Yuri Suhl Papers
Central Archives of Historical Records, Warsaw, Poland
    Kalisz Court Documents, 1826–1828
The Co-operative College, Holyoake House, Manchester, England
    Robert Owen Papers
Łódź Archives, Poland
    Piótrkow Trybunalski Jewish Records
Vassar College Library
    Paulina Wright Davis Archives
    Alma Lutz Papers
    Elizabeth Cady Stanton Archives

NEWSPAPERS

The Beacon, 1836–1846 (New York City)
Boston Investigator, 1835–1904
The Communitist, 1844–1846 (Skaneateles, NY)
The Crisis, 1832–1834 (London)
Deutscher Frauen=Zeitung, 1852 (Newark, NJ)
The Free Enquirer, 1829–1835 (New York City)
The Freethinker, 1892 (London)
Herald of Freedom, 1843 (Manchester, NH)
The Liberator, 1836–1865 (Boston, MA)
National Reformer, 1869–1893 (London)
The New Moral World, 1834–1836 (London)
New York Herald, 1837–1869
New York Times, 1851–1869

New York Tribune, 1841–1869
New York World, 1860–1869
The Phalanx, 1844–1845 (New York City)
The Reasoner, 1847–1872 (London)
The Revolution, 1868–1871 (New York City)
Revue Philosophique et Religieuse, 1856–1857 (Paris)
The Truth Seeker, 1873–1889 (New York City)
The Una, 1853–1855 (Providence, RI)

CONVENTION PROCEEDINGS

(chronological order)

Proceedings of the Second Co-operative Congress, held in Birmingham, October 4, 5, and 6, 1831 and composed of delegates from the co-operative societies of Great Britain and Ireland. John and James Powell, 1831.

Report of the Third Congress of Delegates from Co-operative Societies of Great Britain and Ireland held in London April 23rd to 30th, 1832 under the presidency of Robert Owen. No publication information given.

The Meteor of Light, containing the Minutes of the Proceedings of the Infidel Convention, held in the City of New York, May 4th, 5th, and 6th, 1845. Boston: J. P. Mendum, 1845.

The Proceedings of the Woman's Rights Convention Held at Worcester, October 23rd and 24th, 1850. Boston: Prentiss & Sawyer, 1851.

Proceedings of the Presentation to the Honorable Robert Dale Owen of a Silver Pitcher, on Behalf of the Women of Indiana, on the 28th Day of May, 1851. New Albany, IN: 1851.

The Proceedings of the National Woman's Rights Convention Held at Worcester, October 15th and 16th, 1851. New York: Fowler & Wells, 1852.

Proceedings of the Woman's Rights Convention held at West Chester, Pa., June 2nd and 3rd, 1852. Philadelphia: Merrihew and Thomson, 1852.

Proceedings of the [Third National] *Woman's Rights Convention held at Syracuse, September 8th, 9th, & 10th, 1852.* Syracuse, NY: J. E. Masters, 1852.

Proceedings of the Hartford Bible Convention. [June 1–5, 1853] New York: Partridge & Britten, 1854.

Proceedings of the Woman's Rights Convention, Held at the Broadway Tabernacle, in the City of New York, on Tuesday and Wednesday Sept. 6th and 7th, 1853. New York: Fowler and Wells, 1853.

Proceedings of the [Fourth] *National Woman's Rights Convention, held at Cleveland, Ohio on Oct. 5th, 6th and 7th, 1853.* Cleveland: Grey, Beardsley, Spear, 1854.

Proceedings of the Fifth Annual National Woman's Rights Convention held in Sansom Street Hall, Philadelphia, Penn. on Wednesday, Thursday, and Friday, October 18th, 19th, and 20th, 1854. Published only in *The Liberator*, January 12, 1855: 4.

Proceedings of the Sixth National Woman's Rights Convention, Cincinnati, Ohio, October 22nd and 23rd, 1855. Published in the *New York Times*, October 23 and 24, 1855.

Proceedings of the Seventh National Woman's Rights Convention, held in New York City, at the Broadway Tabernacle, on Tuesday and Wednesday, Nov. 25th and 26th, 1856. New York: Edwin O. Jenkins, 1856.

Minutes of the Infidel Convention, held in the City of Philadelphia, September 7th & 8th, 1857. Philadelphia: Published by the Central Committee, 1858.

For the Eighth National Woman's Rights Convention, May 13, 1858, *New York Herald*, May 14, 1858, p. 3, and a few paragraphs in *The Woman's Rights Almanac for 1858, Containing Facts, Statistics, Arguments, Records of Progress, and Proofs of the Needs of It.* Worcester, Mass.: Z. Baker, Boston: R. F. Walcutt, 1858.

Proceedings of the Free Convention, held at Rutland, Vt., July [*sic*, although the convention actually took place in June] *the 25th, 26th, and 27th, 1858.* Boston: J. B. Yerrinton and Son, 1858.

Proceedings of the Ninth National Woman's Rights Convention Held in New York City, Thursday, May 12, 1859. Rochester, NY: A. Strong & Co., 1859.

Proceedings of the Tenth National Woman's Rights Convention, held at the Cooper Institute, New York City, May 10th and 11th, 1860. Boston: Yerrinton & Garrison, 1860.

Proceedings of the Infidel Convention in Philadelphia, October, 1860 in the *Boston Investigator*, October 31, 1860: 1, and November 7, 1860: 1.

Proceedings of the Meeting of the Loyal Women of the Republic, held in New York, May 14, 1863. New York: Phair & Co., 1863.

Proceedings of the Eleventh National Woman's Rights Convention, Held at the Church of the Puritans, New York, May 10, 1866. New York: Robert J. Johnston, 1866.

Proceedings of the First Anniversary of the American Equal Rights Association held at the Church of the Puritans, New York, May 9 and 10, 1867. New York: Robert J. Johnston, 1867.

For the Second *Anniversary of the American Equal Rights Association* held in New York on May 14, 1868, the *New York Tribune*, May 15, 1868.

For the Third *Anniversary of the American Equal Rights Association* held in New York on May 12 and 13, 1869, see the *New York Times,* May 13 and 14, 1869.

Report of the Proceedings of the Festival in Commemoration of the Centenary Birthday of Robert Owen, the Philanthropist, Held at Freemasons' Hall, London, May 16, 1871. London: E. Truelove, 1871.

Report of a General Conference of Liberal Thinkers, for the "Discussion of Matters Pertaining to the Religious Needs of Our Time, and the Methods of Meeting Them" Held June 13th & 14th, 1878 at South Place Chapel, Finsbury, London. London: Trübner, 1878.

Congrès International des Sociétés des Amis de la Paix, tenu à Paris Les 26, 27, 29 & 30 Septembre et le 1 Octobre, 1878. Paris: Imprimerie Nationale, 1880.

PUBLISHED SOURCES PRIMARY

Barnard, L[emuel]. E. "Ernestine L. Rose." *The Liberator*, May 16, 1856.

Bodensteiner, Keri A. "The Rhetoric of Ernestine L. Rose with Collected Speeches and Letters." 3 vols. Ph.D. Dissertation, University of Kansas, 2000.

Davis, Paulina W. *A History of the National Woman's Rights Movement*. New York: Journeymen Printers' Co-operative Association, 1871.

Doress-Worters, Paula, ed. *Mistress of Herself: Speeches and Letters of Ernestine L. Rose, Early Women's Rights Leader*. New York: Feminist Press, 2008.

Foner, Philip S., ed. *Frederick Douglass on Women's Rights*. 1976. Reprint, New York: DaCapo Press, 1992.

Gaylor, Annie Laurie, ed. *Women without Superstition "No Gods, No Masters": The Collected Writings of Women Freethinkers of the Nineteenth and Twentieth Centuries*. Madison, WI: Freedom from Religion Foundation, 1997.

Greene, A[sa]. *A Glance at New York Embracing the City Government, Theatres, Hotels, Churches, Mobs, Monopolies, Learned Professions, Newspapers, Rogues, Dandies, Fires and Firemen, Water and Other Liquors, &c. &c*. New York: Greene, 1837.

D'Héricourt, Jenny P. "Madame Rose." *La Revue Philosophique et Religieuse*, vol. 5: 129–139. Paris: Bureaux de la Revue, 1856. For a translation, "Madame Rose: A Life of Ernestine L. Rose as told to Jenny P. d'Héricourt." *Journal of Women's History*, vol. 15, #1 (2003): 183–201. Ed., Paula Doress-Worters; trans., Jane Pincus, Mei Mei Ellerman, Ingrid Kislink, Erica Hurth, and Allen J. Worters, with Karen Offen.

Lohmann, Christoph, ed. and trans. *Radical Passion: Ottilie Assing's Reports from America and Letters to Frederick Douglass*. New York: Peter Lang, 1999.

Manual of the Association of all Classes of all Nations, No. 2. London, 1836.

McClymer, John F. *This High and Holy Moment: The First National Woman's Rights Convention, Worcester, 1850*. New York: Harcourt, Brace, 1999.

Palmer, Beverly Wilson, ed. *Selected Letters of Lucretia Coffin Mott*. Urbana: University of Illinois Press, 2002.

Morton, A. L. *The Life and Ideas of Robert Owen*. New York: International Publishers, 1969.

Noyes, John Humphrey. *History of American Socialisms*. Philadelphia: J. P. Lippincott, 1870.

Owen, Robert Dale. *Threading My Way: An Autobiography*. 1874. Reprint, New York: Augustus Kelley, 1967.

Putnam, Samuel P. *400 Years of Freethought*. New York: Truth Seeker Co., 1894.

Rose, Ernestine L. *A Defence of Atheism*. 1861. Reprint, Boston: J. P. Mendum, 1881.

Stanton, Elizabeth Cady. *Eighty Years and More: Reminiscences 1815–1897*. 1898. Reprint, New York: Schocken Books, 1971.

Gordon, Ann D., ed. *The Selected Papers of Elizabeth Cady Stanton and Susan B. Anthony*: vol. 1, *In the School of Anti-Slavery, 1840–1866*. New Brunswick, NJ: Rutgers University Press, 1997.

Gordon, Ann D., ed. Vol. 2, *Against an Aristocracy of Sex, 1866–1873*, 2000.

Stanton, Elizabeth Cady and Susan B. Anthony, *Papers,* ed. Ann Gordon: ecssba.rutgers.edu/pubs/microfilm.

Stanton, Elizabeth Cady, Susan B. Anthony, and Matilda Joslyn Gage, eds. *History of Woman Suffrage*, 4 vols. 1881, 1886, 1902. Reprint, Salem, NH: Ayer Co., 1985.

Stanton, Theodore and Harriot Stanton Blatch, eds. *Elizabeth Cady Stanton as Revealed in Her Letters, Diary and Reminiscences.* 2 vols. New York: Harper & Bros., 1922.

Stoehr, Taylor. *Free Love in America: A Documentary History.* New York: AMS Press, 1979.

Lasser, Carol and Marlene Deahl Merrill, eds. *Friends and Sisters: Letters between Lucy Stone and Antoinette Brown Blackwell, 1846–1893.* Urbana: University of Illinois Press, 1987.

Trollope, Frances. *Domestic Manners of the Americans.* 1832. Reprint, London: Folio Society, 1974.

Underwood, Sara A. "Ernestine L. Rose." *Heroines of Free Thought.* New York: C. P. Somerby, 1876: 255–281.

PUBLISHED SOURCES SECONDARY

Altherr, Thomas L. "A Convention of 'Moral Lunatics': The Rutland Free Convention of 1858." *Vermont History* 69 (Symposium Supplement) (2001): 90–104.

Arnstein, Walter L. *The Bradlaugh Case: Atheism, Sex, and Politics among the Late Victorians.* Columbia: University of Missouri Press, 1983.

Bartel, Israel. *The Jews of Eastern Europe 1772–1881.* Trans. Chaya Naor. Philadelphia: University of Pennsylvania Press, 2005.

Basch, Françoise. *Rebelles Américaines au XIXe Siècle: Mariage, amour libre et politique.* [Ernestine Rose and Victoria Woodhull] Paris: Méridiens Klincksieck, 1990.

Basch, Norma. *Framing American Divorce: From the Revolutionary Generation to the Victorians.* Berkeley: University of California Press, 1999.

Basch, Norma. *In the Eyes of the Law: Women, Marriage, and Property in Nineteenth-Century New York.* Ithaca, NY: Cornell University Press, 1982.

Berkowitz, Sandra J. and Amy C. Lewis. "Debating Anti-Semitism: Ernestine Rose vs. Horace Seaver in the *Boston Investigator*, 1863–1864." *Communication Quarterly*, vol. 46, #4 (Fall 1998): 457–471.

Biale, Rachel. *Women and Jewish Law: An Exploration of Women's Issues in Halakhic Sources.* New York: Schocken, 1984.

Bonner, Arthur and Charles Bradlaugh Bonner. *Hypatia Bradlaugh Bonner: The Story of Her Life.* London: Watts, 1942.

Braude, Ann. *Radical Spirits: Spiritualism and Women's Rights in Nineteenth-Century America.* Boston: Beacon Press, 1989.

Brodie, Janet Farrell. *Contraception and Abortion in Nineteenth-Century America.* Ithaca, NY: Cornell University Press, 1994.

Brown, Marshall G. and Gordon Stein. *Freethought in the United States: A Descriptive Bibliography.* Westport, CT: Greenwood Press, 1978.

Budd, Susan. *Varieties of Unbelief: Atheists and Agnostics in English Society 1850–1960.* London: Heineman, 1977.

Burchell, Kenneth W. "Birthday Party Politics: The Thomas Paine Birthday Celebrations and the Origins of American Democratic Reform." In Ronald F. King and

Elsie Begler, eds., *Thomas Paine: Common Sense for the Modern Era*. San Diego, CA: San Diego State University Press, 2007: 174–189.

Burrows, Edwin G. and Mike Wallace. *Gotham: A History of New York City to 1898*. New York: Oxford University Press, 1999.

Burtis, Mary Elizabeth. *Moncure Conway 1832–1907*. New Brunswick, NJ: Rutgers University Press, 1952.

Ceniza, Sherry. *Walt Whitman and 19th-Century Women Reformers*. Tuscaloosa: University of Alabama Press, 1998.

Claeys, Gregory. "Lewis Masquerier and the Later Development of American Owenism, 1835–1845." *Labor History*, vol. 29, #2 (Spring 1988): 230–243.

Clark, Anna. *The Struggle for the Breeches: Gender and the Making of the British Working Class*. Berkeley: University of California Press, 1995.

Conrad, Charles. "Ernestine Rose." In Karlyn Kohrs Campbell, ed., *Women Public Speakers in the United States, 1800–1925: A Bio-Critical Sourcebook*. Westport, CT: Greenwood Press, 1993: 350–368.

Crawford, Elizabeth. *The Women's Suffrage Movement: A Reference Guide 1866–1928*. [Great Britain] London: UCL Press, 1999.

Diner, Hasia R. *A Time for Gathering: The Second Migration 1820–1880. The Jewish People in America* series, vol. 2. Baltimore, MD: Johns Hopkins University Press, 1992.

Dubois, Ellen Carol. "Ernestine Rose's Jewish Origins and the Varieties of Euro-American Emancipation in 1848." In Kathryn Kish Sklar and James Brewer Stewart, eds., *Women's Rights and Transatlantic Antislavery in the Era of Emancipation*. New Haven, CT: Yale University Press, 2007: 279–298.

Dubois, Ellen Carol. *Women's Suffrage and Women's Rights*. New York: New York University Press, 1998.

Dudden, Faye E. *Fighting Chance: The Struggle over Woman Suffrage and Black Suffrage in Reconstruction America*. New York: Oxford University Press, 2011.

Dynner, Glenn. *Men of Silk: The Hasidic Conquest of Polish Jewish Society*. New York: Oxford University Press, 2006.

Eckhardt, Celia Morris. *Fanny Wright: Rebel in America*. Cambridge, MA: Harvard University Press, 1984.

Endelman, Todd M. *The Jews of Britain, 1656 to 2000*. Berkeley: University of California Press, 2001.

Ernst, Robert. *Immigrant Life in New York City 1825–1863*. New York: Columbia University Press, 1949.

Faulkner, Carol. *Lucretia Mott's Heresy: Abolition and Women's Rights in Nineteenth-Century America*. Philadelphia: University of Pennsylvania Press, 2011.

Freeze, ChaeRan, Paula Hyman, and Antony Polonsky, eds. *Jewish Women in Eastern Europe*, vol. 18, *Polin: Studies in Polish Jewry*. Oxford: Littman, 2005.

Giladi, Ben. *A Tale of One City: Piotrkow Trybunalski*. New York: Shengold, 1991.

Ginzberg, Lori D. *Elizabeth Cady Stanton: An American Life*. New York: Hill & Wang, 2009.

Ginzberg, Lori D. "'The Hearts of Your Readers Will Shudder': Fanny Wright, Infidelity, and American Freethought." *American Quarterly*, vol. 46, #2 (January 1994): 195–226.

Ginzberg, Lori D. "'Moral Suasion Is Moral Balderdash': Women, Politics, and Social Activism in the 1850s." *Journal of American History*, vol. 73, #3 (December 1986): 601–622.

Ginzberg, Lori D. *Women in Antebellum Reform*. Wheeling, IL: Harlan Davidson, 2000.

Griffith, Elisabeth. *In Her Own Right: The Life of Elizabeth Cady Stanton*. New York: Oxford University Press, 1984.

Habermann, Paul and Gisela Habermann. *Friedrich Wilhelm III: König von Preussen Im Blick Wohlwollender Zeitzeugen*. Schernfeld: SH-Verlag, 1990.

Harap, Louis. *The Image of the Jew in American Literature: From Early Republic to Mass Immigration*. Philadelphia: Jewish Publication Society of America, 1974.

Harper, Ida Husted. *Life and Work of Susan B. Anthony*. 3 vols. Indianapolis: Bowen-Merrill, 1898–1908.

Harrison, J. F. C. *Robert Owen and the Owenites in Britain and America: The Quest for the New Moral World*. London: Routledge & Kegan Paul, 1969.

Hersh, Blanche Glassman. *The Slavery of Sex: Feminist-Abolitionists in America*. Urbana: University of Illinois Press, 1978.

Hoffert, Sylvia D. *When Hens Crow: The Woman's Rights Movement in Antebellum America*. Bloomington: Indiana University Press, 1995.

Holcombe, Lee. *Wives and Property: Reform of the Married Women's Property Law in Nineteenth-Century England*. Toronto: University of Toronto Press, 1983.

Hundert, Gershon David. *Jews in Poland-Lithuania in the Eighteenth Century: A Genealogy of Modernity*. Berkeley: University of California Press, 2006.

Hyman, Paula. *The Jews of Modern France*. Berkeley: University of California Press, 1998.

Isenberg, Nancy. *Sex and Citizenship in Antebellum America*. Chapel Hill: University of North Carolina Press, 1998.

Jacoby, Susan. *Freethinkers: A History of American Secularism*. New York: Henry Holt, 2004.

Jeffrey, Julie Roy. "Permeable Boundaries: Abolitionist Women and Separate Spheres." *Journal of the Early Republic*, vol. 21 (Spring 2001): 79–93.

Johnson, Linck C. "Reforming the Reformers: Emerson, Thoreau, and the Sunday Lectures at Amory Hall, Boston." *ESQ* 37 (1991): 235–289.

Kern, Kathi. "'I Pray with My Work': Susan B. Anthony's Religious Journey." In Christine L. Ridarsky and Mary M. Huth, eds., *Susan B. Anthony and the Struggle for Equal Rights*. Rochester, NY: University of Rochester Press, 2012.

Kern, Kathi. *Mrs. Stanton's Bible*. Ithaca, NY: Cornell University Press, 2001.

Kerr, Andrea Moore. *Lucy Stone: Speaking Out for Equality*. New Brunswick, NJ: Rutgers University Press, 1992.

Kirkley, Evelyn A. *Rational Mothers and Infidel Gentlemen: Gender and American Atheism 1865–1915*. Syracuse, NY: Syracuse University Press, 2000.

Kolmerten, Carol A. *The American Life of Ernestine L. Rose*. Syracuse, NY: Syracuse University Press, 1999.

Korn, Bertram W. *American Jewry and the Civil War*. New York: Atheneum, 1970.

Leopold, Richard William. *Robert Dale Owen: A Biography*. Cambridge, MA: Harvard University Press, 1940.

Lowenstein, Steven M. *The Berlin Jewish Community: Enlightenment, Family, and Crisis, 1770–1830*. New York: Oxford University Press, 1994.

Mansel, Philip. *Paris between Empires: Monarchy and Rebellion 1814–1852*. New York: St. Martin's Press, 2001.

McLaren, Angus. *Birth Control in Nineteenth-Century England*. New York: Holmes & Meier, 1978.

McPherson, James M. *Battle Cry of Freedom: The Civil War Era*. New York: Oxford University Press, 1988.

Nethercot, Arthur H. *The First Five Lives of Annie Besant*. London: Rupert Hart-Davies, 1961.

Penny, Sherry H. and James D. Livingston. *A Very Dangerous Woman: Martha Wright and Women's Rights*. Amherst: University of Massachusetts Press, 2004.

Piepke, Susan L. *Mathilde Franziska Anneke (1817–1884): The Works and Life of a German-American Activist including English translations of "Woman in Conflict with Society" and "Broken Chains."* New York: Peter Lang, 2006.

Pilbeam, Pamela M. *The 1830 Revolution in France*. London: Macmillan, 1991.

Post, Albert. *Popular Freethought in America: 1825–1850*. New York: Columbia University Press, 1943.

Primi, Alice. *Femmes de progrès: Françaises et Allemandes engagées dans leur siècle 1848–1870*. Rennes: Presses Universitaires de Rennes, 2010.

Primi, Alice. "Women's History According to Jenny P. d'Héricourt, Daughter of Her Century." *Gender and History*, vol. 18, #1 (April 2006): 150–159.

Pula, James S. "'Not as a Gift of Charity'—Ernestine Potowska Rose and the Married Women's Property Laws." *Polish American Studies*, vol. 58, #2 (Autumn 2001): 33–73.

Riley, Glenda. *Divorce: An American Tradition*. New York: Oxford University Press, 1991.

Roberts, Mary Louise. "Frances Wright and Ernestine Rose: Freethinkers and Feminists." M.A. Thesis, Sarah Lawrence College, 1980.

Rose, June. *Elizabeth Fry*. New York: St. Martin's Press, 1980.

Rzedowska, Anna and Beata Halaczkiewicz. *Historia Piotrkowskich Zydow (do 1939 roku)*. [History of Piortrkow's Jews until 1939]. Piotrków Trybunalski: Nakładem Urzędu Miasta, 2008.

Schwartz, Laura. *Infidel Feminism: Secularism, Religion and Women's Emancipation, England 1830–1914*. Manchester, UK: Manchester University Press, 2013.

Shanley, Mary Lyndon. *Feminism, Marriage, and the Law in Victorian England, 1850–1895*. London: I. B. Tauris, 1989.

Smith, Warren Sylvester. *The London Heretics 1870–1914*. New York: Dodd, Mead, 1968.

Solomon, Martha M., ed. *A Voice of Their Own: The Woman Suffrage Press, 1840–1910*. Tuscaloosa: University of Alabama Press, 1991.

Sorkin, David. *The Transformation of German Jewry, 1780–1840.* New York: Oxford University Press, 1987.

Speicher, Anna M. *The Religious World of Antislavery Women: Spirituality in the Lives of Five Abolitionist Leaders.* Syracuse, NY: Syracuse University Press, 2000.

Spurlock, John C. *Free Love: Marriage and Middle-Class Radicalism in America, 1825–1860.* New York: New York University Press, 1988.

Stampfer, Shaul. "Gender Differentiation and Education of Jewish Women in Nineteenth-Century Eastern Europe." *Polin: Studies in Polish Jewry*, vol. 7 (1992): 63–87.

Sterling, Dorothy. *Ahead of Her Time: Abby Kelley and the Politics of Antislavery.* New York: W.W. Norton, 1991.

Stern, Madeleine B. *The Pantarch: A Biography of Stephen Pearl Andrews.* Austin: University of Texas Press, 1968.

Stewart, James Brewer. *Wendell Phillips: Liberty's Hero.* Baton Rouge: Louisiana State University Press, 1986.

Suhl, Yuri. *Ernestine L. Rose: Women's Rights Pioneer.* 2nd ed. New York: Biblio Press, 1990.

Taylor, Anne. *Annie Besant: A Biography.* New York: Oxford University Press, 1992.

Taylor, Barbara. *Eve and the New Jerusalem: Socialism and Feminism in the Nineteenth Century.* [Great Britain] New York: Pantheon, 1983.

Teller, Adam. "The Shtetl as an Arena for Polish-Jewish Integration in the Eighteenth Century." *Polin: Studies in Polish Jewry*, vol. 17 (2007): 25–40.

Tetrault, Lisa. *The Myth of Seneca Falls: Memory and the Women's Suffrage Movement, 1848–1898.* Chapel Hill: University of North Carolina Press, 2014.

Thistlethwaite, Frank. *America and the Atlantic Community: Anglo-American Aspects, 1790–1850.* New York: Harper & Row, 1959.

Tyrrell, Ian R. "Women and Temperance in Antebellum America, 1830–1860." *Civil War History*, vol. 28, #2 (June 1982): 128–152.

Venet, Wendy Hamand. *Neither Ballots nor Bullets: Women Abolitionists and the Civil War.* Charlottesville: University Press of Virginia, 1991.

Warbasse, Elizabeth Bowles. *The Changing Legal Rights of Married Women 1800–1861.* New York: Garland, 1987.

Warren, Sidney. *American Freethought, 1860–1914.* 1943. Reprint, New York: Gordian Press, 1966.

Wellman, Judith. *The Road to Seneca Falls: Elizabeth Cady Stanton and the First Woman's Rights Convention.* Urbana: Illinois University Press, 2004.

Wellman, Judith. "The Seneca Falls Women's Rights Convention: A Study of Social Networks." *Journal of Women's History*, vol. 3, #1 (Spring 1991): 9–37.

White, Jerry. *London in the Nineteenth Century: A Human Awful Wonder of God.* London: Vintage, 2007.

Yellin, Jean Fagan and John C. Van Horne, eds. *The Abolitionist Sisterhood: Women's Political Culture in Antebellum America.* Ithaca, NY: Cornell University Press, 1994.

Index